Warwick University Caribbean Studies

Land and Development in the Caribbean

Edited by

Jean Besson and Janet Momsen

MACMILLAN CARIBBEAN

First published 1987

Published by Macmillan Publishers Ltd
London and Basingstoke
*Associated companies and representatives in Accra,
Auckland, Delhi, Dublin, Gaborone, Hamburg, Harare,
Hong Kong, Kuala Lumpur, Lagos, Manzini, Melbourne,
Mexico City, Nairobi, New York, Singapore, Tokyo*

ISBN 0-333-45406-5

Printed in Hong Kong

British Library Cataloguing in Publication Data
Besson, Jean
    Land and development in the Caribbean. —
    (Warwick University Caribbean studies).
    1. Land use — Caribbean Area
    I. Title   II. Momsen, Janet Henshall
    III. Series
    333.73′13′091821   HD403.2
ISBN O-333-45406-5

Cover based on a painting by Aubrey Williams presented to
The Centre for Caribbean Studies, University of Warwick.

Series Preface

The Centre for Caribbean Studies at the University of Warwick was founded in 1984 in order to stimulate academic interest and research in a region which, in spite of its creative vitality and geopolitical importance, has not received the academic recognition it deserves in its own right. In the past, the Caribbean has tended to be subsumed under either Commonwealth or Latin American Studies. The purpose of the Centre is to teach and research on the region (which includes those circum-Caribbean areas sharing similar traits with the islands) from a comparative, cross-cultural and interdisciplinary perspective. It is intended that this Pan-Caribbean approach will be reflected in the publication each year of papers from the Centre's annual symposium as well as other volumes.

This comparative study from countries within the Commonwealth Caribbean consists of papers originally presented to the panel on 'Land and Development in the Caribbean' at the 44th Congress of Americanists (Manchester 1982). It challenges outsider models of development and highlights creole inner perspectives. The vitality and creativity of Caribbean peoples in literature, music, dance and the visual arts, drawing much of its inspiration from rural folk, is widely recognized. Less well known are those forms of ancestral wisdom which outsiders tend to despise or ignore as being obstacles to 'progress'. However, the insights of peasants need to be incorporated into the processes of development and we hope that this volume will contribute towards planning specialists taking more seriously the motivations, perceptions and traditional attitudes to land of peasant farmers everywhere.

Prof. Alistair Hennessey
Series Editor

Other titles in this series

Labour in the Caribbean   M Cross, G Heumann
The Powerless People   A Sanders

Acknowledgements

The Editors would like to thank Professor David Lowenthal for his enthusiastic support and encouragement during the preparation of the book. We should also like to thank Professor Alistair Hennessey, Series Editor, for his assistance and advice. The secretaries in the Department of Sociology at the University of Aberdeen and the Department of Geography at the University of Newcastle upon Tyne worked very hard typing various drafts of the manuscript. Olive Teasdale, cartographer, at the University of Newcastle upon Tyne did a magnificent job in preparing our maps. Finally we should like to thank our families who put up with many phone calls between Aberdeen and Newcastle.

The authors and publishers wish to thank the following who have kindly given permission for the use of copyright material:-

Allen and Unwin for *Ethnic difference and peasant economy in British Guiana* from *Capital saving and credit in peasant societies* (1964) by Raymond Smith (editors R. Frith and B.S. Yamey).

American Geographical Society for *The future of traditional agriculture; Focus* by D.Q. Innis. Vol. 30, No. 3 (1980).

The Catholic University of America Press for *Land Tenure and transmission in rural Barbados* by Sidney M. Greenfield: Anthropological Quarterly 33 (4) (1960).

University of the West Indies for *The family system of Jamaica* by W. Davenport: Social Economic Studies 10 (4) (1961) and *Land Tenure and the family in four communities in Jamaica* by Edith Clarke: Social Economic Studies 1 (4) (1953).

Yale University Press for *Crab antics: the social anthropology of English-speaking negro Societies of the Caribbean* by Peter J. Wilson (1973).

Contents

Preface

The genesis of this book may be traced back to a meeting of the
Society for Caribbean Studies in 1981 when Jean Besson, Janet
Momsen and Karen Olwig proposed that a session on Caribbean
Attitudes to Land should be organised for the 1982 Congress of
Americanists held at Manchester University. Janet Momsen put
together this session but Jean Besson and Karen Olwig were prevented
from attending because of illness. Papers were presented by Hymie
Rubenstein and Riva Berleant-Schiller. Michael Craton had planned
to attend but had to withdraw at the last minute. Despite the
difficulties of assembling the contributors at the Americanist
Congress the session aroused considerable interest and so it was
decided to develop the theme into a book.

The present volume contains papers written by Rubenstein and
Olwig for the 1982 meeting and a paper presented by Frank Innes at
another Caribbean session held at the Congress. Berleant-Schiller,
Besson, Craton and Momsen have written new papers specifically for
the book. Brierley, Hanley and McKay were brought in as additional
contributors in order to provide a broader and more balanced
treatment of the theme in both locational and conceptual terms. Thus
most of the essays are based on very recent field and archival research
and all reflect the ideas developed in the discussions in 1981 and 1982.

The editors thank the contributors for their patience and
understanding during the lengthy generation of this volume.

Jean Besson
Janet Momsen

The Contributors

Riva Berleant-Schiller Ph.D. Associate Professor of Anthropology at the University of Connecticut, U.S.A., she has published widely on the peasantry of Barbuda and Montserrat. She is co-editor of *The Keeping of Animals: Adaptation and Social Relations in Livestock-Producing Communities.*

Jean Besson Ph.D. Lecturer in Social Anthropology at the University of Aberdeen, Scotland. Born in Jamaica, Dr Besson has done extensive fieldwork in rural Jamaica and has also published on Caribbean peasantries. She is co-author of *Caribbean Reflections: The Life and Times of a Trinidad Scholar, 1901–1986.*

John S Brierley Ph.D. Associate Professor of Geography at the University of Manitoba, Canada. His regional research interests concern the Canadian Prairies and the West Indies, particularly Grenada. He is the author of *Small Farming in Grenada.*

Michael Craton Ph.D. He became Professor of History at the University of Waterloo, Canada after teaching for six years in the Bahamas. He is the author of *A History of the Bahamas, A Jamaican Plantation, Sinews of Empire, Searching for the Invisible Man* and *Testing the Chains.*

Eric Hanley Ph.D. A Lecturer in Social Anthropology at the University of Edinburgh he is also Head of the Department of Anthropology. He has spent several periods of fieldwork in Guyana and published on Guyanese rice cultivation.

Frank C Innes Ph.D. Professor of Geography at the University of Windsor, Canada. Dr Innes has carried out fieldwork in several parts of the Commonwealth Caribbean since completing his doctoral dissertation on the historical geography of Barbados.

David Lowenthal Ph.D. Emeritus Professor of Geography at University College, London. He has written several books on cultural and historical geography including *West Indian Societies* and most recently, *The Past is a Foreign Country.*

Lesley McKay M. Litt. candidate in Social Anthropology at Aberdeen University, Scotland. She carried out fieldwork in Jamaica in 1985, studying the impact of tourism on the small community of Negril.

Janet Momsen Ph.D. She is presently Lecturer in Geography at the University of Newcastle upon Tyne after several years teaching in Canada and Latin America. She has published on the peasantries of the Commonwealth Caribbean and is co-author of *The Geography of Brazilian Development* and *Geography and Gender*.

Karen Fog Olwig Ph.D. Senior Research Fellow at the Institute for Ethnology and Anthropology, University of Copenhagen, Denmark. She has done extensive fieldwork in Nevis and St John and is author of *Cultural Adaptation and Resistance on St John: Three Centuries of Afro-Caribbean Life*.

Hymie Rubenstein Ph.D. He is a citizen of St Vincent and an Associate Professor of Anthropology at the University of Manitoba, Canada. He has carried out several years of fieldwork in St Vincent and published papers on Caribbean social and economic organization.

Foreword

David Lowenthal

For centuries the Caribbean has been stereotyped as a realm given over to sugar and other agricultural exports and to tropical beaches for tourism. The image is doubly paradisiacal: alike lavishly productive and delectably scenic. The benefits of both production and scenery, it should be noted, accrue not to inhabitants but to outsiders.

The stereotype has some basis in fact. Since Columbus, European planters have exploited Caribbean land, using slaves and indentured labourers from Europe, Africa, and Asia to raise crops for export. And with the decline of plantations, tourism has become an economic mainstay (and also a social scourge) of many islands. But these facts ignore most of the actors on the Caribbean stage. What do the majority of West Indians themselves do with their land and their labour?

This book corrects and overturns the stereotype by supplying that want in our understanding. The received wisdom about Caribbean agriculture has for some time been condemned as incomplete and partisan. Observers of the ways of life and uses of land of rural folk in various parts of the Caribbean have sought to redress the Eurocentric bias.

Their collective insights are here set forth and synthesized for the first time. This book makes it clear that customary folk practices are deployed all over the Caribbean to enhance productivity, sustain resources, reinforce community ties, and strengthen bonds with the land itself. As the editors point out, creative strategies for conserving and adapting local traditions exhibit striking regional convergence. Customary tenurial institutions such as family land, and customary land use practices such as intercropping, help rural folk throughout the Caribbean to win freedom of action and enterprise from a precarious environment and meagre resources, in the face of legal and other institutions weighted heavily against the peasantry, and an entrenched planter mentality that denies the utility of peasant enterprise. The long annals of research at the Imperial College of Tropical Agriculture in Trinidad show how export commodities have dominated imperial minds and purses to the virtual exclusion of crops for local consumption. And Colonial Office directives couple reiterated encouragement to sugar and other planters with disdain for peasant efforts to grow food — efforts maligned as backward, primitive, wasteful, 'African'.

For all its laudable emphasis on successful strategies of local resistance against planters and governments, this book is no polemical celebration of folk virtues. Rather, it details how peasant modes of land use and land tenure function in particular localities with distinctive environments and social histories, assessing the difficulties along with the advantages they portend. The authors paint no rosy picture of rural revival in realms beleaguered by soil erosion and depletion, over-population and under-capitalization. Indeed, they underscore how peasant practices, cherished as a means of securing and keeping control and as modes of insuring against ever-imminent disaster, often exacerbate these very ills.

One other point emerges with poignant clarity from these pages: the deep and abiding attachment of Caribbean people to their land, as a symbol of family and community bonds and as a source not simply of livelihood but of life's meaning. The Caribbean has long been seen primarily as a series of landscapes to be mined for their wealth or enjoyed for their beauty by outsiders. This book demonstrates what West Indian novelists and poets and playwrights have long been telling us, that love of Caribbean land is integral to the identity of its people. Only recently have some of them come into full possession of even a part of that land. Here we see how they, like their dispossessed ancestors, strive by every means at their disposal to strengthen and validate that possession.

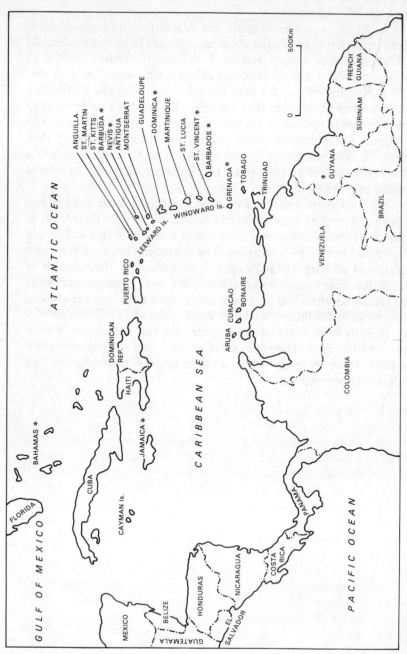

Frontispiece. Map 1 The Caribbean (* Case study areas)

Introduction

Jean Besson and Janet Momsen

In the 150 years since the Emancipation of the slaves, the peoples of the Caribbean have established several indigenous patterns of land occupancy, side by side with the archetypal export-oriented plantation. The plantation alternative takes many forms reflecting differences between islands in cultural traditions, ecological restraints and historical determinants. Since the Second World War political independence, structural change in island economies, and massive emigration have led to a breakdown in traditional man-land relationships. Today the Caribbean is a food-deficit area with a declining production of the export crops on which many of the smaller economies still depend. At the same time, the proportion of uncultivated farm land is increasing. The key to a reversal of this depressed agricultural situation lies in a clearer understanding of contemporary attitudes to land.

This collection of essays addresses this important theme. Drawing on anthropological, geographical and historical perspectives, and on a wide range of case studies from the English-speaking Caribbean, the volume portrays the complexity of attitudes to land resulting from the region's long colonial history. It reveals that land in the Caribbean is viewed as both an economic and a symbolic resource, the use of which is regulated by both legal and customary codes. Against this background theme, the essays uncover a diverse set of adaptive strategies which the peoples of the Caribbean have evolved in the face of both opportunity and constraint. In addition, a strong case is made for the potential of the peasantry in rural development, and for the richness of their local wisdom. The volume thus challenges Eurocentric 'outsider' models of development and highlights the significance of Creole 'insider' perspectives. Within this wider context, the essays are grouped around three interrelated and complementary themes. The first section on traditional attitudes to land is followed by a section on recent political and economic change and its effect on these attitudes and the implications for development. The final section explores the conflicts between 'insider' and 'outsider' views of rural development.

The book focuses on the interrelationships of land tenure, attitudes to land and agricultural production in the Commonwealth

Caribbean. Case studies are drawn from Guyana, Barbados, Jamaica, the Bahamas, the Windward Islands of St Vincent, Dominica and Grenada and the Leeward Islands of Nevis and Barbuda (Map 1). The significance of this volume is not, however, solely regional. The Caribbean, as the oldest colonial sphere, provides a microcosm of many of the attitudes to land found throughout the Third World. Furthermore, 'insider' development perspectives also have a wider relevance beyond the region for other Third World countries where rural people's considerable knowledge is generally an under-utilized resource. Development planners can no longer afford to ignore this local wisdom. These essays, written by an international group of scholars, should therefore be of use to anthropologists, rural sociologists, geographers, economists and planners working on the problems of Third World rural development.

The first section on 'Tenurial Traditions' examines the historical development of systems of land tenure in the region, and the relationship between 'black custom' and 'white law'. The first two essays provide a broad regional coverage of these themes. The section also includes specific case studies drawn from Jamaica, Nevis, St Vincent and the Bahamas. Together these four chapters highlight the customary tenures and attitudes to land which have evolved despite the constraints of slavery, the plantation system and colonial legal codes, in response to both benign neglect and the establishment of free villages and land settlements.

Starting from a Jamaican case study, chapter one explores the paradoxical perceptions of land as both economic and symbolic, limited and unlimited, which have emerged among Caribbean peasantries. Perceptions of land scarcity have generated the customary institution of 'family land' which is seen as serving ever-increasing numbers of descendants in perpetuity. Land so designated within the kin group is therefore seen as unlimited. This paradox reflects the central long-term role of family land, which is primarily symbolic. Such land symbolizes the identity and continuity of the family line as well as its freedom and prestige.

The origins of these attitudes to land lie not in cultural survivals from colonial or ancestral cultures as some theorists suggest. Instead, they can be explained as cultural creations by the peasantries themselves in response to the constraints of Caribbean agrarian relations. This structural theory of family land in turn elucidates the nature and dynamics of Caribbean landholding kin groups, as based on an unrestricted cognatic descent system enabling the retention of inalienable land rights by all descendants and rooted in paradoxical perceptions of land. Thus the existence is uncovered of a kinship system in the Caribbean once thought inoperable by anthropologists and some of the complex reasons behind the so-called 'inefficient' land use practised by the peasantries are revealed. Inequitable agrarian structures rather than peasant land use are identified as the true cause of rural under-development.

The second chapter continues the study of historical and regional perspectives on Caribbean tenure systems and their impact on production. This chapter also introduces a new dimension by focusing on land settlements as a recurring, externally-imposed solution to the intense land hunger of the peasantries. An additional theme which is picked up again in the final section of the book, is that of the ecological constraints of peasant land, for it is clear that the marginal nature of much settlement land has often led to the downfall of land settlements. Yet, in a case study of Nevis, it was found that although settlement land is an inadequate economic resource, in the absence of freehold land it provides a basis for kinship continuity, security and independence. The Nevisian data also shows that settlement farms are less productive than farms held under other forms of tenure, a discrepancy which can only partially be explained in environmental terms. It appears that this difference reflects to some degree the perception of settlers of the role of settlements. In Nevis, where half the settlers are several years in arrears on their rent, such land is often used as a form of common land for extensive grazing of livestock or to supplement either subsistence cultivation on non-settlement land or income from other sources.

Ideological factors also contribute to the under-utilization of Caribbean land in St Vincent as the following chapter demonstrates. St Vincent is one of the poorest countries in the region and yet its rural areas are typified by pronounced under-cultivation, especially in the west coast valleys, where the village studied is located. Three systems rooted in historical precedent regulate tenure, transmission and use of land: an island-wide legal system, a customary folk system including family land, and the modification of both systems through the pragmatic strategies of 'personalism'. This complex situation, which takes account of both the symbolic and economic significance of land, shows in detail how both the customary system and the flexibility of 'personalism' are adaptive strategies designed to cope with the disadvantageous socio-economic conditions defining peasant life, which include the continued inequitable distribution of Vincentian land. Thus this chapter continues the theme of Creole creativity in response to the constraints of Caribbean agrarian relations. The St Vincent study illustrates how voluntary non-use by many claimants, especially through extra-island wage-labour migration, makes productive land use possible by those kin most in need. This strategy reduces the scope for disputes concerning family land while at the same time enabling the retention of inalienable land rights by absentees.

In the fourth chapter the common themes of the first three essays are pursued in a detailed historical analysis of legal and customary codes in the Bahamas where traditions of individual freehold were implanted by early British settlers and American Loyalists, in contrast to the customary common and generational tenures of the slaves and their descendants which drew on African tradition. These customary tenures were most pronounced in the isolated, absentee-owned and ecologically marginal out-islands. There, fortified by the belief that the lands to which they were so attached had been entailed to them by their former owner, the slaves resisted both formal work in favour of subsistence cultivation and their owner's attempts to move them to more profitable plantations.

After the Second World War the increasing pace of development exacerbated the conflict between Bahamian legal and customary codes, exemplified by the Bowe case in Exuma in 1961–2. An examination of this case reveals the interplay between Bahamian tenures and decolonization, showing how this process threatens customary tenures through the adoption of Eurocentric policies. Significantly, independence has stimulated a move towards the legitimation of customary tenures with their focus on kinship and community which are coming to be regarded as features of independent nationhood.

In Section B we look at the recent impact of exogenous forces on traditional attitudes to land. This topic is illustrated by studies of the effect of political change on customary tenure in Barbuda, of the impact of tourism on Negril, a west coast Jamaican village, and of migration on children's perceptions of land in Nevis. All the essays continue the volume's central theme of Creole creativity within the contexts of opportunity and constraint.

In chapter five the distinctive development of Barbuda is attributed to its peculiar history of absentee proprietorship, marginal ecology and the absence of a plantation economy. Slaves were proto-peasants who were able to establish customary tenure in a context of benign neglect and isolation. In Barbuda the problem for ex-slaves was not to find land but to retain it in the face of external attempts to develop commercial agriculture. Barbudan demands for political separation from Antigua (with which it was joined on independence in 1981) stem from the impact of externally-imposed attitudes to land involving private ownership and commercial development, introduced from the larger island.

The parallel with the Bahamas is close as in both instances customary tenures emerged among an isolated proto-peasantry at the margins of plantation society, in a situation of benign neglect. Both groups believed that land had been entailed to them by their former owners, and in both cases these customary tenures have been effective in resisting external attempts to impose commercial agriculture or tourism.

A central theme of the first two sections of the book is that both family land and common land are forms of customary tenure in the anglophone Caribbean created in response to the constraints of agrarian relations and their legal codes. These have emerged at the margins of Caribbean plantation society as well as at its core. One significant feature of this development, which has not been given the recognition it deserves, is the variety of Creole creativity within a common colonial matrix, whether the indigenous response draws on African traditions as in the Bahamian case or derives from a particular history and ecology as in the case of Barbuda.

The example of Negril, a Jamaican village, is different again as there the threat has come from a massive growth of tourism. Instead of being submerged by this intrusion, Negrilians have responded by becoming involved themselves in the informal sector of the tourist industry. An initial rush to sell land in the late 1950s was halted by a sense of guilt at disposing of the family patrimony and by a realisation that land could be protected either by leasing instead of sale or by creating 'family land' through lawyers and wills, rather than by oral bequests as was the customary system. While these strategies have reinforced the primary symbolic significance of land, its secondary economic meaning has changed. Land for Negrilians now has a commercial and not an agrarian importance. Whereas family land was traditionally a means of achieving independence from the plantation, it is now seen as a basis for entrepreneurial activity and as a means of maintaining an interest in a foreign-dominated industry. The Negrilian case shows very clearly how family land still has a role in the contemporary Caribbean and can be used flexibly under many different circumstances.

The final chapter in this Section questions the relevance for Caribbean nationhood of Eurocentric development perspectives which assume that nationhood is rooted in an attachment to native land. This cannot be taken for granted in the case of small islands such as Nevis and St Kitts, where a high proportion of the population live and work abroad, with the result that perceptions about land and its use have been profoundly affected. The study of Nevisian children indicates a closer orientation to migrant relatives in Brixton or

Brooklyn than to their home community, reflecting the significance of migration networks and of remittances.

These negative attitudes may be traced to the legacy of slavery and colonialism which alienated people from the land and encouraged a tradition of migration. With the stranglehold of the plantation system until the 1930s there was little opportunity to establish free villages or peasant cultivation. Emigration has been a well-used response to the constraints of Caribbean agrarian structures, and has reached a point, in the case of the smaller islands, where the population increasingly consists of old people and children subsisting on remittances rather than agriculture.

What is remarkable about the widely different cases studied in Sections A and B is both the creativity and flexibility of Creole responses, revealing that peasants are not passive spectators of inexorable changes but are themselves actors who have the potentiality to participate in and influence the course and shape of development.

The final section of the book shifts the focus from traditional and changing attitudes to land and their impact on development, to a fuller consideration of rural development itself. The three essays highlight the adaptiveness of the peasantry to the constraints of land fragmentation which results from a long history of plantation monopoly, and challenge Eurocentric models of development. In chapter eight which deals with Guyana, it is argued that, unlike the foreign-owned sugar and bauxite industries, rice has always been domestically controlled and based on peasant cultivation. Colonial and national governments, and now international aid programmes, have all shared a 'rice bias' and made rice the major focus of their planning despite the evidence that it is unprofitable for the peasantry. This bias has been perpetuated by the existing infrastructure of drainage and irrigation, by the plantation model of export agriculture, by traditional East Indian attitudes to land and by the political and economic ideologies of colonial and national governments which have all encouraged mechanized agriculture. But, it is argued, rice has kept Guyana dependent and poor as mechanization has evolved within a persisting pattern of small fragmented farms. The path to recovery lies in non-agrarian development in rural areas so as to absorb the workers made redundant by mechanization.

Chapter nine, on Grenada, examines the Caribbean paradox of under-utilized land co-existing with a high level of food imports. One of the root causes has been land fragmentation which has severely limited peasant cultivation and reduced productivity. The extent of this problem seems not to have been fully appreciated even by the revolutionary government of Maurice Bishop. However, the

Grenadan peasantry has evolved adaptive strategies of land use within this constraining situation. Intensity of land use declines with the distance of a plot from the farmer's home. Those crops requiring most attention and most at risk from praedial larceny are cultivated in a kitchen garden in the yard. Tree crops are distributed on the various fragments to fulfil specific functions such as boundary markers, shade, windbreaks and protection against soil erosion. Mixed cropping and interplanting are additional strategies within the framework of fragmentation. As well as this economic rationale, the peasant's fragmented farm also has symbolic significance, for social status is based on its areal extent and not on its productive capacity.

The final chapter calls for a reassessment of development strategies both in the Caribbean region and throughout the Third World in general, and in doing so draws together many of the themes discussed in previous chapters. Current Eurocentric strategies are inadequate, involving either massive applications of not always appropriate technology, and with it dependence on foreign capital and expertise, or limited injections of indigenous resources having very little effect. In the territories of the Commonwealth Caribbean small-holders, who make up over half of all farmers, have available to them generally less than one-quarter of the agricultural land and yet contribute a substantial proportion of the total agricultural product, especially in basic foodstuffs for domestic consumption. Thus, despite land scarcity, contemporary West Indian peasant agriculture has a substantial output and therefore a significant potential for development.

Using examples taken from Barbados, Dominica and Jamaica it is shown how the peasantries have evolved a self-sufficient system of agriculture, reinforced by various adaptive strategies, despite the constraints of Caribbean agrarian systems. Labour-intensive, unmechanized technology utilized by the peasant is well suited to much of the land in small farms. Likewise, the small farmer has taken advantage of fragmentation to reduce environmental risks and to diversify production. In addition a pattern of multicropping, established by the early proto-peasantry, ensures a constant food supply and is ecologically meaningful. Using these methods cultivators not only provision their own households and provide small surpluses for domestic markets, but also deter pests and soil erosion and increase the total crop yield.

Caribbean rural development planning should utilize peasant's local wisdom regarding land tenure and land use and harness the indigenous system of peasant agriculture. Already viable in a context of constraint, it could maximize food production for the region given sufficient opportunity. This would be a more appropriate development strategy than either mechanized or export-oriented agriculture. Caribbean peoples are evolving their own solutions to development and planners should put aside Eurocentric models. The Caribbean experience explored in this volume challenges Eurocentric perspectives and demonstrates the creativity and viability of indigenous development solutions.

Today many of the problems which confronted the region's agriculture at the time of Emancipation remain unresolved. A plethora of 'outsider' solutions, both from metropolitan governments and later from international agencies, have failed to achieve a strong agricultural sector. Food crop and livestock production does not satisfy the nutritional needs of the population, environmental degradation is widespread and peasant farming has not become a significant component of the agricultural system.

The reasons for this depressing situation are inevitably complex but the role of the state in setting or accepting the priorities and strategies for agricultural development is of primary importance. Increasingly it is coming to be recognised that indigenous attitudes need to be considered and that plans must be more farmer-centred. As was observed by the former head of the Caribbean Development Bank:

> Governments and planners must not lose their patience in dealing with the small producer. If they are to guide the process of transformation of small-scale agriculture in the West Indies, they must enter sympathetically into the frame of reference of the small-scale farmer and seek to modify [it] by institutional and social changes in order to make for different behaviour patterns on the part of the small farmer. In the last analysis the perceptions of the small-scale farmer must be altered. He must see his entire social, economic and institutional environment not as something alien and hostile to him, but as something offering hope and the opportunities of upward social and economic mobility ... the small-scale farmer must himself be involved in the formulation of agricultural development plans.[1]

To this end the motivations, perceptions and traditional attitudes to land of peasant farmers in the Caribbean need to be more fully understood. This book provides some of this vital information and so perhaps may be instrumental in encouraging an innovative approach to development based on a productive blending of 'insider' and 'outsider' perspectives. As the role of small-scale agriculture in providing domestic food supplies in the Caribbean, as elsewhere in the Third World, comes to be more fully appreciated the ideas developed here may be seen to have wider application.

Notes

1 Demas, W. G. 1970. The prospects for developing agriculture in the small Commonwealth Caribbean territories: the role of the small-scale farmer. In *Proceedings of the Fifth West Indian Agricultural Economics Conference*. St Augustine, Trinidad, University of the West Indies, 5.

Section A

Tenurial Traditions

CHAPTER 1

A paradox in Caribbean attitudes to land

Jean Besson

This chapter explores a paradox in Caribbean attitudes to land: namely, the perception of land by Afro-Caribbean peasantries as both an extremely scarce, and an unlimited, resource.[1] This paradox was first identified in a Jamaican village, but subsequent documentary research has uncovered its existence throughout the Caribbean region. The first part of the chapter briefly outlines the paradox as it is found in the village of Martha Brae,[2] while the second part generalizes to the wider Caribbean case. A concluding note examines the theoretical and practical implications of the analysis, including its significance for Caribbean agricultural development.

The initial evidence: The paradox in Martha Brae

Martha Brae is a 'reconstituted' negro peasant village (cf. Mintz, 1974a: 132) of some 800 persons in the rural parish of Trelawny, Jamaica (Besson, 1974, 1979, 1984a, 1984b). The villagers are the descendants of African and Creole slaves who once toiled on Trelawny's sugar plantations. After Emancipation in 1838, the villagers' ex-slave ancestors settled the ruined site of the former planter town of Martha Brae, thus establishing the peasant village. The settlement of the village took place within the wider context of the 'free village movement' (Paget, 1964), in which ex-slaves throughout the island left the plantations wherever they could in order to establish peasant communities.

This movement, however, took place in the face of severe planter resistance to peasant settlement (Paget, 1964:39–42; Knox, 1977). Planters generally refused to sell land to former slaves, and legislated to keep them dependent on the plantations as a landless proletariat; a situation which continued for a century after Emancipation. Thus peasant settlement was severely constrained, and most ex-slaves 'remained tenants at will, subject to eviction with a week's notice and firmly bound to work on the estates on which they lived on pain of eviction' (Robotham, 1977:51). Jamaica's contemporary agrarian relations are little changed for, despite the island's transformation from colonial to post-colonial status, most of its fertile land continues to be engrossed by the plantation system (Beckford, 1972:23–28; Robotham, 1977:56; Floyd, 1979:87). Such land monopoly is now reinforced by the bauxite and tourist industries (Beckford, 1975:82; Kuper, 1976:16–25).

This picture of agrarian relations is mirrored in microcosm in Trelawny parish, whose fertile land is dominated by two large plantations, consolidations of the many former slave estates. The Martha Brae villagers are strongly aware of this stranglehold by the plantation system, and regard the lack of 'land room' as their major problem. Thus, in relation to the wider plantation-dominated society, the villagers have a perception of land as an extremely scarce resource. One villager succinctly summed up this general perception as follows:

> The district [Martha Brae] is surrounded by properties [plantations] *still.* So when the properties want workers, they just notify the district and the workers come . . . The majority of the [provision] grounds that you have now, the land belong to the properties still . . . Many people here don't have a square of land to call their own . . . Lack of land space — the people is like you put a pig in a kraal. That's just how plenty a the poor people live, just like a pig in a kraal.

In resistant response to these agrarian relations, the villagers have created and perpetuated the institution of 'family land', which is the central ethnographic feature of the village. This institution, whereby miniscule plots of land are regarded as the inalienable property of all descendants of the ancestor who obtained the land, is a strategy maximizing freehold land rights among the peasantry in response to plantation hegemony (Besson, 1979, 1984a, 1984b). It is in association with such land that the villagers' paradoxical view of land emerges. For these tiny plots of land, generally only a few square chains in size, are imbued with an unlimited capacity for sustaining ever-increasing generations of descendants forever. They 'serve children's children, till every generation dead-out.' Thus as a kinship system, family land is based on a system of 'unrestricted cognatic descent', in which all descendants through both sexes have inalienable land rights (Besson, 1979; cf. Fox, 1967:147–52).

A number of factors reinforce the perception of family land as unlimited, and enable the functioning of this unrestricted kinship system. Firstly, the short-term economic aspects of such land are subordinated to its long-term symbolic role. For the land serves primarily as a symbol of personhood, prestige, security, and freedom for descendants of former slaves in the face of plantation-engendered land scarcity. It also provides a symbol for their family lines (Besson, 1984b). Thus it is the *entitlement* to freehold land which is the crucial aspect of family land, rather than the *activation* of such rights. The kin group therefore functions as an unrestricted dispersed landholding corporation (cf. Goodenough, 1970:52–53; Hanson, 1971; Verdon, 1980:139,144), rather than as the restricted residential multipurpose group more typical of kin-based societies (see Fox, 1967:161). The implications of this for land use are outlined at a later point in this discussion.

The fact that family land is generally undivided, so that co-heirs have joint rights to the land rather than actual pieces of it, reinforces its symbolic role and is therefore a second factor enabling unrestricted descent. Thirdly, the unlimited quality of the land is perceived as relating to its characteristics of permanence and immortality; that is, to its symbolic nature, rather than to its size or productive capacity. It is this enduring nature of the land which is drawn on to symbolize the continuity of the land-holding corporation. Thus when discussing family land, two interrelated contrasts are reiterated by the villagers: the permanence of family land as opposed to the impermanence of man; and the immortality of the kinship corporation in opposition to the mortality of its individual members.

Thus co-existing with the perception of land as a scarce resource in relation to the wider agrarian structure, is a view of family land as unlimited within the kinship corporation. Elaborating and reinforcing this paradoxical view of land is a further factor: the awareness of family land as a scarce economic asset among *living* kinsmen. For such land is recognised as limited in its short-term dimension, for example as a residential site, in contrast to its unlimited capacity in a long-term symbolic role for unborn generations.

This awareness of land as a scarce economic asset among living kinsmen gives rise to two opposing strategies. One is the voluntary non-use of the land by some members of the group, enabling the activation of land rights by those kin most in need. Thus family land is interrelated with a complex of other features which serve as alternatives for enterprising kinsmen. These include resort to other forms of tenure for residence and cultivation (preferably 'bought land', but more usually cash tenancy, 'free land', squatting, rented rooms, and even 'landless farms'); and migration to other parts of the parish, island, and abroad. All such non-resident kin and their heirs, however, retain inalienable land rights. Their claims are symbolized by the acknowledgment that they may pick from the ancestral fruit trees rooted in the land, and may come to live there if in dire need. This retention of multiple claims by absentees is the main factor contributing to the pattern of 'under-production' associated with such land. Thus the strategy of voluntary non-use is entirely consistent with the long-term symbolic role of family land, and provides a fourth factor reinforcing the image of such land as unlimited and the functioning of the unrestricted descent system.

The other strategy is manoeuvring for individual advantage among kin, attempting to claim restricted rights to the land on the basis of some exclusive mechanism such as residence or legitimate birth. Such manoeuvres, or 'crab antics' (cf. Wilson, 1973), draw on the concepts of individual freehold and legitimacy inherent in the island's legal code, but directly contravene the customary ethos of family freehold.[3] Such crab antics are referred to as 'covetousness' and 'contentiousness'; and as 'robbing', 'dishing-out', 'molesting', and 'depriving' kin. This language underlines the negative sanctioning of such attempts to establish restriction in the kinship system, and contrasts with the language used to reflect the 'amity' (see Fortes, 1970:110) of positively sanctioned unrestricted descent. For here the kin group 'moves together', 'lives loving', and 'lives in unity'.

The second part of this chapter demonstrates the existence of this paradoxical view of land as both scarce and unlimited among the negro peasantries of the Caribbean on a regional scale. First, I identify the existence of the institution of family land throughout the region, and highlight its association with a perception of land as scarce resulting from plantation hegemony. Then I explore the regional evidence that family land itself is regarded as unlimited in its long-term symbolic role. Finally, I examine the view of such land as a limited economic asset among living kinsmen, that is in its short-term dimension, and identify the associated strategies which reinforce and contravene the ethos of the unrestricted descent system. This pan-Caribbean focus will encounter and elucidate two controversial regional issues: the explanation of the institution of family land, and the nature of Afro-Caribbean kinship.

The regional paradox

Land as a scarce resource: Caribbean agrarian relations

The institution of family land is not unique to Martha Brae, but exists widely throughout the Caribbean region. Thus the institution, known also as 'children's property' and 'generation property', is not only widespread in Jamaica (E. Clarke, 1953, 1966; Davenport, 1961: 447–53; Edwards, 1961:95–7), but is also found among the negro peasantries of the Bahamas (Otterbein, 1964), Haiti (Larose, 1975), St John (Olwig, 1981), Montserrat (Philpott, 1973:14–8), Dominica (O'Loughlin, 1968:102), Martinique (Horowitz, 1967:29–30, 45–50), St Lucia (Momsen, 1972), St Vincent (Rubenstein, 1975), Barbados (Greenfield, 1960), Grenada (M.G. Smith, 1965a), Carriacou (M.G. Smith, 1956), Trinidad (Rodman, 1973:135–44), Guyana (R.T. Smith, 1971), Surinam (Brana-Shute, 1979:64), Curacao (Henriquez, 1969), Providencia (Wilson, 1973:53–7), and among the Black Caribs of Central America's Caribbean coast (Solien,1959).[4] In addition, Barbudan common tenure (Berleant-Schiller, 1977; Lowenthal and C.G. Clarke, 1979, 1980:296–8) may be an extreme variant of the regional pattern of family land.[5] Family land can therefore be regarded as a pan-Caribbean institution, typifying Afro-Caribbean peasantries in general (Besson, 1984a).

Numerous explanations of the existence and persistence of these institutions of family land have been suggested. Thus Edith Clarke (1966:40,48,71) attributes family land in three Jamaican villages to African survivals; specifically, to the Ashanti cultural heritage of Jamaican slaves. Greenfield (1960) ascribes the Barbadian institution to the English cultural heritage; namely, the English upper class legal technique of the 'settlement' and the associated 'seed to seed' clause. Writers on family land in the Francophone Caribbean, such as Horowitz (1967:29–30) and Finkel (1971:299), attribute it to French culture; notably, to the Napoleonic code of equal inheritance by all children. The Afro-Guyanese institution is traced by R.T. Smith (1971:245,254–5) and Despres (1970:280) to the Dutch cultural heritage; namely, the persistence of the Roman-Dutch property code with its principle of joint rights in undivided land. Wilson (1973:56) attributes family land in Providencia to the islanders' Jamaican (and thus African?) cultural heritage. While M.G. Smith (1956:138, 1960:42) explains the institution in Carriacou as a functional adaptation to the island's social structure.

These explanations are, however, inadequate on a number of grounds (Besson, 1984a). Firstly, they are piecemeal, accounting for the existence of family land in specific Caribbean territories only, whereas pan-Caribbean consideration of the institution is clearly required. Secondly, they conflict, providing no coherent explanation of the institution at a regional level. Thirdly, with the exception of M.G. Smith's account of the Carriacou case, the explanations are couched in terms of the concept of 'cultural heritage', an approach which has two interrelated weaknesses. First, it presents family land as simply a survival of colonial or ancestral cultures; and therefore, second, plays down the socio-economic context of Caribbean society within which the institution emerged and still persists up to the present time.

More valid, and of direct relevance to this essay, is the alternative explanation that the institution throughout the region is a resistant response to Caribbean agrarian relations, as in the case of Martha Brae (Besson, 1984a). In other words, ex-slaves throughout the Caribbean obtained freehold land wherever possible, and created family land to maximize these freehold rights in the face of plantation-engendered land scarcity. For plantations continued to engross the region's land, with planters opposing peasant settlement in order to create a landless proletariat (Marshall & Beckford, 1972:31; Cross, 1979:121). Thus the establishment of Afro-Caribbean peasantries was severely constrained on a regional scale. Within this context, freehold land was not only of obvious economic importance to those ex-slaves who managed to obtain it, giving some independence from the plantations and a bargaining position for higher wages when working on them, but it also had considerable symbolic significance to a people who had not only once been landless, but property themselves. For such land symbolized their freedom, and provided property rights, prestige, and personhood. Family land was also the basis for the creation of family lines and the maximization of kinship ties, in contrast to the kinlessness of the enslaved (Besson, 1984b; cf. Mintz, 1974a:155; 1974b:60). The descendants of such ex-slaves perpetuate the strategy of family land today, in the face of continued plantation hegemony (see Beckford, 1975; Cross, 1979:34).

Thus Afro-Caribbean peasantries, since their inception, have perceived land as a scarce resource in relation to the wider societies in which they are located; a perception which has generated the institution of family land on a regional scale. But co-existing with this perception of land as scarce in relation to the wider agrarian structure, is the view throughout the region that family land itself is unlimited in its symbolic role within the kinship corporation. The next section of this chapter examines this theme, first encountering and rejecting the argument that Caribbean family land is typified by a restricted cognatic descent system; and its corollary that the peasantries thus have a view of land as a purely economic, and therefore scarce, resource.

Land as unlimited: family land and Caribbean kinship

The analysis of Caribbean kinship systems.

Most studies of Afro-Caribbean kinship have focused on domestic organisation and family structure, highlighting the so-called 'matrifocal' family (Wilson, 1973:1). As far as the wider kinship system is concerned, such studies have emphasised 'the general lack of integration of domestic groups in wider corporative kinship contexts' (Marks, 1976:12-13), thus concluding that the kinship system is typified solely by ego-focused, bilateral, non-corporate kindreds (cf. MacDonald & MacDonald, 1978:7).[6] The existence of family land throughout the region, however, provides evidence of ancestor-focused, landholding, cognatic descent corporations[7] co-existing with such kindred organisation. A few anthropologists (Solien, 1959; Davenport, 1961; Otterbein, 1964; and see Besson, 1979) have attempted to analyse this corporate feature, tending to conclude that it is characterized by a 'restricted' cognatic descent system (see Fox, 1967:146-174). In other words, they argue that a regular restricting mechanism (generally an exclusive residence rule, whereby land rights are lost through absenteeism) excludes some descendants every generation, thus restricting the group's size. These interpretations reflect either the traditional anthropological dogma that unrestricted kinship systems are inoperable, due to their structural 'problem' of generating overlapping kin groups of ever-increasing size (Radcliffe-Brown, 1950:43; Leach, 1960:117); or the current view that such systems are theoretically possible but ethnographically rare (Firth, 1963:25-26; Fox, 1967:150-52).[8]

Thus Nancie Solien (1959:578), in a pioneering analysis of the 'nonunilineal' (cognatic) descent group in the Caribbean and Central America based on her own Black Carib material and a reinterpretation of Edith Clarke's (1953) Jamaican study, argues that:

> ... some element other than descent must restrict and define the actual membership of each group. An individual may belong to as many such descent groups as he has ancestors, and without some other determining element such groups could never function as discrete or corporate units in a society.

Consistent with this perspective, Solien searches for regular restricting mechanisms enabling the formation of such discrete groups in both the Carib and Jamaican cases. She suggests that among the Carib these mechanisms are: the failure in practice of some children to inherit equally from both parents, due to conjugal separation and the consequent estrangement of the child from one parent (Solien,1959:579); and the high incidence of migrants who never return because they have succeeded in the non-Carib world. Thus, regarding such migration, Solien (1959:581–82) concludes that 'The fact that many persons never return seems to be essential to the working of the system, for it is in this way that extra inheritors are sloughed off in each generation.' Non-residence through migration, then, is thus interpreted as a regular mechanism of exclusion from such groups.

For the Jamaican case, Solien (1959:581–82) suggests the following restricting mechanisms. Firstly, when a child inherits land rights in two areas, that of the mother and the father, he will generally exert his rights in one area only. Secondly, there is a high incidence of permanent migration of young people from the unproductive family land of the rural areas to Kingston or abroad. Thirdly — and contrary to Clarke's own interpretation, as Solien herself points out — she argues that there is an exclusive residence rule; that is, land rights are forfeited through non-residence.

Davenport (1961:449–50) suggests a similar analysis for Jamaican landholding groups, arguing for the necessity of a restricting mechanism, and attempting to identify this both from Clarke's (1953, 1957) account and his own study of Black Point family land. He is nevertheless forced to conclude, on the basis of Clarke's work, that so far the restricting process in the Jamaican case has not yet been identified:

> If this system [described by Clarke] is projected indefinitely into the future, even for a few generations, the number of persons who could make legitimate claims on any one piece of family land would be staggering. This is all the more significant in view of the fact that family land holdings are generally very small, amounting to only a few acres at best, and many times to less than an acre. Wherever corporate land holding groups are found there is to be found an effective way of limiting the number of eligible claimants at some point in time. This is usually done each generation, by including some and excluding other descendants. So far, however, this limiting mechanism in the case of Jamaican family land has not been discovered. (Davenport 1961:449).

Davenport (1961:449–50) hypothesizes that patrilineal innovations, consolidation of shares, and division and conversion into fee simple holdings could serve as restricting mechanisms.

Although Otterbein (1964), in his comparative discussion of family land in the Bahamas, Barbados, and Jamaica, regards both unrestricted and restricted variants of cognatic descent as feasible, his reinterpretation of Clarke's (1953, 1957) Jamaican study nevertheless closely resembles Solien's and Davenport's. For he suggests that Jamaican landholding corporations are discrete, restricted, residential groups, with regular exclusion of some descendants occurring every generation through an exclusive residence rule and parental choice of residence. His analysis rests on the hypothesis that increasing land scarcity results in greater restriction in kinship systems; and that such increased scarcity has shifted the Jamaican system from unrestricted descent in the post-emancipation era, to restricted cognatic descent at the present time.

These analyses of Caribbean family land, then, present the institution as typified by restricted cognatic descent; and thus as essentially an efficient, 'economic' system of land use and tenure within a context of land scarcity. Recast in the framework of this essay, this perspective suggests that Afro-Caribbean peasantries perceive land not only as scarce in relation to the wider agrarian structure, but also as a scarce resource within their landholding corporations. Thus, the peasantries are regarded as manifesting the view of land as a purely economic, and therefore scarce, resource which typifies capitalist societies.

However, this conclusion overlooks the long-term symbolic role of family land as providing freehold rights for generations in perpetuity in these plantation-dominated societies; and the associated perception of such land as unlimited. Furthermore, the conclusion cannot be sustained in view of the widespread pattern of 'underproduction' associated with family land throughout the region. For, as will be demonstrated at a later point in this discussion, this pattern results primarily from the retention of inalienable rights by absentees and their descendants; that is, from the very *absence* of an exclusive residence rule.

Further weaknesses also typify these arguments (Besson, 1979). Thus Solien's interpretation of Clarke's material is inconsistent with Clarke's own conclusion that non-resident kin and their heirs retain inalienable land rights, as Solien (1959:581) herself concedes. Similarly, Davenport (1961:449–50) is unable to locate conclusively the restricting mechanism in the Jamaican case, neither on the basis of Clarke's extensive study nor his own; and is only able to hypothesize what these might be. Finally, Otterbein's (1964) conclusions on

Jamaica are inconsistent with his interpretation of Barbadian family land, which he argues is typified by unrestricted groups due to the island's intense land scarcity resulting from the region's highest population density. It is also inconsistent with the fact that the dynamics of the Jamaican descent system described by Clarke are identical to those of the Barbadian and Bahamian systems, both of which Otterbein concedes are unrestricted. Thus, not surprisingly, Mintz and Price (1976:39) observe, in a discussion of Caribbean land-holding groups, that 'a good deal remains obscure about the precise nature of the kin groups'; Price (1967:47–48) elsewhere refers to the 'mysteries' of Caribbean land tenure systems; and Mintz (1974a:242) remarks that 'The problems of land tenure and the transmission of land rights among Caribbean peasantries remain largely unsolved.'

The remainder of this section, therefore, develops an alternative interpretation of Caribbean kin groups as *unrestricted* dispersed land-holding corporations,[9] perceived as operating unlimited supplies of land. This alternative interpretation will also elucidate the 'mysteries' of Caribbean landholding groups; that is, the dynamics of their cognatic descent systems. The analysis is based on a wide range of evidence, at present unrelated and scattered in the literature, which highlights the symbolic role of family land throughout the region and the unrestricted nature of its kinship system.

The symbolic role of family land.
We start this regional overview with Edith Clarke's (1953, 1966) pioneering analysis of Jamaican family land. In her discussion of land tenure in three Jamaican villages, Clarke highlights the symbolic significance of freehold tenure and, especially, of family land. Of freehold land in general, Clarke (1966:65) argues that 'Land has not only a real but an almost mystic significance' for the Jamaican peasant, identifying three reasons why this is so:

> First, . . . land acquired during slavery had a social and status value, and, after slavery, became in a sense both the symbol and the reality of freedom. Secondly, the religious asso-ciation of land is strong: the spot on which the ancestors are buried is sacred and land containing their graves should not be permitted to pass into alien hands. Thirdly, in the economy of the Island, ownership of land is believed to be the only real and permanent source of security and of the means of satisfying the normal expectations which operate between men and women as prospective parents and between them and their children. And this has no connection, be it stated, with the income which the land can provide.

More specifically, Clark (1966:64) highlights the role of family land as a symbol of security:

> The possession of an interest in family land or a family house produces a sense of security out of all proportion to the actual economic security, which at best is slight. The word home, as a place one can go back to, may be said to be synonymous with a family holding.... With the increasing scarcity and irregularity of employment and the corresponding insecurity of the wage earner as well as the pressure of population on the land which the small man can buy or rent, a few squares of family land in which one has an interest come to have great importance and the internal forces are all against any division of the family holdings or enforced consolidation. The few pounds received in compensation is no recompense for the satisfaction to be got from the knowledge that there is a place to which a man or woman can go when the worst happens and be permitted 'to build a house and live there'.

Clarke's material also clearly indicates the unrestricted, dispersed nature of the descent corporations associated with family land. For 'any member of the family "through the name or through the blood" [i.e. through unrestricted cognatic descent] has rights of use which are not lost through non-exercise for any period' (E. Clarke, 1966:44). Such kin are 'not only scattered about Jamaica but in other parts of the world' (E. Clarke, 1966:68).

Edwards' (1961) study of small farming in Jamaica likewise highlights the symbolic, as well as economic, significance of land ownership and family land. Thus he refers to the 'very special sentimental value' surrounding freehold land, 'particularly when it contained the family burial plot'; and to the idea that such land provides a home and 'an old-age pension fund' (Edwards 1961:94). He also identifies the notion of the permanence of land: 'Land does not spoil' (Edwards, 1961:94). Edwards' material on family land also supports the interpretation of its kinship system as one of unrestricted, dispersed descent corporations (1961:95).

Raymond Smith (1964:311,316), writing of Guyanese peasantries, similarly notes the symbolic significance of freehold and family land among the negro peasants, a feature which he contrasts with the more economic orientation of the East Indian land-holder:

> The possession of rights in land is of more than purely economic significance; if this were the only consideration more land would be placed on the market instead of being

left idle as it is, particularly in the negro villages. It is generally felt that possession of permanent rights in land provides some sort of independence and security ... Negroes are especially reluctant to part with freehold rights in land, even though it is lying idle and they may have to pay rates on it, often sending the money back to the village from other parts of the country or even from overseas. It is quite common to find large areas of Negro village land under bush, but rare in Indian villages where all available land is generally under rice.... The Negro village tends to be regarded as the physical base, the birthplace, the place where one's 'navel string is buried', from which individuals venture forth to make a living knowing that they can always return to its security and the warmth of its human relationships in time of trouble. The Indian village by contrast is primarily the place where one has a rice farm ...

Smith's evidence also points to the unrestricted, dispersed nature of the descent corporation associated with family land (1971:253–55).

Among the negro peasantry of Texier, St Vincent, Rubenstein (1975:165) identifies similar sentiments regarding the symbolic significance of freehold and family land, including the perception of such land as a permanent resource:

... land is desired in its own right beyond its productive or commercial potential and it is the ambition of nearly every landless villager to own a piece of land. To own land symbolizes individual economic well-being and confers prestige and respectability on the owner. Equally important, land is something permanent and immovable, thereby conferring stability in a social system in which unpredictability and impermanence are constant elements. Finally, land represents a legacy that may be passed on to one's heirs, thus ensuring that one will be remembered by one's descendants.

Rubenstein's analysis also indicates the presence of unrestricted, dispersed, overlapping kin groups associated with family land. For he notes that, due to migration, 'Out of the total of 545 claims to valley land [over one-third of which is family land], only 266, or less than one-half, are represented by claimants currently resident in Texier'; that 'the same person may have claims on more than one piece of land'; and that claims to family land are not well defined (Rubenstein, 1975:159,164).

In Providencia, Wilson (1973:44–68, 224–25) identifies a 'sentimental' or 'philosophical' relationship of man to land, in addition to the latter's economic and social significance, generalizing this theme to other Anglophone Afro-Caribbean societies. His analysis builds particularly on the earlier work of David Lowenthal (1961), whose classic paper on 'Caribbean Views of Caribbean Land' highlights the symbolic significance of freehold land to the West Indian. Such land, notes Lowenthal (1961:4), has symbolized 'freedom, pride, status, continuity, solidarity, sovereignty' from the days of slavery to the present time; sentiments which, Lowenthal demonstrates, are most clearly manifested in the institution of family land.

These sentimental aspects of the relationship of man to land are expressed, in Providencia, in the system of equal partible inheritance; but even more so in the institution of jointly held, undivided, family land:

> The continuity of the relationship between kinsmen and land is more deliberately expressed in the idea and reality of family land ... [The latter] is land that has been cleared or staked out by an ancestor and explicitly designated by him as being for the exclusive use of his descendants, male or female, full or outside. Anyone can so designate his land — it does not have to be a long-dead ancestor. Such land is no longer subject to the dividing process described above. It remains forever undivided and available for the use of descendants. (Wilson,1973:56–57)

Wilson (1973:57) also provides evidence that the landholding group is unrestricted and often widely dispersed, with members 'living half a world away'.

In the formerly Danish Virgin Island of St John, family land traditionally had a strong symbolic content, symbolizing both security and freedom on the one hand, and kin group identity and continuity on the other:

> Though family land was usually not large enough for all children to settle on it comfortably had they chosen to do so, they still appreciated the fact that they had a claim on land and could use this any time they wanted to should it be necessary. Thus no St Johnian with family land need ever be without a place to live, and he/she would always have a place to go in time of need. Many of the older St Johnians expressed very close attachment to the land, which their ancestors had bought for their families, and they were strongly opposed to selling the land which, today, is

extremely valuable. The old people equated owning land
with being free and felt that their ancestors had freed
themselves from slavery or bondage to the plantations by
acquiring land . . .

The claim in the family land tied relatives together into fairly
permanent groups. The common family tie to the land was
concretized in the family's cemetery, which was located on
the family land. The original buyer of the land was buried
here together with the other relatives who had died by this
time . . . (Olwig, 1977:249–50)

The St Johnian landholding groups were unrestricted, dispersed,
overlapping corporations controlling an unlimited, primarily
symbolic, resource rather than exclusive restricted residential groups
(Olwig, 1977:241, 248–51, 1981a:69). The fact that, as elsewhere in
the Caribbean (e.g. R.T. Smith, 1971:245; Horowitz, 1967:30; Larose,
1975:489), such land was undivided so that no heir 'owned a particular
piece of land, but all had a claim in the land' (Olwig, 1977:240) clearly
reinforced this unrestricted descent system.

In both Barbados and the Bahamas freehold land also has strong
symbolic connotations, manifested most clearly in the institution of
family land. Such land, as studies by Greenfield (1960) and Otterbein
(1964) make clear, is regarded as an unlimited resource serving
unrestricted, dispersed, cognatic descent corporations in perpetuity.
Mathurin (1967:10) also provides evidence of similar landholding
groups in St Lucia. Likewise in Haiti, as Larose (1975:494) observes,
the *démembré*, or undivided family land, is 'for all of us' (all
descendants of the founding ancestor). The Haitian descent
corporation is unrestricted and often widely dispersed; and the
démembré 'stands as a powerful symbol of the continuity of the
family group', forming, with its family cemetery, cult house, and trees
(harbouring the *loas* or family spirits), the basic unit of Haitian
peasant religion (Larose, 1975:489–96).

Writing more generally on the Caribbean region, Mintz
(1974a:155, 1974b:62) notes that the significance of land ownership
for Caribbean peasantries 'far exceeds any obvious economic
considerations': symbolizing freedom and 'identity as persons', and
being 'perceived as the key to independence and dignity'. Mintz
(1974a:154–5) demonstrates that these sentiments are most clearly
reflected in family land, which also represents the continuity and
identity of kinship groups or 'family lines'. He develops this theme in
detail in his essay on the house-and-yard, which focuses especially on
the negro peasantries of Haiti and Jamaica (Mintz, 1974a:246–7).

Here Mintz also notes the dispersion of the unrestricted landholding corporation, with absentees retaining rights to undivided family land (1974a:242).

It seems clear from a wide range of evidence, then, that Afro-Caribbean peasantries regard freehold land in a symbolic as well as an economic sense, and that the symbolic element is most pronounced in the institution of family land. Such land is perceived throughout the region as unlimited: controlled by an unrestricted descent corporation, and sustaining ever-increasing generations of kin forever. This interpretation is perhaps most vividly illustrated with material from the Dutch island of Curaçao, where Henriquez (1969) reports a case of family land with 250 living claimants.[10]

In summary, then, Afro-Caribbean peasants in general hold a paradoxical view of land. They view it as both a scarce economic resource in relation to the wider agrarian structure, and an unlimited symbolic one within the kinship corporation. Further elaborating this complex view of land, as will be seen below, is the awareness of family land as a scarce economic asset among living kinsmen: that is, in its short-term dimension, in contrast to its unlimited capacity in its long-term symbolic role. This gives rise to the two strategies of voluntary non-use and crab antics: the former reinforcing the long-term symbolic role of family land and the functioning of its unrestricted kinship system; the latter contravening the basic ethos of the institution. While, as has been noted, attempts to interpret Caribbean family land as a restricted exclusive cognatic system cannot be sustained, it will be seen that such analyses can usefully be re-interpreted within these contexts. We turn, then, to examine these themes.

Family land as scarce among living kin: voluntary non-use and crab antics

Voluntary non-use.

The strategy of voluntary non-use throughout the region is the corollary of the essential theme of family land: namely, that its primary purpose is to provide freehold land *rights* to generations in perpetuity, and that such rights should provide security in time of dire need. Therefore kinsmen who can, resort to means of support other than family land, but still retain inalienable land rights for themselves and their descendants. These absentee claims are sometimes reinforced by the custom of picking from the fruit trees rooted in the land. Such voluntary non-use enables needy members of the corporation to activate their rights to use the land as a short-term economic resource, for example as a residential site. Thus Edith Clark (1953:83,112), discussing Jamaican family land, observes that:

> There is also, in practice, non-exercise by kin of their 'rights' for one reason or another — the fact that they have got on in the world and have better land or prospects elsewhere or that they live too far away to use the land. Even in such cases, we were told that they would have the right to return at any time and build on the site and there were many instances of gifts of produce from family holdings being sent to kindred in Kingston or other parts of the island ...

> It was unequivocally asserted that members who did not exercise their right to live on land did not thereby lose their right to do so at a later period. Non-residential heirs might draw on the land by reaping the fruit of permanent crops on the holdings (such as breadfruit or coconut) or by renting rooms or house sites upon it. And always their right to return and live on it was acknowledged. These privileges also extend to their recognised heirs.

Davenport (1961:448–49), commenting on Clarke's data, reinforces her conclusions regarding the retention of land rights despite non-residence: 'It is ... clear that neither prolonged absence, non-use, nor failure to exert one's legitimate claim on family land nullifies a person's or his descendants' claim on it.' Lowenthal (1961:4), drawing on Clarke's work, also highlights this point; as does Edwards' (1961) study of Jamaican family land. Thus Edwards (1961:111,95) notes that 'Small pieces of land not occupied by houses were sometimes left in the possession of the neediest owner'; but that abstention from using family land does not result in forfeiture of land rights by absentees and their heirs.

Haitian family land is likewise treated as an 'insurance policy' at the economic level, with only the neediest activating rights of use: 'Residence in a "lakou" seems restricted to those who do not have the means to do in a different way' (Larose, 1975:496). However, all descendants through unrestricted descent retain inalienable rights to the land:

> The present occupation of it [family land] is seen as a provisional sharing that could be questioned any time by the coming back of an heir who would have been away ... Anyone who traces genealogical relationship to the ancestor

'who left it for all his children', is entitled to come in and
build up his house. (Larose 1975:494,490)

Family land serves a similar 'insurance' role in Providencia, with
absentees retaining inalienable rights:

> Should a man wish to cultivate family land he informs the
> co-owners. As soon as he has harvested his crop the land he
> used goes back into the pool. He may neither sell nor rent
> any portion of family land, except with the consent of all the
> co-owners, and the sentiment is strong against such a
> practice ... Because there is always a percentage of people
> living away from the island, the actual number actively
> concerned with family land at any one time is relatively
> small. Since it is located in the hilly interior it is not entirely
> suitable for cultivation or even pasture. So family land on
> Providencia is at best an emergency pool of land where a
> man, otherwise landless, can affirm his sense of belonging to
> the island and, if need be, can support himself. (Wilson,
> 1973:57).

In Barbados the theme of voluntary non-use, enabling needy kin
to use family land as an economic resource while absentees still retain
inalienable land rights, is also clear:

> Though all children usually inherited an interest in the family
> property, there was informal agreement that once a son
> purchased land of his own or a daughter married a property
> owner, they and their heirs would not press their claims to
> the family land since they no longer needed the protection it
> offered. In the event that they lost their rights in this other
> land they could then reassert their claims to the family land.
> (Greenfield, 1960:174).

Likewise in Guyana, family land:

> may be divided according to 'need' while the title may be
> retained as joint ownership, so that those who do not need to
> use the land at the time may still retain undivided rights in it
> which they can transmit by will or inheritance to their own
> children ... (R.T. Smith, 1971:253, cf. 254–5).

The retention of family land rights by absentees is also stressed by
Mathurin (1967:10) for St Lucia, where such rights are retained
'whether the individual is resident on the holding or not, and whether
or not he cultivates his share.' A similar theme is also clear for St
John:

... by having a claim, one always had a possibility of settling on the land, and this offered some security to the members of the family. One did not give up a claim by not living on the land, and this claim passed to one's children who could choose whether they wished to reside on the family land ... (Olwig 1977:241; cf. 1977:248, 1981a:69).

The evidence that among Afro-Caribbean peasantries generally family land does not, despite non-use by some co-heirs, become the exclusive property of resident kin, reinforces the conclusion that such land is held through unrestricted descent and is thus regarded as unlimited in its long-term dimension. Thus non-residence on, and migration from family land as referred to by Solien (1959) and Otterbein (1964), may now be seen in their proper context. They are 'pragmatic' or *non-exclusive* modes of effecting the use of the resources of an unrestricted corporation (see Fox, 1967:156), rather than an exclusive mechanism restricting the corporation itself.

Voluntary non-use and under-production.
The above conclusion is further underlined by the pattern of 'under-production' associated with family land throughout the region. For this pattern results primarily from the retention of multiple inalienable claims by absentees and their descendants. Thus Edith Clarke (1966:66) remarks on 'the impracticability of the system [of family land] in the modern social evolution of Jamaica' with respect to land use, but weighs this against the symbolic value of family land:

From the aspect of land use it is inevitably wasteful and incompetent. A good deal of family land is under-used, occupied by the old people, who are physically unable to develop it. Other multiple owned holdings are completely unproductive save for the food trees planted by the ancestors ... Misuse of land in the form of exhaustion or neglect, under-use because of lack of capital, or multiple ownership restricting development, are all practical results which have to be weighed against the strong sentiment and the high values attached to the system. (Clarke, 1966:66–67).

Comitas' (1962:152) observations on family land in Jamaican fishing villages bears out Clarke's conclusions on this 'uneconomic' use of family land:

With families scattered throughout Jamaica and abroad, the claims of individual members are difficult to anticipate by the remaining guardians of the land. This has meant a reluctance on the part of those who have remained on the land to put it into really productive agricultural use. Consequently, as Clarke (1957:44) puts it, 'family land, in the process of transmission and use has, in the main, long ceased to have agricultural value, apart from the economic trees with which it is usually well stocked'.

Edwards (1961:112) also notes the 'reluctance to plant long term crops' on Jamaican family land, due to multiple ownership of such land. While Palmer (1968:42–4) concludes that Jamaican customary tenure 'is a serious obstacle to increased productivity in the agricultural sector'.

Rubenstein (1975:164) identifies a similar pattern of under-production associated with family land in Texier, St Vincent, and elucidates this pattern of land use by referring to similar factors to those outlined for Jamaica:

> The sixty-seven holdings classified as family land account for over one-third of valley acreage. Only sixty percent of these holdings undergo any cultivation despite the fact that nearly all of them have at least one claimant resident in the village. One factor relevant to the under-cultivation of family land has already been mentioned: land is often held by those who have neither the skill nor the interest in working it. But this does not account for the fact that the *same proportion* of holdings in both the inherited and family categories are not utilized despite the residence in the village of less than seventy percent of those owning inherited land. The answer seems to lie in the fact that there is a general reluctance to cultivate land in which the claim is not well defined. For example, the right of various heirs to distinct and separate portions of family holdings is rarely clear except on a year-to-year basis.

Rubenstein's analysis of 'under-production' in St Vincent is even more significant in that it is intended to elucidate the *general* pattern of under-production for the Leeward and Windward Islands (1975:188). This wider pattern is also noted by the Tripartite Economic Survey of the Eastern Caribbean (Sargent, 1967:188), which identifies family land tenure as 'A major obstacle in the way of expanding agricultural production'.

Thus for the Windward Island of St Lucia, Momsen (1972:104) notes that family land tenure 'is a barrier to the adoption of agricultural innovation even where such a short-term crop as vegetables is concerned'. While a team of experts visiting St Lucia (1951:21) reports that in this island, 'Members of the family are more conscious of their rights to reap crops from the land than of their obligations to plant them and this is undoubtedly one of the main reasons for what may be described as completely inefficient land use.' Mathurin (1967:1,2,5), who also identifies St Lucian family land as 'an unfavourable system of land tenure' which is 'stifling agricultural development', elucidates the reasons behind this situation, which closely resembles those for the Jamaican and Vincentian cases:

> There is an understandable reluctance on the part of the peasantry to undertake long term improvement projects and to grow permanent and sometimes even short term crops because of the possibility of having these crops harvested by other family members who appear entitled to do so under the existing system of tenure.

Similarly Finkel (1971:299) describes St Lucian family land as 'a strong deterrent to agricultural development since the more ambitious and enterprising farmers feel it is not worthwhile planting crops' in this situation of 'communal land rights', where all may harvest from the land.

Reference has already been made to the general pattern of under-production in Guyanese Negro villages, in contrast to the Indian villages where all available land is cultivated. This contrast can undoubtedly be attributed to the presence of the institution of family land, and the associated retention of inalienable rights by absentees, among the Afro-Guyanese; and the absence of the institution among Guyana's East Indian population (R.T. Smith, 1964:311, 316; 1971:243–66; cf. Despres, 1970).

Lowenthal's (1972:104) comments on under-production on family land among Afro-Caribbean peasants generally, sums up the regional situation:

> Local authorities condemn 'family land' tenure as un-economic, wasteful, a prime cause of soil exhaustion and erosion, an obstacle to agricultural modernization; but to outlaw it would disrupt kinship ties, multiply litigation beyond court capacities, and jeopardize untold small-holdings. (cf. Lowenthal 1961:5).

Thus undoubtedly the Caribbean pattern of under-production on family land can be directly related to the primarily symbolic role of such land throughout the region; and to its associated unrestricted descent system, which is reinforced through voluntary non-use and the retention of inalienable land rights.

Crab antics.

The second strategy associated with family land as a scarce economic resource among living kinsmen is 'crab antics': manoeuvring for advantage within the kinship corporation. This strategy is seen by the peasantries throughout the region as contravening the ethos of family land. Although the term 'crab antics' was coined by Wilson (1973) in relation to Providencia, an earlier account of this strategy and its negative sanctions can be found in Edith Clarke's (1953, 1966) work on Jamaican family land. There Clarke developed one of the earliest challenges to the 'functionalist' model in anthropology (see e.g. Radcliffe-Brown, 1952) by focusing on the elements of conflict and individual self-interest, as well as cohesion and solidarity, in small-scale communities. Her analysis was cast in the mould of two conflicting systems of land tenure among the Jamaican peasantry: the customary system of family land, and the legal system of individual freehold. In addition to elucidating the symbolic essence of the former, Clarke also demonstrates how self-interested individuals may draw on the legal code to challenge and undermine the customary system. She makes clear, however, that such attacks on the customary system go entirely against the ethos of family land (E. Clarke, 1953:87; 1966:41). References to attempts to exclude kin in the Jamaican case by Solien (1959) and Otterbein (1964) would therefore be consistent with these attempts to draw on the legal system to undermine the customary one, rather than being a valid interpretation of the customary system itself.

Similar self-interested behaviour on the part of individuals in contravention of the ethos of family land forms a major theme in Wilson's later study of *Crab Antics* (1973):

> As noted above, inheritance is an elementary part of the social process where competitive sentiments are mustered; where ideals must sometimes give way before circumstance. People quarrel and spend a lot of time and effort manoeuvring for an advantageous position for themselves, especially in respect of land. This sort of behavior is a sufficiently conscious aspect of reality that it has a special name: *crab antics*...

> Crab antics is behavior that resembles that of a number of crabs who, having been placed in a barrel, all try to climb out. But as one nears the top, the one below pulls him down in his own effort to climb. Only a particularly strong crab ever climbs out — the rest, in the long run, remain in the same place.

Thus in spite of the ideal or even the reality of equal inheritance, the way is always open for some to acquire more land than others. This in turn inspires a reaction on the part of those others to stop them. It might be argued that if, as I have maintained above, land is a primary basis of social identity and of belonging to the island, then owning more of the island is indicative of a greater sense of belonging and ownership — a sign of wealth, power, status and prestige . . . (Wilson, 1973:57-8).

'Crab antics', continues Wilson (1973:58), 'manifest themselves in two attitudes towards land that islanders suggest are ingrained: covetousness and contentiousness'. These Providencian attitudes associated with crab antics underline the negative sanctioning of such behaviour, and highlight the fact that crab antics are regarded as a travesty of the ethos of family land.

While Clarke and Wilson provide the fullest accounts of crab antics associated with family land, echoes of this strategy occur in other sources. Thus Larose (1975:492,493), reporting that 'Misfortune in Léogane [Haiti] is often attributed to a weakening of family solidarity', further remarks that:

> The disease [of a sick family member] may be interpreted as the result of deliberate misbehaviour on the part of some ambitious relatives who disregard family solidarity to promote their own interests at the expense of their kin . . . A large number of sorcery accusations are thus contained within the family and relate to the ways preponderance may be achieved mainly through control of the land by a few members of the family.

Thus in Haiti, too, crab antics exist and are negatively sanctioned. Underwood's (1964) account of land and its manipulation among the Haitian peasantry provides a more detailed account of such crab antics.

In Texier, St Vincent, 'one or more heirs will frequently attempt to take control of the entire property excluding the other claimants in the process' (Rubenstein, 1975:164); a factor which contributes to under-production on family land. For attempts to 'extend or improve cultivation on family land' might be interpreted as signs of such crab antics, and 'may be resented or even resisted by one or more of the other claimants' (Rubenstein, 1975:164).

In Barbados, Greenfield (1960:167-8, cf. 173-4) likewise provides evidence of crab antics:

Two conflicting sets of attitudes were held by the villagers with respect to land tenure. The first, and traditional belief, is that land should be left to and shared by all children without reference to birth order and legitimacy. The peasants say that 'the old people' bequeathed their land in this way; and since they were wise, their example should be followed. This ideal however, is often neglected in practice. The modern tendency toward individual ownership and freedom to alienate the land — which at times leaves some members of the family landless — is in conflict with the older theory and often produces disharmony, and at times, open hostility among kin. The villagers rationalize their present behavior by saying 'if people lived lovin', as they were assumed to have done in the 'old'n days' they all could share. But since others are selfish, they too must be selfish.

Less a case of 'modern' versus 'traditional' systems perhaps, as Greenfield suggests; and more a case of simple crab antics, with resort being made to the legal system of individual freehold in an attempt to undermine the customary system of family land. Olwig (1977:351) also identifies similar crab antics in St John, reporting that, in the 1970s, 'In some cases, disagreements over family land had led to court cases between relatives'; and that 'land disputes have caused cleavages to develop within families'.

The attitudes of Afro-Caribbean peasantries to land in general, then, are as complex and paradoxical as those found in Martha Brae. They perceive land as scarce in relation to the wider agrarian structure of the Caribbean societies in which they are located, and have responded throughout the region by creating and perpetuating the institution of family land. *Within* the kinship corporations associated with such land, however, land is regarded as unlimited in its primarily long-term symbolic role. Co-existing with this perception of family land, and thus elaborating their paradoxical view of land, is the awareness that family land is scarce as a short-term economic asset among living kin. Associated with this awareness are the opposed strategies of voluntary non-use and crab antics. The former reinforces the perception of family land as unlimited in its long-term symbolic role. The latter represents attempts to undermine the essential ethos of customary freehold, by trying to establish restriction in the descent system. The theoretical and practical implications of identifying this paradox on a regional scale are outlined in the concluding discussion.

Conclusion

This chapter has served to identify and explore a paradox in Caribbean attitudes to land. The analysis began by outlining the paradox in the Jamaican village of Martha Brae, and then extending the discussion to Afro-Caribbean peasantries in general. Thus through its methodology, the chapter has sought to contribute not only to the ethnography of a Jamaican village, but also to the study of the Caribbean region. This regional perspective has long been overlooked for, as Mintz (1974c:xii) observes, few Caribbeanists have attempted to generalize beyond a specific territory:

> It is a typically Caribbean fact that few students of the region even attempt to deal with more than one island, or one group of islands (such as the French overseas territories or the Dutch Antilles) or, at best, one language-group (such as Puerto Rico, Santo Domingo and Cuba). Somewhat depressingly, each Caribbean-born scholar tends to concern himself almost exclusively with the island of his birth, thus fulfilling that fondest of European imperialist hopes for the region: that no Caribbean person ever develop a pan-Caribbean outlook ...

This chapter, by contrast, has systematically sought to generalize from a Jamaican case study to the wider Caribbean (cf. Besson 1979, 1984a); drawing together material from the British, French, Dutch, and former Danish territories in order to develop this regional perspective.

In addition, by focusing on *Afro*-Caribbean attitudes to land, manifested especially through the institution of family freehold, the chapter highlights the important variation between the non-Hispanic and Hispanic Caribbean. For, due to the earlier burgeoning of the large-scale plantation in the former variant (Mintz, 1971:37), these countries received larger importations of African slaves (Cross, 1979:103–110). Thus it is within these territories that Afro-Caribbean peasantries have emerged in their sharpest contours (Mintz, 1959, 1971:28–31; 1979); and here that the institution of family land is most pronounced. The contrasting attitudes to land typifying Afro- and Indo-Caribbean populations (R.T. Smith, 1964:311,316; Despres, 1970:280–82) point, in turn, to further regional complexities, not just in the non-Hispanic variant but also within some of its component territories.[11] Thus not only has a pan-Caribbean perspective been developed in this essay, but it has been done while still acknowledging the rich variety of socio-cultural themes existing in the region.

Within these wider contexts, the analysis has encountered and elucidated two controversial regional issues: the explanation of the institution of family land, and the nature of Afro-Caribbean kinship. In the former case, the exploration of the paradox establishes a regional explanation for the existence of family land. This pan-Caribbean perspective replaces conventional theories that are not only *ad hoc*, but conflicting. It also substitutes a structural theory, related to Caribbean agrarian relations, for explanations based on the outmoded concept of cultural survivals (cf. Besson, 1984a). Regarding the nature of Afro-Caribbean kinship, the essay demonstrates the presence of corporate features in the kinship system, namely, the descent corporations associated with family land. It also unravels the 'mysteries' of these landholding groups, elucidating their unrestricted descent system and uncovering, in the Caribbean region, a kinship system once thought inoperable and even now considered rare (cf. Besson, 1979). The clarification of these two interrelated issues in turn highlights Caribbean peasant land tenure and kinship systems as cultural creations in the face of European capitalism (cf. Besson, 1974; R.T. Smith, 1978); and thus extends the evidence for interpreting the region's peasantries as a mode of resistant response to the plantation system and imposed colonial cultures (Mintz, 1974a:132–3; cf. Besson, 1979, 1984a, 1984b).

Finally, the analysis has practical implications for the region's agricultural development, for it identifies the complex reasons behind the so-called inefficient land use practised by the peasantries. These lie in both the history and structure of Caribbean agrarian relations, and in the creative strategies constructed by the peasantries to deal with the constraints of these relations. Thus it is not peasant land use *per se* which is 'stifling agricultural production' (Mathurin, 1967:2), as conventional developers suggest. The 'obstacle to modernization' (Lowenthal, 1972:104) is the agrarian structure, with its inequitable land distribution, persistence of plantation agriculture, and associated export mentality (cf. Beckford, 1972, 1975; Cross, 1979a:34). This essay, therefore, reinforces the strong case now being built in defence of the region's peasantries (Beckford, 1975:86; Mintz, 1983, 1984); a case which also establishes their potential for Caribbean development. The analysis thus highlights the need for agrarian reform on a regional scale (cf. Cross 1979b:xvi),[12] accompanied by agricultural diversification and the promotion of peasant agriculture. It also indicates the necessity for such reform to take account of the cultural values of the peasantries themselves, which focus for historical reasons on the significance of freehold land.

Notes

1   An earlier draft of this essay was prepared for the Social Anthropology Discussion Group, Department of Sociology, University of Aberdeen, May 1983. I wish to thank all those who commented on the draft, especially my colleagues Drs Charles Jędrej, Nicholas Bradford and Juliet du Boulay. Dr du Boulay's own work, (1974, 1980) identifying a similar paradox among the Greek peasantry, has provided strong support for the analysis undertaken in the present essay. I also thank Drs Janet Momsen and Eric Hanley who subsequently offered helpful comments on the draft.

2   The Martha Brae case is explored more fully in a separate publication (Besson, 1986, forthcoming). An early draft of the Martha Brae case study was prepared for the symposium on 'Afro-Caribbean Attitudes to Land' at the 44th International Congress of the Americanists, University of Manchester, September 1982. Fieldwork in Martha Brae was conducted during the period 1968–1985. It was funded in part by the Carnegie Trust for the Universities of Scotland, and the University of Aberdeen Fund for Travelling Allowances. I wish to thank these bodies for their financial assistance.

3   Such crab antics are not, however, the only mode of interplay between the legal and customary systems in Martha Brae. At least three other variants occur. Firstly, some elements of the legal system are imposed by law on customary tenure, such as the requirement to pay land tax. Secondly, individuals sometimes draw on the legal system to reinforce customary tenure; while, thirdly, some aspects of the legal system indirectly reinforce the customary institution of family land. Legal and customary systems in Martha Brae are therefore totally distinct only at the cultural level. The Martha Brae ethnography therefore does not support the plural society thesis of Caribbean land tenure (e.g. M.G. Smith 1965b:221–61; Mason 1970:291), nor the conclusion that the only mode of interplay between legal and customary systems of Caribbean land tenure occurs in terms of conflict (see e.g. E. Clarke, 1953:86–7,116; Greenfield, 1960:167–8). For detailed discussion of these points see Besson, 1974, II:1–113; cf. Besson, 1984a:76, notes 7 and 9. This aspect of the Martha Brae ethnography is further explored in Besson, 1986 (forthcoming).

4   For fuller documentation of the occurrence of family land throughout the Caribbean region see Besson, 1984a:77–78, note 16.

5   This parallel was suggested to me by C.G. Clarke (personal communication, 1982) on the basis of his work on Barbuda (Lowenthal and Clarke, 1977, 1979, 1980). In Chapter 5 of this book Riva Berleant-Schiller rejects this interpretation, which I first put forward in an earlier essay (Besson,1984a:60,78 note 16). She argues that, despite several similarities between Barbudan common tenure and Caribbean family land, the differences outweigh the similarities and are 'qualitative and profound'. This divergence, she concludes, is due to Barbuda's peculiar ecology, history, proprietorship and slave community. However a reconsideration of the Barbudan case, along with new evidence from Nevis and the Bahamas (see Momsen, Craton, Chapters 2 and 4), leads me to reassert and extend the hypothesis linking Barbudan common tenure and Caribbean family land. For the above three cases all have a

mix of customary tenures or attitudes to land involving features of both family land and commonage, and in each case this has been effective in resisting Eurocentric models of development (cf. Besson and Momsen, Introduction). This suggests that, in a regional context, family land and commonage are variants on a theme. Both are customary tenures created in resistance to Caribbean agrarian relations and their legal codes. This resistant response has occurred at the margins of plantation society (Craton, Berleant-Schiller, Chapters 4 and 5) as well as at its core (Besson, Momsen, Rubenstein, Chapters 1–3).

In support of this hypothesis I offer a brief complementary perspective on the Barbudan case in addition to that presented in Berleant-Schiller's essay. I suggest that Barbuda's unusual proprietorship, slave community and history may be seen as variations on the regional theme of colonial domination and resistance, with especially strong parallels in the Bahamian case (cf. Lowenthal and Clarke, 1977; Craton, 1978). For, despite the absence of plantations due to its marginal ecology, Barbuda was not totally divorced from the regional plantation scene. The Codringtons, Barbuda's proprietors from 1680–1870, had extensive plantation holdings in Barbados and Antigua and 'used Barbuda as an annex to their [Antiguan] sugar estates' (Lowenthal and Clarke, 1977:510; 1979:143). Although Christopher Bethel Codrington's hopes that Barbuda might become a nursery for Negroes for his Antiguan plantations did not materialise, there were some labour transfers from Barbuda to Antigua (Lowenthal and Clarke, 1977). The Barbudan slaves were property like other slaves, and were aware of the Antiguan threat for 'they refused to be sent away' and 'died when removed by force to Codrington estates in Antigua' (Berleant-Schiller, Chapter 5; cf. Craton, Chapter 4). Their proto-peasant slave community was thus a variation on a regional theme (cf. Lowenthal and Clarke, 1979:145), for proto-peasantries emerged throughout the Caribbean in adaptive resistance to the slave regime (Mintz, 1974a:151–2; Olwig, 1981a, 1981b). Even in their unusual isolation the Barbudan proto-peasants were paralleled by those of Exuma (Lowenthal and Clarke, 1977; Craton,1978 and Chapter 4) and by maroon communities (Price, 1973; Mintz, 1974a:152–4). Indeed, the central theme of Barbudan history emerges as resistance to attempted domination (see Lowenthal and Clarke, 1977; Berleant-Schiller, 1978).

Within this alternative perspective the differences of origin, form and function between the Barbudan commons and Caribbean family land (Berleant-Schiller, Chapter 5) appear less 'qualitative and profound'. Thus despite its formal post-emancipation origin family land, like the commons, is rooted in a proto-peasant past. For the post-emancipation peasantries are mainly of proto-peasant origin, and family land perpetuates the proto-peasant attachment to yard, ancestral graves and provision ground (see Mintz, 1974a:152, 209–9, 237; cf. Paget, 1964:40; Farley, 1964:52). The interrelationship between proto-peasants, family land and commonage is further borne out by the Exumian case (Craton, Chapter 4). Regarding differences of form, while Codrington Village is 'not a [cognatic] descent group ... [but] a set of overlapping kindreds' (Berleant-Schiller, Chapter 5), it is 'essentially one consanguineous community' reinforced by isolation (Lowenthal and Clarke, 1977:515) and this is reflected in its common lands (Lowenthal and Clarke,

1979:147–8). Also, as the community is 'composed of a few interrelated families' (ibid:147) and since house and yard may be inherited through cognatic descent (Berleant-Schiller, 1977:264), the Barbudans may have overlapping cognatic descent groups as well as overlapping kindreds. In addition, contrary to Berleant-Schiller's argument, the Exumian case (Craton, Chapter 4) demonstrates that the principles of family land can be applied to an extensive system of land use. For on the Rolle estates in Exuma, over 4,000 kin defined by cognatic descent have rights to 5,000 acres of commonage. The functional differences between the commons and family land identified by Berleant-Schiller may also be qualified. Like the commons, family land may bolster island equality as demonstrated in Providencia (Wilson, 1973); and like family land, the commons may engender conflict as shown by changing attitudes to Barbudan land (Berleant-Schiller, Chapter 5). Finally, while family land is 'under-productive' from a capitalist perspective, 'voluntary non-use' may enable its efficient exploitation, like the commons, within the framework of peasant values (cf. Rubenstein, McKay, Chapters 3 and 6). Indeed, Barbudan common tenure, like family land, has also been condemned as 'under-productive' from a capitalist perspective (see Berleant-Schiller, 1978).

6   Such kindreds consist of circles of relatives, traced through both parents, surrounding each individual. A kindred dissolves on the death of the focal individual.

7   In contrast to the kindred, such corporations share descent, traced through both sexes, from a common ancestor. They persist in perpetuity despite the death of the focal ancestor.

8   Unrestricted descent systems exist in relation to a 'specific situation' only: that is, in relation to either a specific resource such as land, or a specific occasion such as a kinship gathering (Firth, 1963:25–6; Fox, 1967:150–52). Their overlapping kin groups of ever-increasing size contrast with the discrete, restricted, residential, multi-purpose groups which are regarded as the building blocks of kin-based societies. At present the few unrestricted systems which have been recognized are mainly in the Pacific region. See Besson (1979) for a fuller discussion of these points.

9   Thus in the Caribbean case the unrestricted descent system operates in relation to a 'specific resource' only, i.e. family land. (See note 8 above).

10   I am grateful to Dr Ank Klomp of the University of Utrecht for providing an English summary of Henriquez' article (personal communication, 1978).

11   Guyana and Trinidad have the largest East Indian populations in the Caribbean. While this essay has focused on the contrast in the Guyanese case, Freilich (1960) also identifies a variation between Afro- and Indo-Caribbean attitudes to land in a Trinidadian village. However, his interpretation differs from R.T. Smith's on Guyana. Freilich contrasts the 'future time orientation' of East Indians with the 'present time orientation' of the Creoles, and applies this to material on landholding. He demonstrates that the Creoles have lost land to East Indians and argues that this is due to these contrasting perspectives, predicting that this process will continue until the Creoles are no longer peasant farmers. Thus his analysis implies that Trinidadian Negro peasants have little

regard for land. However, Freilich's own material elsewhere (Freilich & Coser, 1972:4) suggests that Afro-Trinidadians in fact place a strong symbolic value on freehold land, which lends support to Smith's interpretation of the Guyanese case. (cf. Rubenstein, 1975:165–66) for a critique of the 'present-time orientation' as applied to Afro-Vincentian peasants in the context of land tenure; and see Hanley in this volume (Chapter 8) for a further discussion of Afro- and Indo-Guyanese attitudes to land).

12 The obvious exception to this generalization is Cuba, which has embarked on extensive agrarian reform (Pollitt, 1982). However, even here plantation agriculture dominates the scene (ibid; Beckford 1972:5, note 2). Furthermore, Pollitt's analysis (1982:21–2) highlights the potential of the Cuban peasantry in comparison with the large-scale state farms.

References

Beckford, George L. 1972. *Persistent poverty: underdevelopment in plantation economies of the third world.* London: Oxford University Press.

1975. Caribbean rural economy. In G.L. Beckford (ed.). *Caribbean economy,* Kingston, Jamaica, Institute of Social and Economic Research, University of the West Indies.

Berleant-Schiller, Riva. 1977. Production and division of labor in a West Indian peasant community. *American Ethnologist,* 4(2):253–72.

1978. The failure of agricultural development in post-emancipation Barbuda: a study of social and economic continuity in a West Indian community. *Boletin de Estudios Latinoamericanos y del Caribe,* 25:21–36.

Besson, Jean. 1974. *Land tenure and kinship in a Jamaican village.* 2 vols. Ph.D. dissertation. University of Edinburgh.

1979. Symbolic aspects of land in the Caribbean: the tenure and transmission of land rights among Caribbean peasantries. In Cross, Malcolm and Marks, Arnaud (eds.). *Peasants, plantations and rural communities in the Caribbean.* Guildford, University of Surrey, and Leiden, Royal Institute of Linguistics and Anthropology.

1984a. Family land and Caribbean society: toward an ethnography of Afro-Caribbean peasantries. In Thomas-Hope, Elizabeth M. (ed.). *Perspectives on Caribbean regional identity.* Liverpool, Liverpool University Press.

1984b. Land tenure in the free villages of Trelawny, Jamaica: a case study in the Caribbean peasant response to emancipation. *Slavery & Abolition,* 5(1):3–23.

1986. Agrarian relations and perceptions of land in a Jamaican peasant village. In Brierley, John and Rubenstein, Hymie (eds.). *Small farming and peasant resources in the Caribbean.* MS. Forthcoming.

Brana-Shute, Gary. 1979. *On the corner: male social life in a Paramaribo creole neighborhood.* Assen, Van Gorcum.

Clarke, Edith. 1953. Land tenure and the family in four communities in Jamaica. *Social and Economic Studies,* 1(4):81–118.

(1957) 1966. *My mother who fathered me: a study of the family in three selected communities in Jamaica.* (2nd ed.). London, Allen and Unwin.

42   Land and Development in the Caribbean

Comitas, Lambros. 1962. *Fishermen and co-operation in rural Jamaica.* Ph.D. dissertation. Columbia University.

Craton, Michael. 1978. Hobbesian or Panglossian? The two extremes of slave conditions in the British Caribbean, 1783 to 1834. *William & Mary Quarterly*, Third Series, XXXV(2):324–56.

Cross, Malcolm. 1979a. *Urbanization and urban growth in the Caribbean: an essay on social change in dependent societies.* Cambridge, Cambridge University Press.

1979b. Introduction. In Cross, Malcolm and Marks, Arnaud (eds.). *Peasants, plantations and rural communities in the Caribbean.* Guildford, University of Surrey, and Leiden, Royal Institute of Linguistics and Anthropology.

Despres, Leo A. 1970. Differential adaptations and micro-cultural evolution in Guyana. In Whitten, Norman E. and Szwed, John F. (eds.). *Afro-American anthropology.* New York, Free Press.

Davenport, William. 1961. The family system of Jamaica. *Social and Economic Studies* 10(4):420–54.

Du Boulay, Juliet. 1974. *Portrait of a Greek mountain village.* Oxford, Oxford University Press.

1980. Limited and unlimited good: two ways of thinking about the Greek peasantry. (Paper presented to the Greek Study Group, Centre for European Studies, Harvard University).

Edwards, David. 1961. *An economic study of small farming in Jamaica.* Kingston, Jamaica, Institute of Social and Economic Research, University of the West Indies.

Farley, Rawle. 1964. The rise of village settlements in British Guiana. *Caribbean Quarterly*, 10 (1):52–61.

Finkel, Herman J. 1971. Patterns of land tenure in the Leeward and Windward Islands. In Horowitz, Michael M. (ed.). *Peoples and cultures of the Caribbean: an anthropological reader.* Garden City, N.Y., Natural History Press.

Firth, Raymond. 1963. Bilateral descent groups: an operational viewpoint. In Schapera, Isaac (ed.). *Studies in kinship and marriage.* London, Royal Anthropological Institute.

Floyd, Barry. 1979. *Jamaica: an island microcosm.* London, Macmillan.

Fortes, Meyer. 1970. *Kinship and the social order.* London, Routledge and Kegan Paul.

Fox, Robin. 1967. *Kinship and marriage.* Harmondsworth, Middlesex, Penguin Books.

Freilich, Morris. 1960. Cultural models and land holdings. *Anthropological Quarterly* 33(4):183–97.

Freilich, Morris and Coser, Lewis A. 1972. Structured imbalances of gratification: the case of the Caribbean mating system. *British Journal of Sociology*, 23(1):1–19.

Goodenough, Ward H. 1970. *Description and comparison in cultural anthropology.* Cambridge, Cambridge University Press.

Greenfield, Sidney M. 1960. Land tenure and transmission in rural Barbados. *Anthropological Quarterly*, 33(4):165–76.

Greenwood, R. and Hamber, S. 1980. *Emancipation to emigration.* London, Macmillan.

Hanson, F. Allan. 1971. Nonexclusive cognatic descent systems: a Polynesian example. In Howard, Alan (ed.). *Polynesia: readings on a culture area.* Scranton, Chandler.

Henriquez, E.C. 1969. Familiegronden (tera di famia) en oude fideicommissen (filocommis) op het eiland Curaçao. In Quint, S. Gonda and En Zoon, D. Brouwer (eds.). *Honderd jaar codificatie in de Nederlandse Antillen.* Arnhem, Het Huis de Crabbe.

Horowitz, Michael M. 1967. *Morne-Paysan: peasant village in Martinique.* New York, Holt, Rinehart and Winston.

Knox, A.J.G. 1977. Opportunities and opposition: the rise of Jamaica's black peasantry and the nature of planter resistance. *Canadian Review of Sociology and Anthropology,* 14(4):381–95.

Kuper, Adam. 1976. *Changing Jamaica.* London, Routledge and Kegan Paul.

Larose, Serge. 1975. The Haitian *lakou*; land, family and ritual. In Marks, Arnaud F. and Romer, Rene A. (eds.). *Family and kinship in Middle America and the Caribbean.* Curacao, Institute of Higher Studies in Curaçao, and Leiden, Royal Institute of Linguistics and Anthropology.

Leach, E.R. 1960. The Sinhalese of the dry zone of northern Ceylon. In Murdock, George Peter (ed.). *Social structure in southeast Asia.* Chicago, Quadrangle Books.

Lowenthal, David. 1961. Caribbean views of Caribbean land. *The Canadian Geographer,* 5(2):1–9.

1972. *West Indian societies.* London, Oxford University Press.

Lowenthal, David and Clarke, Colin G. 1977. Slave-breeding in Barbuda: the past of a negro myth. In Rubin, Vera and Tuden, Arthur (eds.). *Comparative perspectives on slavery in New World plantation societies.* New York, The New York Academy of Sciences.

1979. Common lands, common aims: the distinctive Barbudan community. In Cross, Malcolm and Marks, Arnaud (eds.). *Peasants, plantations and rural communities in the Caribbean.* Guildford, University of Surrey, and Leiden, Royal Institute of Linguistics and Anthropology.

1980. Island orphans: Barbuda and the rest. *Journal of Commonwealth and Comparative Politics,* XVIII(3):293–307.

Macdonald, John Stuart and Macdonald, Leatrice. 1978. The black family in the Americas: a review of the literature. *Sage Race Relations Abstracts,* 3(1):1–42.

Marks, A.F. 1976. *Male and female and the Afro-Curacaoan household.* The Hague, Martinus Nijhoff.

Marshall, W.K. and Beckford, G.L. 1972. Peasant movements and agrarian problems in the West Indies. *Caribbean Quarterly,* 18(1):31–58.

Mason, Philip. 1970. *Patterns of dominance.* London, Oxford University Press.

Mathurin, D.C. Emerson. 1967. An unfavourable system of land tenure: the case of St Lucia. (Paper read at the Second West Indian Agricultural Economics Conference, St Augustine, Trinidad, April, 1967).

Mintz, Sidney W. 1959. Labor and sugar in Puerto Rico and Jamaica, 1800–1850. *Comparative Studies in Society and History,* 1(3):273–81.

1971. The Caribbean as a socio-cultural area. In Horowitz, Michael M. (ed.). *Peoples and cultures of the Caribbean: an anthropological reader.* Garden City, N.Y., Natural History Press.

1974a. *Caribbean transformations.* Chicago, Aldine.

1974b. The Caribbean region. In Mintz, Sidney W. (ed.). *Slavery, colonialism and racism*. New York, Norton.

1974c. Foreword. In Hagelberg, G.B. *The Caribbean sugar industries: constraints and opportunities*. New Haven, Yale University Press.

1979. Slavery and the rise of peasantries. *Historical Reflections*, 6:213–42;

1983. Reflections on Caribbean peasantries. *Niewe West Indische Gids*, 57(1/2):1–17.

1984. *From plantations to peasantries in the Caribbean*. Washington, D.C., The Wilson Centre.

Mintz, Sidney M. and Price, Richard. 1976. *An anthropological approach to the Afro-American past: a Caribbean perspective*. Philadelphia, Institute for the Study of Human Issues.

Momsen, Janet D. 1972. Land tenure as a barrier to agricultural innovation: the case of St Lucia. *Proceedings of the Seventh West Indian Agricultural Economics Conference*, 103–9. Grand Anse, Grenada.

O'Loughlin, Carleen. 1968. *Economic and political change in the Leeward and Windward Islands*. New Haven, Yale University Press.

Olwig, Karen Fog P. 1977. *Households, exchange and social reproduction: the development of a Caribbean society*. Ph.D. dissertation. University of Minnesota.

1981a. Women, 'matrifocality' and systems of exchange: an ethnohistorical study of the Afro-American family on St. John, Danish West Indies. *Ethnohistory*, 28(1):59–78.

1981b. Finding a place for the slave family: historical anthropological perspectives. *Folk*, 23:345–58.

Otterbein, Keith F. 1964. A comparison of the land tenure systems of the Bahamas, Jamaica and Barbados: the implications it has for the study of social systems shifting from bilateral to ambilineal descent. *International Archives of Ethnography*, 50(1):31–42.

Paget, Hugh. 1964. The free village system in Jamaica. *Caribbean Quarterly*, 10(1):38–51.

Palmer, Ransford W. 1968. *The Jamaican economy*. London, Frederick A. Praeger.

Philpott, Stuart B. 1973. *West Indian migration: the Montserrat case*. London, Athlone Press.

Pollitt, Brian H. 1982. The transition to socialist agriculture in Cuba: some salient features. In *Agriculture, the peasantry and socialist development*. Sussex, Institute of Development Studies Bulletin 13(4):12–22.

Price, Richard. 1967. *Studies of Caribbean family organization: problems and prospects*. (MS. Department of Anthropology, the Johns Hopkins University).

(ed.). 1973. *Maroon societies: rebel slave communities in the Americas*. Garden City, N.Y., Anchor Books.

Radcliffe-Brown, A.R. 1950. Introduction. In Radcliffe-Brown, A.R. and Forde, Daryll (eds.). *African systems of kinship and marriage*. London, Oxford University Press.

1952. *Structure and function in primitive society*. London, Cohen & West.

Robotham, Don. 1977. Agrarian relations in Jamaica. In Stone, Carl and Brown, Aggrey (eds.). *Essays on power and change in Jamaica*. Kingston, Jamaica, Jamaica Publishing House.

Rodman, Hyman. 1971. *Lower-class families: the culture of poverty in negro Trinidad*. London, Oxford University Press.

Rubenstein, Hymie. 1975. The utilization of arable land in an eastern Caribbean valley. *Canadian Journal of Sociology*, 1(2):157–67.

Sargent, J.R. 1967. *Report of the tripartite economic survey of the Eastern Caribbean*. London, H.M.S.O.

Smith, M.G. 1956. The transformation of land rights by transmission in Carriacou, *Social and Economic Studies*, 5(2):103–38.

1960. The African heritage in the Caribbean. In Rubin, Vera (ed.). *Caribbean studies: a symposium*. (2nd ed.) Seattle, University of Washington Press.

1965a. *Stratification in Grenada*. Berkeley, University of California Press.

1965b. *The plural society in the British West Indies*. Berkeley, University of California Press.

Smith, Raymond T. 1955. Land tenure in three negro villages in British Guiana. *Social and Economic Studies*, 4(1):64–82.

1964. Ethnic difference and peasant economy in British Guiana. In Firth, Raymond and Yamey, B.S. (eds.). *Capital, saving and credit in peasant societies*. London, George Allen and Unwin.

1978. The family and the modern world system: some observations from the Caribbean. *Journal of Family History* 3(4):337–60.

Solien, Nancie L. 1959. The nonunilineal descent group in the Caribbean and Central America. *American Anthropologist*, 61(4):578–83.

St. Lucia. 1951. *The agricultural development of St Lucia. Report of a team of experts on a visit in March and April, 1951*. Castries.

Underwood, Frances W. 1964. Land and its manipulation among the Haitian peasantry. In Goodenough, Ward H. (ed.). *Explorations in cultural anthropology*. New York, McGraw-Hill.

Verdon, Michel. 1980. Descent: an operational view. *Man*, 15(1):129–50.

Wilson, Peter J. 1973. *Crab antics: the social anthropology of English-speaking negro societies of the Caribbean*. New Haven, Yale University Press.

CHAPTER 2

Land settlement as an imposed solution

Janet Momsen

After Emancipation the ex-slaves had to compete for land with the plantation owners who were long established on the best agricultural lands in the region. For the plantocracy land was wealth but for the former slaves the desire for land transcended economic considerations. The freed slaves sought to acquire plots of land not primarily as a means of production but for security and as tangible evidence of their escape from bondage. As Lowenthal (1961:4) indicates 'it is not surprising that "Freehold" and "freedom" have come to be closely linked in the West Indian mind.' Thus a peasantry developed as a reaction to the plantation system and as a form of resistance to externally imposed styles of life (Mintz, 1983:8).

Two external forces controlled access to land in the post-emancipation West Indies — the plantocracy and the State. For much of the time their attitudes to the peasantry converged and indeed membership of the two bodies overlapped, but there were vital periods of divergence. The metropolitan powers caused the slaves to be freed against the wishes of the plantocracy but did little to encourage the development of a new society. Not until 1897 did a Royal Commission look into the affairs of the British West Indies and declare that 'we do not hesitate to say that no other reform offers the same prospects of permanent, though possibly moderate prosperity, and of political stability to the West Indies as the settlement of the native population as proprietors and cultivators of small portions of land.' (Norman, 1898:117). Thus began the government land settlement schemes which in many parts of the region have been, and continue to be, the main source of land for the peasantry.

This chapter examines how the 'reconstituted' peasantry (Mintz, 1961) reacted to a positive external solution to land hunger. Comparisons are made between different types of land settlements and their relationship to changes in State perceptions of the role of land settlement. Finally, data from land settlements in Nevis is used to examine how, over time, the settlers came to adapt the legal, externally imposed tenure system to their customary attitudes to land.

Peasant agriculture before land settlements

Contemporary peasant agriculture in the Caribbean has its origins, to a large extent, in the cultivation by slaves of provision grounds on the plantations. The Consolidated Slave Acts in the British Territories provided for the right to a 'provision ground', for allowances for farm tools, for the use of food grown around the slave hut or on provision grounds, and also granted the right to the use of every Sunday and every other Saturday for cultivation of the slave's personal food crops. In some cases slaves were allowed to sell their produce and keep the profits from their trading (Mintz, 1964a). This growth of marginal production and internal trading among slave households led to the development of what Mintz (1974) has termed a proto-peasantry which, though largely self-sufficient in food, controlled neither the land nor their time or labour. However, these plantation practices did pave the way for the development of a post-emancipation peasantry for whom subsistence agriculture was a part-time occupation to be combined with plantation labour.

Under the plantation sugar economy based on slavery the Caribbean region had presented a very uniform picture of land use and settlement. The development of an economy based on free labour allowed inter-island variations to appear. The most important variations are usually represented as being functions of the amount of unoccupied land available for settlement by former slaves. In general the plantocracy tried to prevent the former slaves gaining access to land. 'Having successfully opposed the emergence of the white, small-scale farmer in the period of slavery, the sugar industry logically endeavoured to prevent the emergence of the Negro small scale farmer on the abolition of slavery' (Williams, 1954:2). In many islands the planters tried to prevent the former slaves moving off the plantations by providing a small plot of land on condition that the occupant continued to work for the landowner. In this way the provision ground of slavery was perpetuated. In Barbados, the Masters and Servants Act of 1840, under which this 'located labourer' system was introduced, was not abolished until 1937. Tenancy was also important in Barbados and it was said that 'on many estates the labourers are possessors of allotments of land ... from one-quarter to one-half acre for which they pay a weekly rental of a bit and half to four bits' (Parliamentary Papers, XXII, 1842 Enc. 3), but there was no security of tenure and ejections were commonplace (Packer, 1848).

In those islands where unoccupied Crown Lands existed many former slaves became squatters (Parliamentary Papers, XXIX, 1842). In reaction, the planter dominated legislatures adopted strict laws against squatting on Crown Land and a minimum size for Crown Land sales which effectively put this land beyond the reach of most former slaves (Craton, Ch.4). In addition, the practice of requiring costly licences for the sale of small quantities of manufactured sugar and coffee and for the production of charcoal and firewood, was instituted and land taxes were levied which discriminated against owners of smallholdings (Marshall, 1968). Thus the colonial government had imposed a metropolitan solution to slavery by the Emancipation Act but local elites in the West Indies successfully resisted the creation of a new society of farmers.

The types of tenure that developed in the mid-nineteenth century reflected in some measure the relative importance of the two antecedents of the peasant farmer: the slave with the provision ground on the plantation; and the runaway or manumitted slave living outside the plantation economy. In those islands, such as Jamaica and Trinidad, where runaway slaves were numerous before emancipation, the freed slaves tended to squat, or sometimes buy or rent land, in the inaccessible rugged interiors where previously escaped slaves had established settlements. It was said that 'The new interior towns or villages created since the abolition of slavery in this parish, (St Andrew, Jamaica), exhibit little or no organisation or arrangement, they are rather to be considered farm settlements ... The lands thus occupied are generally of an inferior description, but the people buy or rent them readily.' (Parliamentary Papers XXIX, 1842 Enc 5.) Elsewhere in Jamaica the non-conformist missionaries bought land where ex-slaves were able to purchase lots and create free villages around the Church and mission school, as in the parish of Trelawny (Besson, 1984). In other islands, where such a focus did not exist and the planters were heavily in debt, many estate owners reduced their labour costs by offering plantation land to former slaves to be cultivated on a share basis, with the land owner taking one-third to one-half of the crop grown. Share-cropping became an important form of land tenure in Martinique, St Lucia, Tobago and Nevis in particular. Where land was most difficult to obtain, as in the older sugar islands of Barbados, St Kitts and Antigua, the freed slaves were limited to land offered for sale by manumitted slaves and the few white planters who were willing to allow the fragmentation of their plantations.

Economic factors also led to inter-island variation in the post-emancipation land use and settlement pattern. The most important of these factors were land values and the availability of capital in the peasant sector. Land values were at first very closely related to the supply of unoccupied land, being lowest in Jamaica and Trinidad and highest in Barbados, although they could vary greatly within each island. There was a gradual adjustment to the new market situation and the inter-island range decreased, with the increase in prices in Jamaica being most noticeable. In this immediate post-emancipation period capital accumulation in the peasant sector was dependent on profits from the sale of food crops and on the level of wages paid for agricultural labour. Peasant farming in Barbados grew very slowly because few of the freed slaves could afford to pay a minimum price of £80 sterling per acre while wages for agricultural labour were only five to eight pence per day. Yet in Jamaica and Trinidad wages ranged from 2s 6d to 5s sterling per day and land was readily available at £1 per acre. By 1851 there were 3,537 peasant proprietors in Barbados, forming 2.9 per cent of the total population (Colonial Office Papers, C.O. 27,1851). In Jamaica 6.3 per cent of the population were small land owners in 1844 (Colonial Office, C.O. 137,1844) rising rapidly to 11.3 per cent in 1860 and 17.5 per cent in 1890 (Eisner, 1961). These new peasant farmers represented, 'a reaction to the plantation economy, a negative reflex to enslavement, mass production, monocrop dependence, and metropolitan control. Though these peasants often continued to work part-time on plantations for wages to eke out their cash needs, their orientation was in fact antagonistic to the plantation rationale,' (Mintz, 1964:xx).

The introduction of a land settlement policy 1897–1916

As Shephard has pointed out 'It has been shown that the Act of Emancipation conferred on the bulk of the population of the British West Indies for the first time the civil right to acquire land, but that both the British and local Governments discouraged the development of peasant agriculture by placing restrictions on the acquisition of Crown Lands with the object of ensuring an adequate supply of wage-earning labourers for the sugar estates.' (Shephard, 1947:68). The resistance to the growth of a peasantry was most successful in St Vincent and the problems on this island were considered by the 1897 Royal Commission to be so severe that the Commission felt the situation merited a unique solution. In order to give the St Vincent labourer an opportunity to cultivate his own land Sir H. Norman's Commission recommended that the government of the island should purchase small estates and parcel them out in lots to former slaves. In this way the colonial power introduced the concept of land settlement to the West Indies.

In St Vincent the development of peasant agriculture faced even more obstacles than were generally found in the region. Before emancipation free coloured people had not been allowed to own land in St Vincent, consequently, after 1834, there was no coloured land-owning class around which the newly-freed slaves could cluster. Furthermore, Vincentian planters were very loath to sell land to ex-slaves with the result that by 1897 only 1,360 acres were in holdings of less than 20 acres as compared to a small farm area of 7,973 acres in St Lucia and 15,569 in Grenada (Norman, 1898). Crown Land had been offered for sale to peasants between 1890 and 1896 but the land was very steep and far from markets and in 1896 heavy floods swept away most of the cultivation which had been attempted.

In 1898 the Colony of St Vincent was given an Imperial grant of £15,000 and the land settlement scheme was launched, under the provisions of the Land Settlement Ordinance of 1899. The 1897 Royal Commission had suggested that 'the government should acquire fertile lands round the sea coast belonging to holders who were unable to cultivate them or who were unwilling to sell them in small lots at a reasonable price.' (Colonial Report, 77, 1911). Land was available for this scheme because of the collapse of the sugar industry in the early 1890s. The decline of plantation agriculture was exacerbated by the severe hurricane of 1898 which blew down the cocoa trees which had been planted to replace sugar, and by the eruption of the Soufrière Mountain in 1902 which killed some 2,000 people and ruined much fertile land around Georgetown on the east coast and north of Chateaubelair on the west coast (Anderson and Flett, 1902). Camden Park and Rutland Vale estates were used for resettling the evacuees from the volcano and were purchased from the Eruption Fund (Colonial Report, 1911).

During the period 1899 to 1915 a total of 7,327 acres was acquired for land settlement (Map 2). Applicants were chosen on the basis of their ability to pay 25 per cent of the value of the lot rather than on their farming knowledge. Expansion of settlement continued to be related to the purchasing power of the peasantry.

> The prosperity of the peasant class appears just at this time (1911) to have been considerably improved, owing probably to the inflow of money from the Canal Zone. The Lands Department was inundated with applications from all directions and to satisfy some of these the best portions of the reserves in the Linley Valley and Clare Valley, which had not been apportioned owing to their apparent unfitness for agricultural purposes, were offered for sale and found ready purchasers (Colonial Report, 90, 1915).

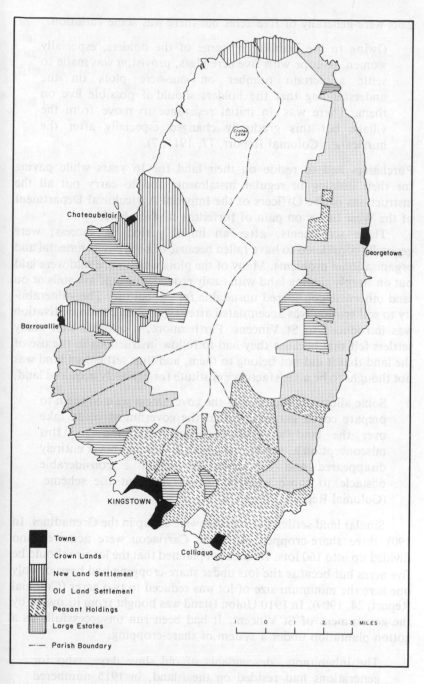

Map 2   Saint Vincent: Land occupance 1966

Lots were generally of five acres but there was some variation.

> Owing to the inability of some of the holders, especially women, to cope with five acre plots, provision was made to settle a certain number on one-acre plots on the understanding that the holders should if possible live on them. There was an initial resistance to move from the village but this gradually changed especially after the hurricane. (Colonial Report, 77, 1911, 7).

Purchasers had to reside on their land for 16 years while paying for their holding in regular instalments and to carry out all the instructions of the Officers of the Imperial Agricultural Department of the West Indies on pain of forfeiture of their land.

These settlements, after an initial period of success, were generally considered to have failed because of both environmental and organizational problems. Many of the plots which were sold were laid out on steeply sloping land with easily eroded, volcanic ash soils or on land otherwise considered unsuitable for agriculture. The vulnerability to soil erosion was accentuated after 1906 when cotton cultivation was introduced to St Vincent. Furthermore, it appears that many settlers felt that because they had to follow instructions in the use of the land that it did not belong to them, and thus settlement land was not thought to be a satisfactory substitute for privately acquired land.

> Some allottees thought that the government wanted them to prepare cocoa gardens so that the government could take over the land as a large cocoa plantation ... this misconception as to the true object in view has never entirely disappeared and has been throughout a considerable obstacle to those engaged in carrying out the scheme. (Colonial Report, 77, 1911).

Similar land settlement schemes were set up in the Grenadines. In 1901 three share-cropped estates in Carriacou were acquired and divided up into 160 lots. It had been planned that the lot size should be five acres but because the lots under share-cropping had been of only one acre the minimum size of lot was reduced to two acres (Colonial Report, 24, 1909). In 1910 Union Island was bought from its owner by the government of St Vincent. It had been run unsuccessfully as a cotton plantation under a system of share-cropping.

> The inhabitants, descendants of old slave days, who for generations had resided on the island, in 1915 numbered about 1800. They resided in two closely packed villages of

squalid wattle and daub huts without the least regard for privacy or sanitation. They were not allowed to grow provisions, except in special localities where the soil was sandy and almost worthless for cultivation, nor were they allowed to keep any stock larger than goats. By 1914 the squalid villages were disappearing and the allottees were building wooden houses ... In 1915 the cotton crop had increased from 42 bales in 1910 to 117 bales and there were 87 cattle and horses belonging to the allottees. (Smith, 1915:9).

It is clear that although these early settlements were viewed with suspicion as imposed solutions to landlessness they were perceived as offering greater independence than existed under share-cropping. After full ownership was attained by the settlers these settlement areas became indistinguishable from other areas of smallholdings.

Land settlement 1929–1960

Interest in land settlement waned as prosperity returned to the sugar industry following the price rises during the period of the First World War. But prosperity was short-lived and the renewed economic weakness of the plantocracy allowed the reimposition of a metropolitan solution. The two Royal Commissions appointed to look into the problems of the West Indies during the depression of the 1930s both reiterated the need for land settlement. The Sugar Commission of 1929/30 noted that the recommendations of the 1897 Commission had been acted upon very effectively in St Vincent, Trinidad and Jamaica but that nothing had been done in the oldest sugar islands of Barbados and St Kitts. The Commissioners went on to say that: 'We are convinced, however, that while schemes of land settlement cannot relieve the present emergency, the increased settlement of labourers on the land as peasant proprietors offers the best prospect of establishing a stable and prosperous economy in the West Indian colonies.' (Olivier, 1930:68). The Moyne Commission of 1938–9 saw land settlement as a solution to the unemployment problems of the period.

The social unrest of 1938 set the stage for subsequent action. Agricultural occupation was to be used to stem the flow of the unemployed from the rural areas of the cities, hence the rapid build-up of the land settlement schemes. (McFarlane et al, 1968:24).

In 1944 the Director of Agriculture in Montserrat wrote to the Colonial Secretary saying that:

It is beyond any doubt that extensive land settlement schemes will be necessary for the efficient development of the island's agriculture. The present system of share farming and the relegation of the peasantry to a rental system on the poor lands based on 'good understanding' and without security of tenure calls for revision in that it is iniquitous and not conducive to good farming. (Robert Johns, quoted in Wilson, 1972).

In Jamaica the colonial government was thinking along similar lines. The governor, Sir John Huggins, said, in 1949, that: 'I think it can fairly be said that no single side of Government's activities is of more significance to the future of the country than the land settlement programme.' (Redwood, n.d.). By 1950 Jamaica had redistributed almost 150,000 acres to some 26,000 purchasers constituting one-twelfth of the population (Redwood, n.d.). Puerto Rico had distributed almost 120,000 acres to some 60,000 individuals since 1921 (Lewis, 1951). In Trinidad 4,120 acres were made available to 2,940 settlers between 1933 and 1948 (Lewis, 1951). In the Windward Islands, (Map 1) where land settlement had first started, about 16,500 acres had been purchased for settlements by 1952 (Momsen, 1969). In the Leeward Islands interest in land settlement developed later, and only about 10,000 acres were included in land settlements by 1950 (Lewis, 1951; Wilson, 1972 and Nevis, 1978).

Land settlement since 1960

During this period new external influences came to bear on attitudes to land settlement. The influence of the colonial power waned as independence was achieved by the British West Indian colonies. At the same time the intellectual climate in the Caribbean became dominated by events occurring within the Western hemisphere: in particular the agrarian changes in Cuba following the Revolution in 1959 and the general spread of interest in land reform throughout Latin America displayed in the Punta del Este Declaration of 1961. Gomes (1985) sees the foundation of West Indian attitudes to this new approach to rural development being laid at the West Indian Agricultural Economics Annual Conference in Jamaica in 1968. These ideas were clarified two years later in Dominica when the Fifth Conference held a work-shop on land settlement (Momsen, 1970) and in 1972 the Seventh Conference in Grenada took land reform as its theme and focused on operational aspects. Attention had now turned to a more holistic approach to planning, with careful choice of settlers and the provision of plots large enough to provide more than bare subsistence. Settlements were increasingly seen as a means of agricultural development rather than as a panacea for welfare problems (Momsen, 1970).

Lessons were learned from the difficulties experienced by the earlier settlements. A study in Jamaica showed that in 1949, 65 per cent of owners of settlement land were absentees (Redwood, n.d.). In Grenada it was found that there were also many absentee settlers and 35 per cent of the settlements were uncultivated in 1945, many lots were too small to be viable and between 33 and 60 per cent of production was consumed at home (Brizan, 1984:231). A government committee set up in 1947 to examine Grenada's land settlements ruefully concluded that 'Experience has shown that land settlements which have been initiated merely as a result of popular demand — or for the purpose of relieving unemployment have invariably led to disappointment and failure.' (Brizan, 1984:232).

Other changes in the region gave a renewed urgency to the need for land settlements. Migration from the West Indies was becoming more difficult because of increasingly restrictive laws in many industrialized countries (Momsen, 1986) and thus population pressure in the West Indies became more marked. Rising expectations and the fast expanding tourist trade combined to produce a realisation that land, for both food production and housing, was a scarce resource in the Caribbean islands.

Since 1960 attempts to meet these needs have led to a proliferation of new types of land settlements. The government of Jamaica has established a variety of co-operative farming schemes which have been generally dependent on high inputs of training and supervision (Dale, 1977) and with stress increasingly being laid on environmental protection and improved nutrition (Chaney, 1985). Both Grenada and St Vincent have experimented with collective forms of production, operating land settlements as state farms (Brierley, 1985 and Le Franc, 1980).

On the new settlements in St Vincent (Map 2) the government was determined to avoid the problems experienced with the early settlements where freehold redistribution of land had been followed by fragmentation and soil erosion. It was planned that the estates intended for land settlement should be operated as a unit until the purchase price of the land had been recovered, when they would be handed over to the labourers on a leasehold basis. At first, production on the estates trebled under state operation and the labourers benefited from higher bonuses and more provision grounds than were found on private estates. By 1966 the idea of subdividing the land had been abandoned because it was feared output per acre would fall. In addition, a new factor appeared to complicate the issue. With the advent of an elected legislature, productivity on government estates declined as the workers adopted the view that the land belonged to them. The externally imposed goal of commercial, export-oriented production was resisted and the workers concentrated their efforts on their subsistence provision grounds. Thus the project was perceived by the government to have failed because of poor communication between the state and the populace. Today these settlements are cultivated in small plots by farmers generally without legal land rights. The collapse of these settlements may be seen in terms of the assertion of customary attitudes to land by a peasantry resistant to externally imposed solutions to landlessness.

Sources of land for settlement are also becoming more disparate. The 1963 Réforme Foncière in the French Antilles established a maximum size for plantations, thus releasing land for peasants. Other countries have made land available for agricultural settlement by taking over under-utilized estate land as in Jamaica (Dale, 1977) and Grenada (Brierley, 1985). In Trinidad 20,000 acres of unused Crown Lands were used to create 2,400 small farms in 1964 (Harewood, 1966). These farms were planned with the aim of increasing domestic food production and providing a reasonable level of living for the farm family. There was careful selection of the settlers, training and financial assistance (Alleyn, 1972). Yet Pollard (1979) found that milk production had declined steadily after 1972, and Harry (1980) established that in most cases the male farmer had been forced to take an off-farm job to supplement the family income, leaving the dairy cattle to be cared for by the women on the farm. In several instances multinational companies have provided land for peasant settlement. In Jamaica, the bauxite companies allowed small farmers to rent land until it was needed for mining and in 1969 such land amounted to 76,000 acres (Johnson et al, 1972). The Shell oil company relinquished its leases on some areas of Crown Land in Trinidad so that the land could be used for a land settlement project (James, 1969). More recently in St Lucia, Geest Industries contributed 1,600 acres of banana plantation land in 1983 to St Lucia Model Farms for the settlement of 175 farmers on five to ten acre lots around a nuclear farm. This project has been so successful in terms of providing a high income to the settlers through central control of cultural practices, purchasing of inputs and marketing, that by mid-1985 there were 800 applicants for the 100 plots then available (Leonce, 1985). It remains to be seen if the St Lucian peasantry will be any more willing than the Vincentian settlers to accept such supervision in the long term.

Today all shades of politicians still see land settlement as a panacea. Bishop's government in Grenada talked of 'Idle Lands for Idle Hands' (Brierley, 1985) and Miss Charles in Dominica sees rural resettlement as 'aimed at bringing under-utilized land into cultivation and improving the standards of living in rural areas' (Insight, 1985). However, increasingly the planners are realizing that the attitudes of the settlers must be taken into account. In 1972, when settlements were being revitalized in Montserrat, settlers were asked what type of land tenure they preferred. At that time 32 per cent of the settlers wished to purchase their holdings, 44 per cent wanted long term leases and 24 per cent were undecided. Eventually most settlers were offered annual leases because many of them were quite elderly (Wilson, 1972). Although the majority of the farming population is still elderly and therefore thought to be incapable of carrying out the hard physical work of land preparation (Bass, 1984) the government of Montserrat is now planning to encourage improvement in agriculture 'by assigning legally secure leases of long term duration on farmer's plots, these leases to be passed on from father to son or from one user to another, but without permitting fragmentation of land holdings.' (Bass, 1984:11). Thus official attitudes to tenure on these land settlements have changed to the position of the majority of the settlers. If West Indian farmland is to be both conserved and utilized most efficiently it is clear that a better understanding of the interaction between official and folk attitudes to land is needed. To this end, I shall look in detail at the development of land settlement in one island, Nevis, in the Leewards.

Land settlement in Nevis

On emancipation the planters in Nevis did not encourage the ex-slaves to become self-provisioning. The planters continued to supply food for their labourers either through imports or by growing food crops on the estates. However, estate owners on Nevis found themselves at a disadvantage in relation to planters elsewhere in the post-emancipation West Indies. Nevis had always been considered less fertile than St Kitts and on this small colony the steepness and stoniness of the land made the introduction of labour saving devices uneconomic. Nevisian planters were able to pay only very low wages and consequently many ex-slaves left for other islands especially St Kitts and Trinidad, where wages were higher. It is estimated that by 1842 almost half the freed slaves had left the island and the Nevisian sugar industry faced marked labour shortages. Sugar production had declined from its pre-emancipation level more than in any other

British colony except Montserrat (Williams, 1970:340). This decline was accelerated by a devastating earthquake in February, 1843 which destroyed several sugar mills and all the public buildings in Charlestown, Nevis (Richardson, 1983:96). Following the collapse of plantation sugar in 1847, Nevisian planters introduced share-cropping on their estates. Under this system land was allocated to individuals who planted and cultivated the cane in return for a proportion of the value of the crop. Richardson suggests that this early introduction of sharecropping gave Nevisians a greater personal stake in the land than their counterparts in other sugar islands such as St Kitts and Barbados (Richardson, 1983:99). The sharecroppers were similar to Mintz' proto-peasants in that they produced their own food but did not have title to the land they worked. Differences soon became apparent, however, as their control of their time and labour allowed them increasing management of the cropping patterns of the land, although land use was ultimately dependant on the approval of the land owner. By 1864 sharecroppers in Nevis were planting larger proportions of their land in food crops than was common in other islands (Nevis Blue Book, 1864:292).

Migrants, returning to Nevis with money earned overseas, found it impossible to invest in land as there was very little for sale. Instead they bought livestock and so by 1857 parts of the island were already looking overgrazed. (Richardson, 1983:103). Ecological degradation continued as the sugar industry declined because the planters in Nevis were too poor to afford to invest in modern equipment. Sea-island cotton began to replace cane after 1900 and by 1920 was the island's main export. A hurricane in 1924 which reduced cotton yields to record low levels was followed three years later by a disastrous fall in prices. Cotton growing added sheet erosion to the environmental damage suffered by Nevis and by 1930 plantation-based export agriculture was no longer viable. Estates were sold and broken up into small plots and the peasantry finally took control of the land itself. In 1929 there were only 292 holdings of less than ten acres, five years later, after Hamilton Estate had been purchased as the island's first land settlement, the number of smallholdings had risen to 363 compared with only 11 on St Kitts (Blue Book, 1934:2). In 1938 the Royal Commission praised the tenacity of these settlers and called for the conversion of sharecropped estates into land settlements (Engledow, 1945:54). The Commission also noted that there were 230 peasants on government land settlement schemes in Nevis, 200 peasants on their own land and 1,200 sharecroppers. (ibid, 193). As in St Vincent access to land enabled the peasantry to concentrate on food production and reject export agriculture and the island became self-sufficient in foodstuffs. Richardson suggests that lower death rates in Nevis, as compared to St Kitts, were related to the more dependable food supply in the smaller island (Richardson, 1983:125).

Nevis took note of the Commission recommendations and by 1950 the colony had bought out nine estates for a total of 3,455 acres, of which approximately 300 acres had been made available to peasants on lease purchase, and nearly 1,200 acres were rented out in small plots (Map 3). By 1985 the government of Nevis owned 5,375 acres on 15 estates of which 31 per cent was rented or leased to peasant farmers.

According to the 1975 Census of Agriculture Nevis had 1,750 farms of less than ten acres, constituting 85 per cent of the total number of farms while the larger island of St Kitts had only 1,634 farms of less than ten acres, forming 66 per cent of the total number of farms. In St Kitts sharecropping was practised by 55 per cent of small farmers and virtually all farms were rented (Mills,1974) while in Nevis sharecropping no longer existed and one-quarter of the small farms were rented on government land settlements.

The development of small farming in Nevis is almost entirely due to the intervention of the State. The colonial power, through Royal Commissions, encouraged the development of land settlements. A study of the records of these land settlements over the last half century allows us to see how the peasantry has recreated its customary attitudes to land within the formal structure of the land settlement, despite the lack of freehold tenure or even long leases.

There has been considerable discussion in the Caribbean as to the relative merits of freehold and leasehold tenure on land settlements and this argument is still alive today particularly in relation to the settlements in Montserrat and Nevis, and the new Model Farm project in St Lucia. It has often been suggested that the West Indian small farmer insists on freehold land settlements, and the Royal Commissions of 1897 and 1929 both proposed peasant proprietorship, but Lewis (1951) felt that there was little evidence to support this view. The contemporary situation indicates that although full legal title to land is not essential, land occupance must offer the peasantry the security and independence generally associated with freehold land. Governments require that the productivity of the land on a settlement should be maintained and most governments have attempted to build in controls to ensure this. However, whether in the early settlements in St Vincent where land was sold to the farmers over a long period, or in Nevis where most settlement land is on annual rental, the state has rarely taken land away from unsatisfactory farmers. Attempts to retain the benefits of economies of scale in cultivation and marketing

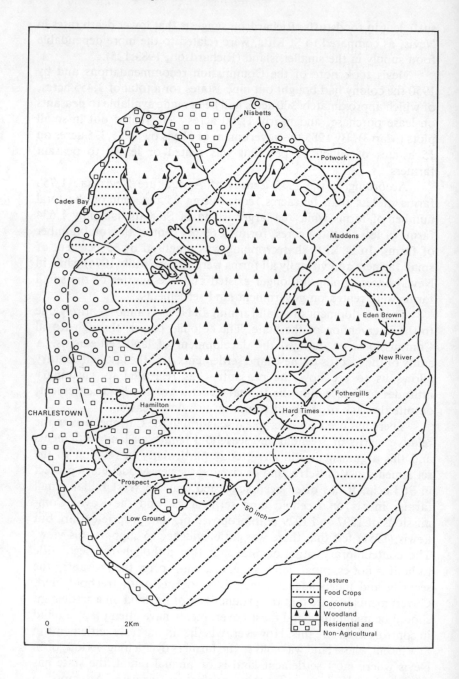

Map 3 Nevis: Land use and land settlement in 1985

by co-operative cultivation of land, have generally been unsuccessful. The Lucky Hill settlement in Jamaica (Dale, 1977), the Proportional Profit Farms of Puerto Rico (Lewis, 1951), the recent attempt to form a co-operative among small farmers in Dominica (White, 1977) and the new settlements in St Vincent (Le Franc, 1980), all suffered from failures of communication between management and worker members due, on the whole, to poor and authoritarian management and untrained workers. Beckford (1972) argued that under freehold tenure the distribution of landholdings would inevitably become unequal and he favoured government ownership of existing estate lands and their distribution to farmers under long-term arrangements. However, Zuvekas (1978) suggests that farmers generally do not regard even 20-year leases as providing sufficient security for making long term investments.

Yet, in Nevis, as Finkel (1964:166) pointed out for the sister island of St Kitts, farmers express little interest in land ownership on settlements. Annual rental allows both government and peasant farmers to move in and out of land occupance as conditions dictate. On Cades Bay estate, bought in 1939 by the government, 112 acres were rented to farmers until 1951 when they were taken back and operated commercially in sugar cane and later cotton. In 1978 this was rented to the Nevis Co-operative Society but has not been very successful and in 1985 only 51 acres were occupied by 29 farmers. Spring Hill estate, also purchased in 1939, has 97 acres of arable land which was originally rented to small farmers. In the 1970s half of this area was put under improved pasture and used for a small herd of Senepol cattle. The last small farmer had his land taken over in 1980 and the remaining land is now used only for house-spots. Potwork Estate, purchased in 1955 was used by the Department of Agriculture for vegetable, sugar cane and cotton growing, and improved pasture. From 1973 onwards land was rented to small farmers and by 1985 the estate had 32 settlers operating plots of an average size of 1.75 acres.

Figure 1 shows the fluctuations in land occupance on Nevisian settlements since 1940, based on data collected from the rent books kept by the Department of Agriculture. The peak year for take-up of land on settlements was 1945, when the ending of the War and the availability of land on Hamilton, New River, Hardtimes, Nisbett and Prospect Estates encouraged 61 people to rent land on these settlements. A second peak came in 1973 as the increasing inflation of this period forced people into self-sufficiency in food production. A third peak occurred between 1980 and 1983 when recession in North America and Europe and the prospect of independence encouraged return migration and a search for land for house sites as well as

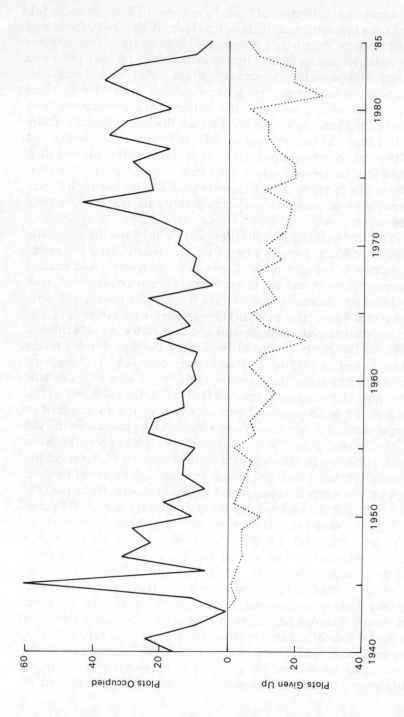

Fig 1   Fluctuations in occupation of land settlement in Nevis

for subsistence cultivation. The growing importance of land for subsistence needs, particularly for mothers supporting young children, is indicated by the gradual feminization of Nevisian agriculture with 29 per cent of settlers in 1950 being women, rising to 34 per cent in 1978 and 38 per cent by 1985.

Withdrawals from settlements were most closely related to opportunities for overseas migration. The first peak year was 1963 when Nevisians left for the United Kingdom in large numbers in order to avoid the restrictive immigration laws about to be imposed by the British government. A second peak came in 1981 as migration flows focused on North America and the Virgin Islands. This was also the time when many of those who had first taken up land in the 1940s were retiring and passing on their land to relatives and friends. Although settlement lands are only rented, of the 341 changes in occupant registered in the official rent books between 1950 and 1985, 20.5 per cent involved transfers of land to a designated heir. According to the Director, the Department of Agriculture never refuses to allow land to be passed on according to the wishes of the previous occupant (Nisbett, 1985). In 57 per cent of the transfers no reason was given and no successor designated. In the remaining cases 13.5 per cent gave up because of ill-health or death, with the loss of life in the sinking of the inter-island steamer in 1970 being noticeable in the records. In 5.6 per cent of the cases emigration was the stated reason for giving up renting land on the settlements. This reason is most commonly noted during the 1950s and 1960s but in the 1980s there is some evidence that settlers are continuing to rent their land even when they go overseas, especially to North America. This may indicate changes of perceptions in relation to the length of time the migrant expects to stay away from Nevis and to the strength of attachment to the land. Only in 12 cases did the government take land away from settlers. This action was not related to failures in the farming skills of the settler but to changes in land use on government estates or the need for land for community use, and the dispossessed settler was always able to obtain alternative land.

This high rate of turnover at first sight appears to support Olwig's (Chapter 7) interpretation of attitudes to agriculture. However, in many cases these changes merely reflected individuals exchanging one plot on an estate for another nearby or adding another neighbouring plot to their farm. In a sample survey of small farmers carried out in 1979 I was told on several occasions that farmers could trace their family's presence on a particular estate back through the period of sharecropping to slave days. Thus government land settlement in Nevis was in many cases not redistribution of land *per se* but a legal recognition of land occupance patterns of long standing. As long as there is adequate land to meet demand then short term leases are acceptable. Rental charges are very low being increased to $6.00EC for mountain land and $12.00EC for low ground in 1978 after many years of stability. Even at this level, in 1985, 49.8 per cent of the settlers owed more than two years rent. Difficulties in collecting the rent owed and the time and cost involved were forcing government to think in terms of moving to freehold ownership of land on the settlements (Nisbett, 1985) although there did not appear to be any demand from the settlers for this change. Indeed the long term trend has been towards an increase in the number of people renting land on the settlements, from 193 in 1949 to 354 in 1979 and 407 in 1985. Some of the latest expansion is a result of illegal subdivisions, mainly for house-spots, rather then a greater rate of take-up of agricultural land. However, the growth of tourism on the island is making it more difficult for peasants to rent land from private land-owners. There have been instances recently of long-term renters of private land being given notice to quit by landlords who then sold the land for commercial development.

Land settlement is an externally imposed solution to land occupance and so it might be expected to produce farms that are distinctive when compared with farms developed without government assistance. Both types of holding were surveyed in Nevis in 1979 and their characteristics compared. Small farms in Nevis typically consist of a piece of land near the coast, close to the house, and another piece in the wetter, hilly interior of the island, and this pattern is recognised in the settlement rental schedule. There is an ecological rationale for such structural fragmentation in an island where drought is a constant threat. The mean number of fragments was slightly greater for the settlement farmers at 2.73 as compared to 2.37 on the non-settlement farms. Most farmers occupied land under several forms of tenure but on the settlements only 11 per cent held more than half their land in other forms of tenure while of the private farmers 48 per cent owned the major part of their holding and 40 per cent occupied pre-dominantly privately rented land. The most marked differences are in land use and accessibility. The settlement farms had an average of only 33.6 per cent of their land in crops while the non-settlement farms surveyed had an average of 52.9 per cent of land cropped. This difference in part reflects the fact that the settlements tend to be on poorly-watered land which was sold to government because the planters could not cultivate it profitably (Map 3). Principal components analysis of the data showed that land on government settlements was characterized by greater distances to markets and water sources than was freehold and privately rented land. This differential accessibility would tend to discourage intensive cropping and commercialization of production on government settlements. However, settlement farmers were more likely than other farmers to live near to medical clinics and schools, probably because the post-emancipation villages in which these services are located tended to be founded close to those marginal estates which first went into sharecropping and later were sold to government. The analysis also showed that land settlement was least likely to be associated with farmers who had spent long periods out of Nevis since the rented land did not represent an investment into which a returned migrant might wish to put his savings. Thus settlement farms tended to have a lower level of capital investment than other farms and there is no evidence that this was compensated for by greater government assistance on settlements.

It is clear that there are differences between settlement farms and non-settlement farms in Nevis and that these differences are related to two aspects: location and tenure. Both these aspects which hinder productivity on settlement farms could be overcome by government action in improving access to water supplies and markets and by attracting capital into settlements either by changing the type of tenure or by making credit more easily available.

Conclusion

Most farmers on land settlements in Nevis also have land which they own or rent privately. This non-settlement land is usually cultivated more intensively than the settlement land, and these differences in land use cannot be entirely explained in terms of environmental variation. There is some indication that, because rents are so low, enforcement of payments so lax, and exchange of parcels within a settlement so easily done, the peasantry see the settlement land as a form of communal land on which they may graze their animals and supplement their subsistence production or their income from a non-farm job. Thus it appears that the folk perception of the role of land settlements in Nevis is very different from the role perceived by the state for them.

Land settlement is an externally imposed solution to land re-distribution, yet in many instances the peasantry has re-created its traditional attitudes to land within the formal structure of the land settlement. Even without land ownership settlers have often attempted to ensure that their heirs, resident or absentee, are allowed to take over occupance of the settlement plot. Land made available for settlements has generally been agriculturally marginal, with a past typified by sharecropping of squatting by ex-slaves, rather than a history of a strong and successful plantation economy. So in many cases the establishment of a land settlement may be little more than the formal recognition of the *status quo ante* rather than a redistribution of land *de novo*. As a consequence of ecological constraints land settlements have rarely achieved the productive prosperity hoped for by the 1897 Royal Commission. Settlement land as an economic resource is clearly inadequate but it has acquired a symbolic role as a substitute for individual land ownership. This role is similar to that seen for family land by Besson (1979) and is particularly important in those territories, such as Nevis, in which there has been little opportunity for the development of family land. Repeatedly settlers have shown that the freedom provided by land occupance must be accompanied by freedom of decision making and that land management by a central authority is not acceptable. The traditional antagonism of the peasantry to the plantation method of land operation has led to the downfall of many settlement schemes. As Craton (1978) has shown for Jamaica, in the Caribbean, continuities often outweigh changes in the socio-economic system.

Acknowledgements

I am grateful to Jean Besson for her helpful comments on an earlier draft of this chapter. Fieldwork on Nevis was funded by the Social Sciences and Humanities Research Council of Canada in 1979 and by the Nuffield Foundation in 1985.

References

Alleyne, E. Patrick 1972. *A review of the Crown Lands Development Project.* Trinidad and Tobago, Mimeo.

Anderson, T. and Flett, John S. 1902. Preliminary Report on the Recent Eruption of the Soufrière in St Vincent and of a visit to Mont Pelée, in Martinique. Communicated by the Secretaries of the Royal Society. *Proceedings of the Royal Society*, 70:423–445.

Bass, J.B. 1984. *Agricultural Development Plan,* Ministry of Agriculture, Trade and Lands and Housing, Montserrat, Mimeo.

Beckford, G.L.F. 1972. Land Reform for the Betterment of Caribbean People. *Proceedings of the Seventh West Indian Agricultural Economics Conference.* Trinidad, University of the West Indies.

Besson, Jean 1979. Symbolic Aspects of Land in the Caribbean: The Tenure and Transmission of Land Rights among Caribbean Peasantries. In *Peasants, Plantations and Rural Communities in the Caribbean*. Malcolm Cross and Arnaud Marks (eds.). Guildford, University of Surrey, and Leiden, Royal Institute of Linguistics and Anthropology: 86–116.

1984. Land Tenure in the free villages of Trelawny, Jamaica: a case study in the Caribbean peasant response to emancipation. *Slavery and Abolition*, 5(1):3–23.

Brierley, J.S. 1985. Idle Land in Grenada: A Review of its causes and the PRG's Approach to Reducing the Problem. *The Canadian Geographer*, 29(4):298–309.

Brizan, George I. 1984. *Grenada: Island of Conflict*. London, Zed Books.

1979. *The Grenadian Peasantry and Social Revolution 1930–1951*. Working Paper No 21, Jamaica, ISER, University of the West Indies.

Chaney, Elsa M. 1985. Women and Food Production: Variations on a Perennial Theme. In *Women Creating Wealth: Transforming Economic Development*. R.S. Gallin and Anita Spring (eds.) Washington D.C., Association for Women in Development:61–64.

Colonial Office. 1844. C.O. 137–*Jamaica*. London.

1851. C.O. 27–*Barbados*. London.

1909. *Colonial Reports No 24 — Grenada*. Report on Land Settlement in Carriacou, London.

1911. *Colonial Reports No 77 — St Vincent*. Report on the Administration of the Roads and Land Settlement Fund, London.

1915. *Colonial Report No 90 — St Vincent*. Report on the Administration of the Roads and Land Settlement fund from 1st January 1911 to 31st March 1914, London.

Craton, Michael 1978. *Searching for the Invisible Man*. Cambridge, Harvard University Press.

Dale, E.H. 1977. *Spotlight on the Caribbean, a Microcosm of the Third World*. Regina Geographical Series No. 2, Department of Geography, University of Regina, Saskatoon.

Eisner, G. 1961. *Jamaica, 1830–1930: A Study in Economic Growth*. Manchester, University Press.

Engledow, F.L. 1945. *West India Royal Commission. Report on Agriculture Fisheries, Forestry and Veterinary Matters*. London, H.M.S.O.

Finkel, H.J. 1964. Patterns of Land Tenure in the Leeward and Windward Islands and their Relevance to Problems of Agricultural Development in the West Indies. *Economic Geography*, 40:163–172.

Gomes, P.I. (ed.) 1985. *Rural Development in the Caribbean*. London, C. Hurst & Co.

Harewood, A. 1966. Land Settlement in Trinidad and Tobago. *Proceedings of the First West Indian Agricultural Economics Conference*. Trinidad, University of the West Indies: 80–110.

Harry, Indra Sita. 1980. *Women in Agriculture in Trinidad*. Unpublished M. Sc. Thesis, University of Calgary, Canada.

Insight, 1985. July, London, West India Committee.

James, L.J. 1969. *Lot 10*. The Introduction of a small farm project in an oilfield area. Trinidad, University of the West Indies.

Johnson, I.E., Strachan, M. and Johnson, J. 1982. A Review of Land Settlement in Jamaica. *Proceedings of the Seventh West Indian Agricultural Economics Conference*. Trinidad, University of the West Indies: 110–132.

Le Franc, E. 1980. Grenada, St Vincent and St Lucia. In *Small Farming in the less Developed Countries of the Commonwealth Caribbean*. Prepared by Weirs Agricultural Consulting Services. Barbados, Caribbean Development Bank.

68   Land and Development in the Caribbean

Leonce, L.M. 1985. Project Manager, St Lucia Model Farms Ltd, Personal communication.

Lewis, W.A. 1951. Issues in Land Settlement Policy. *Caribbean Economic Review* III(1 & 2):58–92.

Lowenthal, David 1961. Caribbean views of Caribbean Land. *Canadian Geographer* 5(2):1–9.

McFarlane, R., Singham, N. and Johnson, I. 1968. *Agricultural Planning in Jamaica*. Paper read at the Third West Indian Agricultural Economics Conference, Jamaica, April, Mimeo.

Mills, Frank L. 1974 Production relationships among small-scale farmers in St Kitts. *Social and Economic Studies* 25 (June):153–167.

Mintz, Sidney W. 1961. The question of Caribbean peasantries, a comment. *Caribbean Studies* 1(3):31–34.

1964. The employment of capital by Haitian market women. In R. Firth & B. Yamey (eds.), *Capital, saving and credit in peasant societies*. London, George Allen & Unwin.

1964a. Foreword to Ramiro Guerra y. Sanchez. *Sugar and Society in the Caribbean*. New Haven, Yale University Press: xi–xliv.

1983. Reflections on Caribbean Peasantries. *Nieuwe West-Indische Gids*. 57(1/2):1–17.

Momsen, Janet D. 1969. *The geography of land use and population in the Caribbean*. Ph.D. dissertation, University of London.

1970. Small-scale Farm-Planning and Land Settlement. *Proceedings of the Fifth West Indian Agricultural Economics Conference, Dominica*. Trinidad, University of the West Indies: 174–176.

1986. Migration and Rural Development in the Caribbean, *Tijdschrift voor Economische en Sociale Geografie*. 77(1):50–58.

Nevis 1864 *Blue Book* (1864), London.

1934 *Blue Book* (1934), London.

1978 *Land Settlement Records*. Nevis, Department of Agriculture.

Nisbett, E. 1985. Personal communication. Nevis.

Norman, Sir. H. 1898. *Report of the Royal Commission on the West Indies, 1897*. Cmd. 8655, 3635 and 8699, London.

Olivier, Lord. 1930. *Report of the West Indies Sugar Commission, 1929/30*. Cmd. 3517. London. HMSO.

Packer, Edward, 1848 On the Present Condition of the Island of Barbados and the Causes which have led to it. *Simmonds Colonial Magazine*, XIV (May–August): 36–40.

Parliamentary Papers XXIX(1842); XXII(1842), London.

Pollard, J. 1979. *Variations in agricultural performance in Trinidad*. Paper presented at the Annual Meeting of the Association of American Geographers, Philadelphia, Pa, April.

Redwood, Paul, n.d. *Statistical Survey of Government Land Settlements in Jamaica, B.W.I. 1929–1949*. Kingston, Mimeo.

Richardson, B.C. 1983. *Caribbean Migrants*. Knoxville, University of Tennessee Press.

Shephard, C.Y. 1947. Peasant agriculture in the Leeward and Windward Islands. *Tropical Agriculture* XXIV(4 & 6):61–72.

Smith, G.W. 1915. Report on the Land Settlement Scheme at Union Island, 28 May 1914. In *Colonial Report No. 90 St Vincent*, London.

White, M.G. 1977. Survey of Castle Bruce Co-operative Project. *Proceedings of the Eleventh West Indies Agricultural Economics Conference.* Trinidad, University of the West Indies: 54–61.

Williams, Eric. 1954. The Importance of Small Scale Farming in the Caribbean In *Small Scale Farming in the Caribbean.* Selected from the Documentation & Report of the Conference on Education and Small Scale Farming in Trinidad, October 6–15, 1954.

1970. *From Columbus to Castro: The History of the Caribbean 1492–1969.* London, André Deutsch.

Wilson, M.J. 1972. *The New Otway Farms. A Land Use Plan for the Otway Estates, Montserrat,* Montserrat, Department of Agriculture, Mimeo.

Zuvekas, Clarence Jr. 1978. *A Profile of Small Farmers in the Caribbean Region.* General Working Document No. 2. Washington D.C., Rural Development Division, Bureau for Latin America and the Caribbean, Agency for International Development, Mimeo.

CHAPTER 3

Folk and mainstream systems of land tenure and use in St Vincent

Hymie Rubenstein

A perennial economic problem throughout the West Indies is the under-utilization of farmland. This occurs even in those countries where agriculture is the mainstay of the economy (see Augelli, 1962:438; Finkel, 1971:298; O'Loughlin, 1968:100–104; Philpott, 1973; Rubenstein, 1975). Although there are a few reports which document some of the factors producing this situation (e.g., Brierley, 1974; Edwards, 1961; Finkel, 1964), little has been done to systematically describe and interrelate the various features which have yielded a particular land use pattern in a given West Indian territory. Both theoretical and practical considerations call for such a study.

In an earlier attempt to address this problem, I presented an analysis of the under-exploitation of arable land in a Black peasant village in St Vincent (Rubenstein, 1975). Twenty-five discrete factors, organized under four headings — demography, ecology, economy, and ideology — were identified as accounting for the extant pattern of local land use. Least attention was paid to the ideological factors — the beliefs, values, aspirations, and attitudes — which contributed to the under-cultivation of farmland in the community. This chapter aims to elaborate upon these ideological concomitants so that their role in agricultural decision-making can be more clearly seen. In particular, I am concerned with the motives for acquiring land, the norms and practices for transferring property from one generation to another, and the set of ideas determining land use. In retrospect, the earlier analysis presented a catalogue of variables affecting cultivation the links between which were not precisely traced. The analysis fell short of its goal, namely a systematic multi-variate examination of the existing pattern of valley land use. This discussion represents a step towards the realization of that goal.

The island background

The acquisition, distribution, tenure, and use of island land are the end product of over 300 years of historical forces and events (see Rubenstein, 1977). In conjunction with local environmental potentialities and limitations, they have yielded a distinct system of folk ideology and practice in matters pertaining to the physical landscape. St Vincent is a hilly island, covering 120 square miles, in the Eastern Caribbean. Its inaccessible, densely forested interior reduces by over one-half the island's occupied land and forces most of its 90,000 inhabitants to live along or near the coastal belt. Most Vincentians are the descendants of Black slaves who were transported to the island during the 18th and 19th centuries to work as labourers on the large sugar plantations that dominated the local economy. Since the freeing of the slaves in 1838, the economic life of the island has featured the disappearance of sugar as an export crop, a gradual but sustained decrease in the number of large estates, a continuous increase in the importance of small-scale peasant cultivation, and short periods of economic stability based on the overseas sale of cash crops such as arrowroot, bananas, cotton, various starchy tubers, and, most recently, tobacco.

St Vincent is one of the poorest countries in the West Indies. A report published in the late 1960s stated that the per capita income of islanders '. . . is probably the lowest in the Western Hemisphere with the possible exception of Haiti' and that:

> most of the people on the island are living in a way which, in terms of material and environmental conditions, could scarcely be far removed from the situation as it was under slavery. (University of the West Indies Development Mission 1969:4,9).

A World Bank study of the Commonwealth Caribbean (Chernick, 1978:87) found that 'St Vincent and St Kitts seem to suffer the most acute cases of extreme poverty in the region.' The island is sometimes referred to as the 'Third World's third world' (Starbird, 1979:402).

Over 90 per cent of Vincentians may be classified as belonging to the island lower class. Most of them are Black, rural residents, barely subsisting by means of peasant cultivation, agricultural wage labour, petty retailing, fishing, unskilled manual labour, and semi-skilled independent trades. A large proportion of the teenage and young adult population and much of the adult female population are unemployed. Under-employment is even more serious and affects all segments of the lower-class work force.

Despite the diminished economic role of the plantocracy and the disappearance of sugar as a major export commodity, the legacy of monocrop cultivation is still evident in the distribution of landholdings. Those properties over 100 acres account for less than one-half of one per cent of the country's 10,465 pieces of land but

*Table 1   Distribution of agricultural holdings in St Vincent**

Size of holding (acres)	Number of Holdings			Area of Holdings		
	No.	%	Cumulative %	No. of acres	%	Cumulative %
0– 1	4,453	42.6	42.6	1,362	3.5	3.5
1– 5	4,762	45.5	88.1	9,521	24.1	27.6
5– 10	828	7.9	96.0	5,071	12.8	40.4
10– 25	320	3.1	99.0	4,611	11.7	52.1
25– 50	52	0.5	99.5	1,789	4.5	56.6
50–100	18	0.2	99.7	1,250	3.2	59.8
100–200	8	0.1	99.8	1,105	2.8	62.6
200–500	16	0.2	99.9	5,195	13.2	75.8
500 +	8	0.1	100.0	9,571	24.2	100.0
Total	10,465	100.0		39,475	100.0	

*Source: University of the West Indies Development Mission 1969:75

make up 40 per cent of all Vincentian farm acreage (Table 1). The eight estates over 500 acres alone account for nearly one-quarter of the arable land in St Vincent. Translated into human terms, one per cent of the population owns nearly 50 per cent of the land (Hourihan, 1975:30). Nonetheless, both the extent and intensity of estate cultivation have decreased dramatically over the past 150 years and agricultural production for overseas sale, inter-island trade, domestic markets, and subsistence is now dominated by the peasant sector. Of all holdings, 96 per cent are under ten acres and these represent 40 per cent of total farm acreage (Table 1).

The more intensive cultivation of peasant holdings is a relative matter and many small-scale producers make far from optimal use of their lands. Under-cultivation is a serious problem in both the plantation and peasant sectors, particularly given the small proportion of arable land in the country. Of the 39,475 acres of farmland, only 26,000, or 66 per cent, are suitable for crops and pasture. Of this 26,000 acres, 6,300, or 24 per cent, are idle or under-utilized, a situation the World Bank (1979:14) called 'a luxury the country can ill afford.' Idleness and under-cultivation are especially acute in the valleys along the island's western coast. Leeward Village (a pseudonym) is located in one such valley.

Table 2   Distribution of holdings in Leeward Valley

	Number of holdings			Area of holdings		
Size of holding (acres)	No.	%	Cumulative %	No. of acres	%	Cumulative %
0–½	16	5.5	5.5	2.7	0.2	0.2
½– 1	51	17.6	23.2	30.7	2.1	2.3
1– 2	93	32.2	55.4	125.9	8.8	11.1
2– 3	53	18.3	73.7	115.9	8.1	19.2
3– 5	40	13.8	87.5	154.5	10.8	30.0
5–10	17	5.9	93.4	111.0	7.7	37.7
10–50	15	5.2	98.6	350.6	24.5	62.2
50+	4	1.4	100.0	542.3	37.8	100.0
Total	289	100.0		1,433.6	100.0	

Source: Fieldwork

Land tenure and use in Leeward Valley

Situated at the foot of the long, narrow Leeward Valley, the community of Leeward Village contains a population of 2,200, nearly all of whom are Black members of the island's lower class. Villagers dominate such unremunerative and low status occupations as peasant and wage-labour agriculture, small-scale commercial fishing, petty-commodity retailing, semi-skilled and unskilled trades, and government manual wage-labour. Paralleling the national situation, many potentially productive persons are regularly unemployed and almost always underemployed.

Located between the lateral spurs of hills branching off from the island's north-south mountain range, Leeward Valley contains nearly 1,500 acres of privately owned land divided into 289 separate holdings (Table 2). Agriculture is the single most important village economic activity with some 30 per cent of the adult working population being employed in commercial and peasant farming. Despite this predominant role of agriculture, only 58 per cent of the 289 holdings in the valley contain any cultivation other than fruit trees. Moreover, most holdings which are worked are seriously under-utilized. The net result is that less than 20 per cent of the 1,500 acres of valley land is farmed at any given time. While short- and long-term fallowing account for some of this under-cultivation, a variety of less obvious but more significant factors are also involved. These have already been discussed elsewhere (Rubenstein, 1975) and include the migration of landowners and agricultural wage workers, soil erosion, holding fragmentation, inexperience at farming, low agricultural prices and unreliable market conditions, praedial larceny, the alternate uses to which land can be put, and an aversion to agricultural work.

Most cultivated plots contain a variety of subsistence and cash crops, the former headed by starchy tubers, especially yams, tannias, and sweet potatoes, the latter including arrowroot and bananas, both of which are exported.

The mean size of holdings is five acres. Nearly 90 per cent are below the average and one-third are between one and two acres (Table 2). The four largest holdings account for nearly 40 per cent of valley acreage and are the remnants of the once flourishing estate system (see Rubenstein, 1977).

Villagers distinguish between three forms of land tenure. Nearly one-half of land is *bought land*, property purchased by the present owner. The remaining holdings are nearly equally divided between *inherited land*, property transmitted at death to a single heir, and *family land*, undivided holdings jointly bequeathed to two or more people. Joint inheritance produces a multiplicity of proprietary rights to *family land* and there are 545 separate claims to the 289 pieces of land. Since many villagers have rights to more than one piece of family property, it is estimated that no more than 400 people hold the 545 claims.

Attitudes towards land

Land in Leeward Village is significant beyond its cultivability and this fact explains much of its under-utilization. As elsewhere in the West Indies, land and its possession are valued in and of themselves. The possession of a piece of land has many connotations: pride in the ownership of something that is valuable; prestige in being a propertied person in a community characterized by material poverty; continuity with the past when land has come down from the 'old parents' [ancestors]; immortalization through the bequest of land to future generations; security against the loss of other income-generating sources; real estate speculation; and freedom from the regimentation and low status of estate wage-labour.

Although it is the ambition of most villagers to own some land, members of only one-third of village households have been able to realize this goal. For the rest, acquisition of a piece of land is a long-term objective, an aim which even accounts for the wage-labour migration of many villagers (cf. Otterbein, 1966; Wilson, 1973). Even persons in their early twenties, including overseas residents, are eager to acquire some land, if only for future house-building or to signal their relative economic prosperity. While land may be mortgaged to finance some commercial venture or to effect removal abroad, it is rarely sold even in cases of severe financial pressure. Only those who have left the island with no intention of returning will voluntarily dispose of their holdings. This does not preclude real estate speculation and several villagers have profited from the purchase, subdivision, and sale of idle estate lands in the valley.

All of this suggests that in Leeward Village owning land and farming land are not the same thing. Hourihan (1973:29–30) has correctly pointed out that there is in St Vincent '... a widespread aversion towards agricultural work by Vincentian youths' and that, generally, white collar work is preferred to any kind of manual labour. In a questionnaire concerning educational and occupation choice administered to nearly 200 children in the village primary school, I found that not a single student cited agriculture as a desirable activity. Conversely, when asked to name the worst village occupation for men and women, agriculture was ranked second to street cleaning and employment on a road repair gang.

While 'working a hoe' is an unpopular activity, it is not the occupation of agriculture which is denigrated. Rather, it is the actual physical labour which is seen as repugnant and agricultural workers are occasionally referred to by other villagers by the old slave pejorative, 'field nigger'. In short, given the low status in which 'hoe and cutlass work' is held, whether it is based on estate wage-labour or small-scale independent farming, most people try to avoid it if they can and accept nearly any vocational alternative that is available. Still the scarcity of alternatives makes escape from farm work impossible for many.

With so many referents — peasant cultivation, subsistence, wage-labour, economic security, real estate investment, sentimentality, prestige, freedom, pride, continuity, etc. — it is no wonder that villagers are so possessive of their properties and react strongly and swiftly to any infringement, actual or perceived, of their customary or legal rights. Praedial larceny, trespass, crop destruction, boundary disagreements, inheritance disputes, squatting, and other 'land affairs' are a popular topic of village conversation and one of the most common causes of civil litigation. Legal squabbles even involve *family land*, that category of property meant to go from generation to generation without formal partition. As a legacy from the 'old parents', *generation to generation land* is supposed to symbolize familial continuity and solidarity. But as elsewhere in the West Indies (cf. Clarke, 1966:65), impartible inheritance runs counter to both the codified legal system and the ambition of most villagers for unencumbered individual land ownership.

Folk and jural systems of transmission

This contrast between a local folk system of tenure and transmission of property and an overarching societal jural system has been reported throughout the English-speaking Caribbean (cf. Clarke, 1971:200–242; M.G. Smith, 1965:221–261; R.T. Smith, 1971:243–266). In Leeward Village, as elsewhere in the region, the legal heirs of an intestate married man are his wife and legitimate children and of an unmarried man, his brothers and sisters. The customary system differs from the jural system in two ways: (1) it recognizes the right of certain categories of illegitimate or 'bastard' issue and extra-legal spouses to inherit property and (2) it observes verbal declarations, the personal circumstances of potential heirs, and the affective relation that existed between the deceased and these heirs. The village's folk system of transmission finds its closest counterpart in the Carriacouan model described by M.G. Smith (1965:250):

> Where a male landholder dies intestate leaving children of different birth status, the legitimate heirs have a right to inherit, while the illegitimate only have a claim of conditional character. Where there are no legitimate children of an intestate male, his illegitimate issue inherit without hindrance. . . . The illegitimate children of intestate women inherit equally with the legitimate. During their lifetime, the widows of intestate landholders exercise complete control over their husbands' land, but may not alienate it.

The customary system in Leeward Village differs in two ways from the Carriacouan one. First, a man's illegitimate children produced prior to his marriage to their mother inherit equally with the legitimate or 'lawful' issue of the union. Second, where there are no 'lawfuls', a man's 'bastard' children inherit 'without hindrance' only if the following conditions are met: (1) the property is not *family land* and (2) the deceased was himself illegitimate, or, if legitimate, his 'lawful' siblings chose not to exercise their legal claim. Conversely, if the land is of the *generation to generation* type, the joint male owner was 'a lawful', he married and produced legitimate offspring, and his 'outside children', as they are called, were produced in a long defunct or short-lived union, then these illegitimate children will not be entitled to a portion of the inheritance. In either of these two polar situations, disposition of property, supported by community sentiment, is straightforward. At times, however, disputes and controversy may break out, as, for example, when an almost forgotten brother suddenly arrives from overseas to press his legal claim to his brother's land, 'disinheriting' the dead man's consensual mate of many years. In these cases, village sympathy usually rests with the common-law wife and the man's illegitimate children.

Land disputes

Villagers are well aware that according to formal Vincentian jurisprudence illegitimate children and consensual mates are not entitled to inherit except by testamentary disposition but, as the following cases illustrate, they also believe that blood ties and years of cohabitation should not be ignored.

The first case involves Godfrey Wilson (a pseudonym) who died intestate leaving behind a house, house-spot, and a two-acre piece of *bought land*. Wilson, who had lived alone during much of his adult life, had most of his meals provided by an unmarried sister, Adelle, who also lived alone. A long-lived non-cohabitational union between Wilson and Lena Jones had produced two children, both of whom Wilson had always supported and with whom he had 'lived loving' [been on amiable terms] right up to his death. But Wilson was legitimate as were his three full sisters and a half-sister, the product of his father's first marriage. After his death, Wilson's half-sister's husband, a man with considerable experience in 'land affairs,' took charge of the disposition of the dead man's property. Two acres of agricultural land were given jointly to the three full sisters; the house was put up for rent and the proceeds earmarked for Adelle, the poorest sister and the one who had provided her brother's meals; two cows and a calf were taken by the administrator on his wife's behalf; the clothing and other personal effects were given to one of the half-sister's sons; and the household furniture was transferred to one of the other sisters. Nothing was given to Wilson's children. Although no one expected Lena Jones to be granted part of the inheritance because their union had terminated many years before, villagers believed that the children who had enjoyed Wilson's faithful support and affection should have been included in the distribution. Although he did not involve his wife in the transmission of the most valuable part of the inheritance, the two acres of land, the administrator, an East Indian in an Afro-Caribbean village, was termed a 'robbery "Coolie" bitch' for leaving Wilson's children out.

'Robbery' may take more dramatic forms than a contradiction between societal jural and local folk norms. It often involves what villagers call *thief land*, property which is viewed as having been fraudulently acquired by the standards of both systems. *Thief land* is obtained in one of two ways: a resident agent or caretaker placed in charge of the land by a migrant owner claims that the land has been abandoned or that the former proprietor has died without any legal heirs; or, as is more common, one or more family heirs obtains a title deed which excludes the other customary owners. As two of the following cases indicate, those who have been dispossessed are often prevented from gaining legal redress because of the large expense involved in what are normally protracted and unpredictable juridical battles.

The first example of *thief land* involves Martha Hadaway who purchased nearly three acres of Crown land during the early years of this century. She bequeathed the land in a will to her three daughters, one of whom, Linda, acquired title to the property after the death of the other sisters. Linda then transferred the land in a deed of gift to one of her sons. A son of one of the excluded beneficiaries consulted a lawyer but did not have the funds to pursue the matter.

A similar situation occurred when Tracey Bowen died intestate and left behind two acres of land. According to legal and customary usage, the property belonged to his two 'lawful' daughters, Nancy and Laura. Nancy, however, took possession of the whole piece, worked it for many years, and willed it to her daughter Verene. Laura, Bowen's other daughter, died, leaving six children, one of whom frequently complained about his mother's and siblings' dispossession. In 1970, Verene, in an apparent attempt to legitimize her control over the land in a manner which would partially recognize the claims of her collateral kin, secured its legal administration into two equal portions with one of Laura's daughters.

Even seizure of a piece of land by a non-heir sometimes occurs. Lawrence Adams had still not paid off his two-acre piece of land when he died in the 1940s. His brother, Christopher, took over the land, completed the payments, and acquired a title deed. Upon migrating to the United States in the late 1940s, he placed a friend, Janet Deare, in charge of the land. A few years later Janet transferred responsibility for the land to Paul Phillips, an enterprising farmer, who began to cultivate it in accordance with the traditional right of anyone who is 'response for' [in charge of] a piece of land. In 1969, Phillips filed the following statutory declaration:

'I Paul Phillips ... do solemnly and sincerely declare as follows:

(1) Christopher Adams was seized of a parcel of land situated in Leeward Village....

(2) The said Christopher Adams resided in the United States of America for many years.

(3) By a letter dated 8th January 1952, I was put in possession of this parcel of land by the said Christopher Adams.

(4) Christopher Adams died in America in the month of March 1955 and was survived by his wife who also died in the same year.

(5) That from the same year 1955, I have been in uninterrupted possession and have paid all the taxes for the said parcel of land.

(6) That I am unaware of anyone other than myself who has made any claim to the said parcel of land or any part thereof or any interest therein.'

In fact, Phillips was wrong on two grounds. First, he was put in charge of the land by Janet Deare, not Christopher Adams. Second, while Adams had no children of his own, he had a 'lawful' sister whose son, William, had tried to exercise his claim by repeatedly 'trespassing' on the land, thereby indicating that Phillips was not in unmolested occupation of it. After making some preliminary inquires concerning his legal rights, William was forced to drop the matter because of a lack of funds.

Deviations from the folk model

Acquiring *thief land* is not the only way the folk norms of the disposition of land and other property are ignored or circumvented. Indeed, 'exceptions' to both traditional and jural norms of transmission seem to be the rule in Leeward Village. If there is a structural principle at work informing the process of actual transmission, it is perhaps best labelled 'personalism,' a notion developed by Rodman (1971:159) to describe the quality of family relations among lower-class Black peasants in Trinidad. Personalism in kinship behaviour refers to ' ... the extent to which the content of a kinship relationship grows out of interaction (instead of being prescribed by the formal tie)' (Rodman 1971:159). The role of personalism in Leeward Village inheritance patterns is most evident in the case of testamentary disposition where the choice of heirs is a product of the quality of the relationship between property owner and various potential beneficiaries. In some cases, a legal heir may be excluded because of a dispute with the testator; in other cases, a distant relative or even non-kin may be granted some or all of the legacy because of the nature of the relationship with the donor; in still others, kin of equivalent genealogical distance may receive unequal allotments based on their differing social circumstances and perceived material needs. The following cases are illustrative of each of these possibilities.

The first case involves Albert Simmons, a farmer who disinherited his two sons, the legitimate issue of his first marriage, because of a long-standing dispute. Naming the younger son, a village resident, the beneficiary of 'a penny and a glass of water' (to protect himself from the charge that he had left the son out by accident), Simmons willed all the property, including a valuable piece of agricultural land, to his childless second wife. The elder son, who was living in England when his father died, returned several years later and challenged the bequest. Although his step-mother had transferred the land to a nephew by this time, his court action was successful and he and his brother are now in undisputed possession of the piece of land.

The second case involves Paul Phillips, the owner of the *thief land* discussed above. When Phillips died he left behind three pieces of land and a house. His will bequeathed none of this property to his three 'outside' children, presumably because he had never been on good terms with them. Instead, he left one piece of land — the *thief land* — to the servant who had cared for him during his painful death from cancer. Most of the remaining property was assigned, in trust, to the two offspring of one of the 'outside' children to be given to them at jural adulthood. Nothing was left to the other grandchildren since he was also not on speaking terms with them. In fact, he had never met the two grandchildren who were to inherit the bulk of his property, but at least he had never quarrelled with them.

Differential distribution need not involve strained family relations. In his will John Millington parcelled up his two and a half acre plot of land among his seven legitimate children. Alex, the eldest, received the largest share, three-quarters of an acre, because he was a married man with a family. Two other sons, both unmarried, received half acre plots each. The four daughters were jointly allotted three-quarters of an acre because they were women and because Millington believed that they would be less likely to farm the land than their brothers.

Less than ten per cent of land and other property is disposed of in wills. Choice, however, continues to hold even in intestacy and its operation may be seen, in part, through the proposed transmission of land by its owners. In a non-random sample of 44 village landholders (Table 3), the following consignment intentions were given: 18 persons

Table 3   Intended transmission of land

Intention	Number
Undecided	18
To children	12
Unequal distribution	10
On the basis of economic assistance	4
Total	44

had not yet decided or were otherwise uncertain about the disposal of their property; 12 proposed to leave it to their children; ten planned some sort of unequal allocation amongst children and other kin; and four intended conveyance on the basis of economic assistance given to them by children or non-kin.

Those who planned equal filial transmission had most or all of their children still living with them. Among males, all of these issue were legitimate; among females, both 'lawful' and 'bastard' children were included. Viewed alongside the unequal distribution in the other categories and the dependent status of most of the children involved, this suggests that these parents had not yet had the opportunity to test their children's loyalty or magnanimity. Like their counterparts elsewhere in the West Indies, villagers look forward to economic assistance from their children in old age as part of the parent-children relationship. While they recognize that this personalized filial obligation is not always met — some children are just 'bad-minded'; others are too poor to help; and still others have family obligations of their own which demand most of their resources — Leeward Villagers believe that if it is fulfilled, then it should be rewarded through the bestowal of any property that is present. Among the ten landowners in the unequal distribution category in Table 3, three proposed leaving their land to their wives alone (in fact, two of the three are childless); one planned to allot it jointly to his wife, two of his many children from various extra-marital unions, and to a foster son; one intended to transfer it to one of his sons on the basis of a request from his dead brother from whom he acquired the land and who was the godfather of the prospective heir; one aimed to allocate it only to some of her grandchildren but has not decided on which ones; one proposed to leave it to his first son and eldest child; one intended to bequeath it to her two daughters, her only children still at home; and one suggested that he would hand it down to two of his sons.

Especially instructive of the economic basis of land transfers and the way they are rooted in personalism are the intentions of the four landholders who cite material aid as their main consideration. One planned to leave her estate to 'the nearest one who takes care of me'; another 'according to treatment' received from his children; a third to 'who will "mind" [support] me'; and a fourth to one of her sons in England because 'he is the one who has me "standing up" [alive and well]. The others don't "notice" [care about] me.'

The intended transmission among most of these 44 villagers may not be carried out in the manner in which they would like since, if they follow past community practice, they are unlikely to formalize their choice through testamentary disposition. Yet it is just as unlikely that the actual conveyances will, in most cases, conform precisely to·the folk model of intestate inheritance. Again, one or more of the customary heirs (and occasional non-heir) may 'walk in and take all'. More likely, the heirs themselves may informally partition the property in terms of their own relative needs and interests. As a consequence, *family land* often loses many of its claimants, sometimes even being transformed into *inherited land* in the process. There are a variety of reasons why some of the legitimate heirs do not exert rights in the land: they are engaged in a more remunerative economic activity and have no interest in farming; they have migrated from the island and do not intend to return; they view the piece of land as a reward to those of their co-heirs who took care of the landowner during old age; they see the plot as too small or unproductive to bother with; they do not want to get embroiled in the confusion of a multitude of claims when there has been two or more generations of transmission; they have other more valuable holdings; and they do not want to interfere with the long time cultivation of the land by one or more of their peers.

The productive utility of family land

Such deviations from the customary transfer of *family land* suggest the need to re-evaluate the traditional view concerning the productive utility of undivided family property. Several observers have described family land in negative terms: on the one hand, it is said to be either abandoned or under-utilized '... because working it would arouse family antagonism' (Brierley, 1974:90); on the other, it is argued that multiple ownership retards its agricultural development even in cases where it is cultivated (Clarke, 1966:66; Finkel, 1971:299; Lowenthal, 1961:5). Clarke (1971:221), for example, has argued that in Jamaica:

the possibility of members of the family living in other parts of the island, returning to exercise their claim, either to cultivate the land, or erect their home on it, or to reap the produce of the trees, acts as a deterrent on economic use.

In St Lucia the norms of *family land* use appear to be taken even further:

the '*rights*' to [*family*] land are equally shared, and the legacy of the land becomes the communal property of the entire family. Thus, for example, if one of the heirs clears a field and plants a crop on it there is nothing to prevent all the other members of the family (including brothers, sisters, nephews, and nieces) from harvesting the crop when it is mature. This arrangement of communal land rights within the family serves as a strong deterrent to agricultural development since the more ambitious and enterprising farmers feel that it is not worthwhile planting crops under these conditions (Finkel, 1971:299).

Given these and other considerations, *family land* is said to have little beyond sentimental significance.

From the aspect of land use it [*family land* in Jamaica] is inevitably wasteful and incompetent. A good deal of family land is under-used, occupied by the old people, who are physically unable to develop it. Other multiple owned holdings are completely unproductive save for the food trees planted by the ancestors.... Misuse of land in the form of exhaustion or neglect, under-use because of lack of capital, or multiple ownership restricting development, are all practical results which have to be weighed against the strong sentiment and high values attached to the system (Clarke, 1971:240–241).

Such views do not generally apply to Leeward Village family holdings. The 67 family plots in the valley have a total of 317 joint owners, but only 128, or 40 per cent, of them are village residents. Most owner absenteeism is a product of extra-island wage-labour migration (see Rubenstein, 1979) and results in an average of only two claimants per parcel of land. While there is some reluctance to farm *family land* when there are a large number of claimants present or when rights to the property are in dispute (Rubenstein, 1975:164), for family members who are otherwise landless the migration of heirs often proves beneficial. Not only does it make more land available to those left behind who wish to cultivate (M.G. Smith, 1965:240–241), it also reduces the scope for family disputes regarding access to and use of communal property. Even when all family heirs are absent — a regular occurrence in Leeward Village — the property is never abandoned. Caretaking arrangements are always made and this enables otherwise landless villagers, kin and non-kin alike, to work a plot of land without the expense and constraints of leasehold and sharecrop transactions. Part or all of 14, or 21 per cent, of the 67 family holdings are also farmed by renters and sharecroppers. The net result of work by family heirs, caretakers, renters, and sharecroppers is that a larger proportion of family holdings than bought or inherited plots — 61 per cent as opposed to 57 per cent — are cultivated, a difference which is magnified when account is taken of the somewhat smaller size and relatively lower subsistence and commercial value of *family land*. Conversely, for many of those who migrated *family land* was used as security for borrowing the funds to finance their overseas removal. Even in cases of non-cultivation, the productive potential of *family land* is not forgotten and its possession can be considered a form of security against adversity. In this regard, Clarke's (1971:208) finding for Jamaica applies equally to Leeward Village:

> temporary non-exercise of a claim on family land does not, in the traditional system, preclude a subsequent exercise of that right. For example, a brother may return to the family land, occupied by his other brothers and sisters, after years of residence elsewhere and it would still be recognized by his family that he had the right 'if he had the need', to erect his house on the land and share in the crops of any of the fruit trees planted by his forbears on the property.

In Leeward Village, as in rural Jamaica (Clarke, 1971:238), produce from several family holdings, especially tree crops, is also distributed to heirs not engaged in the plot's cultivation, including relatives living in other parts of the island.

Conclusion

The various behavioural and ideological features of Leeward Village land tenure, transmission, and use are features of a system which functions to allocate land rights on the basis of individual need and changing conditions (cf. M.G. Smith, 1965:259). The transformation of land rights is governed, in the first instance, by a distinction between an island-wide legal system and a peasant-specific folk system. But even the folk system, which presents a set of rules for disposing of land more in keeping with local economic conditions than its national jural counterpart, is itself often overridden by the practical exigencies of individual cases. There are, then, three extant systems of tenure in the community: a nationally-rooted and codified jural system; an ideal folk system based on socially accepted alternative norms to the legal system; and a situationally-specific set of practical guidelines for coping with the behavioural restraints of the other two systems. Members of the community are aware of, have internalized, and manipulate all three systems. Will-making, informal departures from folk rules of transmission, caretaking, and even the fraudulent seizure of property often ensures that those who are in greatest need of land or will most fully realize its productive potential are in temporary or permanent control of it. Given the economic situation facing most villagers — low returns from self-employed or wage-labour activities, high rates of unemployment and under-employment, and an overall low level of material well-being — a rigid system of land tenure and use would merely add an additional layer of moral and behavioural constraint. Stated otherwise, a fluid and malleable form of land ownership and transmission allows villagers a certain measure of economic choice by permitting them to adjust their behaviour in accordance with existing circumstance (see Rubenstein, 1976, 1980, 1983; cf. Rodman, 1971:171–173,195–198). This system, by allowing choice, personalism, and situational factors to determine access to land, increases the scope for manoevrability in social and economic arrangements. By doing so it helps many villagers cope with the generally disadvantageous conditions defining their lives.

Acknowledgements
I am grateful to John Brierley and H. Christoph Wolfart for helpful comments on an earlier draft of this paper. Fieldwork in St Vincent was carried out between September 1969 and October 1971, between April and August 1972, and between June and August 1980. Research was made possible by a Canada Council Doctoral Fellowship, a University of Toronto, Centre for International Studies, Fellowship and Research Grant, a Province of Ontario Graduate Fellowship, and a Social Sciences and Humanities Research Council of Canada Leave Fellowship.

References

Augelli, John P. 1962. Land Use in Guadeloupe. *The Geographical Review*, 52:436–438.

Brierley, John S. 1974. Small Farming in Grenada, West Indies. *Manitoba Geographical Studies* 4. Winnipeg, Manitoba, Department of Geography, University of Manitoba.

Chernick, Sidney E. 1978. *The Commonwealth Caribbean: The Integrative Experience.* Baltimore, John Hopkins University Press.

Clarke, Edith 1966. *My Mother Who Fathered Me: A Study of the Family in Three Selected Communities in Jamaica,* Second Edition. London, Allen and Unwin.

1971. Land Tenure and the Family in Four Selected Communities in Jamaica. In *Peoples and Cultures of the Caribbean: An Anthropological Reader,* Michael M. Horowitz, (Ed.):201–242. Garden City, New York, Natural History Press.

Edwards, David T. 1961. *An Economic Study of Small Farming in Jamaica.* Kingston, Jamaica, Institute of Social and Economic Research, University College of the West Indies.

Finkel, Herman J. 1964. Attitudes Towards Land as a Factor in Agricultural Planning in the West Indies. *Caribbean Studies* 4:49–53.

1971. Patterns of Land Tenure in the Windward and Leeward Islands and their Relevance to the Problems of Agricultural Development in the West Indies. In *Peoples and Cultures of the Caribbean: An Anthropological Reader,* Michael M. Horowitz, (Ed.):291–304. Garden City, New York Natural History Press.

Hourihan, John J. 1973. Youth Employment: Stubbs. In *Windward Road: Contributions to the Anthropology of St Vincent,* Thomas M. Fraser, Jr., (Ed.):29–34. Amherst, Massachusetts, Department of Anthropology, University of Massachusetts.

1975. *Rule in Hairoun: A Study of the Politics of Power.* Ph.D. Dissertation. Department of Anthropology, University of Massachusetts.

Lowenthal, David 1961. Caribbean Views of Caribbean Land. *The Canadian Geographer,* 5:1–9.

O'Loughlin, Carleen 1968. *Economic and Political Change in the Leeward and Windward Islands.* New Haven., Yale University Press.

Philpott, Stuart B. 1973. *West Indian Migration: The Montserrat Case.* London School of Economics Monographs on Social Anthropology No. 47. London, Athlone Press.

Rodman, Hyman 1971. *Lower-Class Families: The Culture of Poverty in Negro Trinidad.* London, Oxford University Press.

Rubenstein, Hymie 1975. The Utilization of Arable Land in an Eastern Caribbean Valley. *Canadian Journal of Sociology,* 1:157–167.

1976. Incest, Effigy Hanging, and Biculturation in a West Indian Village. *American Ethnologist,* 3:765–781.

1977. Economic History and Population Movements in an Eastern Caribbean Valley. *Ethnohistory,* 24:19–45.

1979. The Return Ideology in West Indian Migration. *Papers in Anthropology,* 20:21–37

1980. Conjugal Behaviour and Parental Role Flexibility in an Afro-Caribbean Village. *The Canadian Review of Sociology and Anthropology,* 17:330–337.

1983. Caribbean Family and Household Organization: Some Conceptual Clarifications. *Journal of Comparative Family Studies,* 14:283–298.

Smith, Michael G. 1965. *The Plural Society in the British West Indies.* Berkeley University of California Press.

Smith, Raymond T. 1971. Land Tenure in Three Negro Villages in British Guiana. In *Peoples and Cultures of the Caribbean: An Anthropological*

Reader, Michael M. Horowitz, (Ed.):243–266. Garden City, New York, Natural History Press.

Starbird, Ethel A. 1979. St Vincent, The Grenadines, and Grenada: Taking It as It Comes. *National Geographic,* 156:399–425.

University of the West Indies Development Mission. 1969. *The Development Problem in St Vincent.* Kingston, Jamaica, Institute of Social and Economic Research, University of the West Indies.

World Bank [International Bank for Reconstruction and Development] 1979. *Current Economic Position and Prospects of St Vincent.* Report No. 2438-CRB. Latin American and Caribbean Regional Office.

CHAPTER 4

White law and black custom
The evolution of Bahamian land tenures

Michael Craton

The special conditions which shaped the history of the Bahamas and its people determined that an unbridgeable dichotomy developed between popular customary and official legal systems of land tenure. More fundamentally, it can be argued that popular customs and concepts — particularly those of 'common' and 'generational' land — stem from African roots, whereas all more formal legal concepts — including squatters' rights and sharecropping as well as leasehold and freehold tenures — derive from Europe. While it was natural that such a counterpoint should evolve in a colony of failed plantations, ruled by whites but with a majority of African slaves and their descendants, it is somewhat paradoxical that, in attempting to resolve current confusions over land tenures, a predominantly black, and purportedly populist regime should veer towards an essentially European and legalist rather than African customary, or even a syncretic 'Creole' solution.

After a brief discussion of the historical roots of the concepts of real estate and common land, this chapter examines in specific detail the evolution of the conflict between them in the Bahamian case. A section describing the origins of formal tenures between 1629 and 1846 is followed by others examining, respectively, the effects of the arrival of the Loyalists and their slaves in the 1780s, and of the resettlement of Liberated Africans and slave emancipation between 1825 and 1838. The situation at the end of the colonial period is illustrated chiefly through a discussion of the Bowe case in Exuma (1961–2), after which a concluding section deals with the problems relating to formal and informal tenures faced by the independent Commonwealth of the Bahamas since 1973.

Real estate and common land: The basic conflict

Whether or not such concepts as real estate, freehold property and inheritance were peculiar to Europe, the fictive construct of individual entitlement to land was the basis which made the creation and expansion of European politics possible, leading successively to feudal kingdoms, empires and modern bourgeois states. As the etymology of the phrase implies, the very concept of real estate was originally based upon the territorial suzerainty of a royal line. As the Germanic tribes settled among the ruins of the Roman Empire, stability and security depended upon military protection, and the integrity of an aristocratic protector class upon the possession and exploitation of land, and its transmission by inheritance. No land was to be without its lord, but no petty lord could hold his land or expect to transmit it to his lineal descendants without a superior power and authority for tenure and inheritance. Thus, absolute and permanent ownership was invested in a monarchy, a hereditary line of kings, whose power was originally established through conquest or 'surrender and regrant', recognised by a renewable act of personal submission — later commuted into nominal rent — and delimited by the effective radius of their legal writ.

The reciprocal advantages of the 'feudal contract' — particularly the practices that allowed faithful 'tenants-in-chief' to become hereditary landowners, and their younger sons to acquire lands under similar terms outside traditional boundaries — led to the creation of ever-larger states and, eventually, overseas empires. The Crown long retained the tradition of absolute sovereignty, maintaining as long as it could the claim that all land was essentially Crown Land and remaining, through its monopoly of the legal system, the ultimate authority for all tenures, and rarely, and reluctantly, alienating land altogether.

Against this basic system, however, as centuries of stability led to commercial expansion and the emergence of a bourgeois class (planters as well as merchants), a demand for freehold property developed and extended into the ownership of land, as part of that crucial growth of 'possessive individualism' of which C.B. McPherson writes.[1] The Crown, as we have argued, held the only original freehold. The dissemination of freehold tenures, strictly speaking, was an invasion of the royal prerogative, though it was at the same time part of that partnership between bourgeois individualism and royal authority that made modern states and empires possible. It also required a complex evolving structure of conveyance, inheritance, survey and registration. It was no coincidence that the profession of lawyer itself changed from that of being part of the royal bureaucracy to one of the most bourgeois (and thus acquisitive) of avocations.

Similar features and functions may have evolved separately outside Europe, but certainly, in most of the world beyond (and in much of Europe itself before feudal times) the traditional system was very different. Land belonged to the community, be it tribe, clan, chiefly state or confederation of village units, with the chief or elders simply apportioning use, or *usufruct*, to heads of households, according to need. Land was common to — in fact, along with the lineage itself, it defined — the political unit. Whatever transmission occurred in authority and customary usage was through the common lineage. All land and almost all property, was for the use of the household, but properly belonged to the extended family, the lineage, the tribe; that is, to 'the people'. This was the tradition that obtained, in classic form, throughout most of pre-colonial Africa, including the entire catchment area from which the millions of slaves carried to European New World colonies, were derived.

The origins of formal tenures in the Bahamas, 1629–1846

Fittingly, the Bahamas began as a British colony with a quasi-feudal system of tenures. The archipelago was claimed by the King by right of conquest or first effective Christian settlement.[2] The abortive grant to Sir Robert Heath (1629) specified that the islands were to be held after the manner of the County Palatine of Durham 'in free and common socage', while the marginally more effective charter given to six of the eight Proprietors of the Carolinas (1670) specified that lands be held in the form of socage customary 'in our Manor of East Greenwich in the County of Kent'.[3] This meant in effect that the Proprietors, as tenants-in-chief of the King, could grant acreages as large as they wished to any individuals, provided that the holders paid an annual quit rent — usually less than a penny per acre. The land could be escheated if not developed or if the quit rents were not paid. But if developed, it would be regarded as virtually freehold property, and could be transmitted to family heirs, bequeathed to others, or even sold — as long as the annual quit rents continued to be paid.[4]

From the beginning, though, the Bahamian system was not quite so simple. The first actual settlement in the islands occurred in the interval between the 1629 and 1670 grants, which coincided with the republican Interregnum in England. A trickle of settlers from Bermuda arrived after 1648, drawn either by the possibility of political and religious freedom (after which their main refuge was named Eleuthera) or by the promise of unencumbered land, contained in a preliminary broadsheet and incorporated in formal Articles in July

1647. In return for an investment of £100, 'adventurers' in a colonial company would be entitled to 300 acres in the 'main settlement' plus 35 acres for each additional member of their household, as well as no less than 2,000 acres outside the main settlement. Time-expired indentured servants were to be granted 25 acres apiece. These provisions were clearly a combination of the shareholder concessions as established for the Adventurers of Bermuda and the 'headright' system already found throughout the mainland colonies.[5]

Thus, the original Bahamian settlers, who by 1670 were established in New Providence as well as northern Eleuthera, Harbour Island and Spanish Wells, came to regard themselves as having absolute property rights, not just in their house-lots in the settlements (an analogue of the 'burgage' tenures in New England towns), but over the farming land needed by their households for subsistence as well. Since the Articles of the Eleutherian Adventurers specified that farmland be worked in common for the first three years or more, there may also have been the germ of the idea that all adjacent farmland was for common use — which for the Harbour Islanders at least became a legal reality between 1783 and 1842.[6]

For their part, the Proprietors attempted to augment their revenue by asserting their rights to quit rents from established settlers, and by attracting new colonists with generous grants of quit rent land. These moves, however, were doomed to failure by the immigration of the pirates, who condemned New Providence to anarchy, isolated the settlements of northern Eleuthera, and made the rest of the Bahama Islands an extremely insecure prospect for potential settlers.

Order, if not prosperity, was restored with the Crown's assumption of political control in 1718, though by a curious compromise the Proprietors retained the right to collect quit rents until 1787.[7] Significantly, one of the first acts passed after the creation of an Assembly in 1729 was aimed at settling claims on land, particularly (in what may have been the majority of cases) that which was 'never laid out, since deserted, never surveyed or titles and patents lost'. In the absence of a valid counter claim, those who could prove possession for a mere three years, with improvements made, were promised clear title, 'confirmed to them and their heirs for ever, any law, usage or custom to the contrary notwithstanding', subject only to the payment of an annual quit rent of 3/– per 100 acres to the Lords Proprietor.[8] An even more vital enactment was the Registry Act of 1764. This required the registration of the deeds or conveyances of all 'lands, tenements or hereditaments, negroes, vessels, goods or effects', in order to prevent the confusion and frauds which had followed from a rapid turnover of lands and mortgages, and the operations of 'many evil minded persons' taking advantage of 'bad and insufficient titles and securities'.[9]

The condition of tenures and titles remained confused until the coming of the American Loyalists in the 1780s changed the demographic and socio-economic condition of the Bahamas. The purchase of lands by the Crown between 1784 and 1786 and the final buying out of the Lords Proprietor in 1787 for a total of £16,000, and the passing of another act to establish the validity of land claims in 1789[10] were necessary parts of the process whereby the British government compensated the Loyalist refugees with grants of land, at the rate of 40 acres for each white head of household, plus 20 acres for every dependant, including slaves.[11] Following the migration of some 1,600 whites and their 6,000 slaves, several hundred such grants were made, totalling perhaps 100,000 acres. Most of the larger Bahamian islands were settled for the first time, with the intention of developing cotton plantations or salinas, producing solar salt.[12]

The Loyalist land grants were free of initial charges and of quit rents for the first ten years, but the Crown had no intention of giving up the principle that these were conditional tenures, dependent upon the development of the land. A comprehensive Quit Rent Act was passed in 1802, calling for the surrender and regranting of all lands allocated by the Crown since 1787, subjecting them to the payment of annual quit rents of 5/– for each town lot and 2/– for every 100 acres of developed land.[13] Theoretically at least, lands were to be escheated either for non-payment or for non-development. Even more important, a new Registration Act in 1805 decreed that not only were all deeds and conveyances to be registered, but registered documents had priority over all others, even those of a prior date.[14]

Thus, as a result of government action between 1787 and 1805, the basic principles of Bahamian land tenure law were fixed; that all unalienated land belonged to the Crown, that Crown grants were not easily to be converted into absolute freehold, and that no land tenures — including freeholds — were secure without duly registered title. After 1805 sundry minor changes occurred, such as different forms of lease for salina, farming or building land, and the distinction made between Public Land, leased by the Crown to the government for public purposes, and true Crown Land. But the only substantial change before the twentieth century was the abolition of the quit rent system by the Commutation Act of 1846.[15] This allowed for the conversion of quit rent tenures for house-lots and lands into absolute freehold, on the payment of arrears dating back for up to 16 years. This undoubtedly increased the number of freeholds, especially in New Providence and the other older settlements. Yet since the act required payment within three months and the production of valid documentation, the net effect was a very large increase in official Crown Land through default in all the most recently settled islands, and the weakening of tenure wherever ownership had been, or became, obscure.

Loyalist landowners and slave proto-peasants

The changes made to official Bahamian tenure law as a result of the Loyalist influx bore little relation to realities, particularly once plantations decayed, white planters deserted the outer islands, and slavery was ended. From the beginning, the Loyalists found conditions very different from those they had left behind on the American mainland. The islands were scattered and infertile, and the sense of community and interdependence which stemmed from the migration of masters with their slaves was reinforced by isolation and the difficulties of combining export crops with subsistence food production.

Where masters remained resident on their lands this produced self-contained units more like late medieval manors or the extended households of Tudor times than the classic model of labour- and land-intensive export-oriented slave plantations. As demonstrated by the most studied of all such units, the Farquharson Estate on Watling's Island, resident masters and their slaves lived very close together in every respect.[16] The master held the legal title to the land, but all inhabitants developed a communal sense of attachment or belonging, that was quasi-proprietorial. This was signified by the voluntary adoption by many slaves of their owners' names, and by the retention of the names of former plantations (not infrequently named after their owners) as the names of the subsequent settlements of free black peasant farmers. Once the master's family left, or through generations of miscegenation folded into the majority (as seems to have happened commonly in parts of Eleuthera and Long Island), the land was regarded as belonging to the former community and its descendants, in custom if not in law. The title might have lapsed, or been long forgotten, or claimed by a coloured descendant of the original owner, but it was almost invariably challenged by all family heads still living in the settlement.[17]

The senses of community, reinforced by actual and fictive kinship, of an attachment to a particular location amounting to a communal quasi-proprietorship, and of being what Sidney Mintz has termed proto-peasants rather than praedial slaves, occurred even earlier, and with greater intensity, on the increasingly large number of Out Island plantations owned by absentees.[18] Under the management of a poor white or even free coloured overseer, these operations were initially concerned with extracting whatever profit could be made from cotton and salt. They therefore lacked the manorial ambiance of Farquharson's Estate and were characterized by separation and tensions between managers and slaves. The slaves' sense of community, though, was aided by their isolation, a common ethnicity and ever-tightening kinship ties. Moreover, as the prospects of plantation or salina profits faded, the slaves, while constrained to live within a regulated settlement and limited in their mobility by the boundaries of their owner's estate, were increasingly left to their own devices, and encouraged to subsist for themselves by slash-and-burn agriculture and small stock raising. The result was the closest replication possible in the new environment of an African-style village-based peasantry.

The most outstanding, and best-known case was that of the Rolle estates on the island of Great Exuma.[19] Denys Rolle, a Devonshire magnate turned Florida planter, was among the most substantial of the Bahamian Loyalists, settling his 140 slaves on two of the better tracts of Great Exuma in 1784, which were appropriately called Rolleville and Rolletown. This holding was later augmented to 5,000 acres by the addition of three more parcels, the chief of which was christened Stevenstone (later Steventon) after the family seat in Devonshire.[20] The Rolle slaves, who were predominantly creoles with a healthy balance of the sexes, living (seemingly by choice) in nuclear family households, flourished exceedingly in the new environment, their numbers rising by natural increase to 254 in 1822 and 374 in 1834. By then they were owned by the absentee son of Denys Rolle, John, Lord Rolle (raised to the peerage by William Pitt in 1797), and being managed by a single white overseer living at Steventon, and an attorney living in Nassau.

In its peak year, 1791, the Rolle estates produced 60,000 pounds of cotton, worth about £3,000. Yet by the 1820s, cotton production had almost faded away and attempts by Rolle's agents to squeeze profit from other activities were equally unsuccessful. By 1828, Lord Rolle was complaining that he had spent £5,000 over the previous ten years to maintain his slaves, for a return of £130. For reasons of control, attempts were made to concentrate the slaves in Steventon village, but this proved impractical because of their numbers. The slaves on the other four holdings were almost unsupervised, but all of Rolle's slaves had comparative freedom and mobility. Encouraged to be as self-sufficient in food as possible, they resisted formal work for their owner in favour of working their family allotments and building up their herds. Far from toiling in gangs from sun-up to sun-down, they were assigned daily or weekly tasks which were annually more difficult to enforce. Apart from periodic trips to the salinas under the eyes of black drivers, slaves went off on their own for days at a time, working distant grounds, herding sheep and goats, fishing, or even shooting ducks, doves, agouti or iguana with guns of their own.

Between 1824 and 1828 Lord Rolle made several appeals to be allowed to shift his slaves to more profitable areas (Trinidad, Demerara, Jamaica or even Cuba), but these were rejected by the Colonial Office, even when Rolle promised that the slaves would be allowed to buy their own freedom by instalments.[21] For their own part, Lord Rolle's slaves vigorously resisted any attempts to move them even within the Bahamas, mutinying on several occasions between 1828 and 1834. 'There is a most insistent impression here,' wrote Governor Lewis Grant in December 1828,

> that the immediate predecessor in possession of them (to Lord Rolle) had either entailed them, or left them under some very particularly favourable provision for them, in his will. The slaves themselves are completely under this impression and have been the more confirmed in it, that their treatment in every respect for many years past, has been of the most indulgent kind.

Besides, very few of Rolle's slaves had availed themselves of opportunities to 'work out their freedom', not just because money was extremely difficult to come by in Exuma, but because they felt it was unnecessary, being virtually free peasants already.[22]

The first serious disturbance happened in November 1828, when a new agent read out to the slaves a letter from Lord Rolle which hinted at a removal to Trinidad, and threatened punishment if the slaves did not work harder. The slaves responded either by refusing to work at all, or by pretending to comply, but quitting the fields as soon as the overseer's back was turned, to go to 'their own plantations'. Each Sunday they paraded in squads under eight ring-leaders — all heads of households — drilling and target-shooting with 45 muskets. The Governor sent down a detachment of the 2nd. West India Regiment in the sloop-of-war H.M.S. *Monkey,* but the slaves were only subdued by a promise that they would not be removed to Trinidad, or anywhere else against their will, and by a long overdue issue of clothing.[23]

Another disturbance took place in 1829, when military force had to be used to shift several Rolle families to Grand Bahama (perhaps the ring-leaders of 1828), despite arrangements being made for them to sell their small stock and receive reimbursement for their unharvested crops.[24] The most determined refusal to be separated from their lands, however, occurred in 1830, when a 32-year old slave called Pompey led resistance to a plan to shift 77 slaves from Exuma to Cat Island. Eight families first fled to the bush, then appropriated Lord Rolle's salt boat and sailed to Nassau to lay their case before the Governor, the allegedly sympathetic James Carmichael Smyth. They were flogged for their boldness but won their case, returning to Steventon in triumph two months later.[25]

Thereafter, extracting formal work from the slaves became almost impossible for Rolle's beleaguered overseer, and troops had to be sent down to Exuma on more occasions between 1830 and 1834. The slaves officially became Apprentices on August 1, 1834, but very shortly afterwards an exasperated Lord Rolle wrote from Devonshire to the Colonial Secretary that his 'slaves' still would not work,

> except the Soldiers are on the spot — the Moment the Troops leave the Island they are again in a State of Insubordination as before — in Consequence of this ... I am inclined to send out Instructions to discharge the Negroes from their Apprenticeship but first to request through you the Cooperation of Government — My Instructions would be in my Power of Attorney that it should contain full Powers to convey the lands for the use of the Negroes during their Apprenticeship.[26]

This disingenuous plan to cut losses was disallowed, but Rolle's ex-slaves were ever-ready to exploit any sign of generosity or weakness on the part of their master. Like a majority of Bahamian blacks, Rolle's ex-slaves served a merely nominal Apprenticeship, and when they were declared fully free on August 1, 1838 they took over Rolle's five tracts of Exuma and set up a well-regulated system of commonage based on the villages of Rolleville, Steventon, Mount Thompson, Ramsey's and Rolletown, despite the absence of a formal deed of conveyance from their former owner.[27] More as a statement of community and a form of identity than as an expression of gratitude (let alone the result of massive miscegenation), they all took the surname Rolle. Thenceforward, in an absolute converse of the system of primogeniture upon which aristocratic European tenures depended, any person with the surname Rolle — today more than 4,000 persons — or anyone who could prove descent from a Rolle on the male or female side — a veritable host — could theoretically claim house-plot and subsistence allotment upon the 5,000 acres of Exumian common land.

Though less well-studied, similar processes occurred in other Out Islands. There were 'proto-peasant' disturbances during the 1830s in Eleuthera, Cat Island, Crooked Island and Ragged Island,[28] and informal commonage systems were established in several islands, particularly Eleuthera. In that island, conditions were in several respects similar to those in Exuma; with the presence of sizeable well-integrated communities of ex-slaves able to take possession of abandoned estates, but constrained within certain boundaries by the comparative scarcity of other unappropriated lands. The Eleutheran commonages based upon the black settlements of The Bluff, Savanna Sound, Tarpum Bay and Rock Sound were also doubtless aided by the creation of the first official Bahamian commonage, granted on the mainland of northern Eluethera to the inhabitants of Harbour Island, allegedly for their assistance in the 'recapture' of Nassau from the Spaniards by Andrew Deveaux in 1783 — though not formally authorised until 1842.[29]

All established Bahamian commonages were eventually regulated by the Commonage Act of 1896.[30] This legislation was inspired by the Common Law relating to ancient English commonages, which originated from the common rights held by ordinary tenants in medieval manors over certain areas of woodland and grazing land. But the majority of Bahamian commonages, involving lands for all phases of peasant subsistence, clearly stemmed from an entirely different, and non-English tradition.

Formal and informal tenures after slave Emancipation

The process of Emancipation, with the black majority of the Bahamian population instantly changed from being property to owning it, was a crucial but difficult transition for masters and slaves alike. With the continued bankruptcy of the plantation economy and the insensible growth of *laissez-faire* principles, the imperial government was no more inclined to help the freed slaves in the Bahamas than those in the true West Indian colonies, while the local regime, fearful that black liberty might turn into licence, had even less motive to aid the ex-slaves. The best that the Bahamian blacks could hope for was benign neglect, and in fact, though they were not directly helped, they were rarely molested. In consequence, they were able to develop customary tenure patterns of their own, subject only to the countervailing interests of the remaining private landowners.

A useful model for government resettlement schemes had been promoted from 1825 by the imperial authorities for the Africans liberated from illegal slave traders and landed in the Bahamas. In the more distant reaches of New Providence, Governors Grant and Carmichael Smyth had founded the villages of Headquarters (later Carmichael), Adelaide and Gambier, each consisting of a row of small house-lots, surrounded by farming plots of a size (5–10 acres) regarded as sufficient for a family's subsistence. These were to be sold for £1 an acre, payable in easy instalments. For the Liberated Africans who could not be settled in the outlying villages or who preferred to live closer to town, a 200-acre development called Grant's Town was laid out just 'Over-the-Hill' to the south of the older part of Nassau. Here only leaseholds were granted at first, but on the eve of slave emancipation freehold house-lots of a quarter of an acre were sold for 10/- and garden plots for £2 an acre.[31]

Faced by the socio-economic uncertainties of Emancipation in 1838, the Bahamian ruling class opposed such generosity towards the 10,000 ex-slaves. As far as they followed any theory, they favoured the ideas put forward by Edward Gibbon Wakefield; that Crown Land should be jealously conserved, made available only in sizeable parcels, at a price sufficient to ensure its development by those with capital, to keep a reservoir of labourers dependent upon wage employment, and to bring substantial revenue into the Treasury. Permission to sell Crown Lands for as little as £1 an acre was given by the Colonial Office in 1836, but in the Bahamas tracts were only released for sale by auction (with £1 thus the minimum, or 'upset' price), and in 1839 the minimum size of lots was restricted to 40 acres. Although the size and price of lots were later reduced to 20 acres at 12/- an acre, even this was beyond the means of most ex-slaves, especially in the Out Islands.[32]

The only formal scheme to settle ex-slaves was a semi-philanthropic private venture at Fox Hill, New Providence, three miles east of Nassau. There in 1840, Judge Sandilands subdivided his estate into 100 lots of one to ten acres for modest prices, forming a village that was named after him in 1849.[33] The great majority of ex-slaves were left to fend for themselves, with those who spurned peasant subsistence farming and wished to live close to Nassau having particular difficulties. Some of these joined with Liberated Africans (mainly Yoruba) in a settlement called Bain Town, after its black developer, G.H. Bain.[34] But a far greater number crowded into Grant's Town, which for a century after 1850 was to contain more than half of Nassau's population. The price of house-lots multiplied regularly, while most were divided and divided again. A common pattern was for the original owners to become landlords, with tenants even moving their wooden houses from lot to lot.

Yet the gradual emergence of classes did not Europeanize even the nearest of Nassau's black suburbs before the twentieth century. Many white visitors commented on the African appearance of Grant's Town, Bain Town and the outlying villages, and on the persistence of African customs. And beneath the exotic surface was a community structure that continued to owe more to African notions of family, kinship, property ownership and inheritance, than to the master culture and official legal system. These characteristics resulted not only from the presence of many native Africans who had never been enslaved, but from the arrival of ex-slave migrants from the Out Islands, who from the mid-nineteenth century formed transplanted mini-communities owing more to island and family connexions than to the new urban environment.

For what obtained for New Providence applied with even greater force to the Out Islands, where the ex-slaves were proportionately even more cut off from the cultural and legal, as from the socio-economic, influences of the colonial metropolis. With the Commutation Act of 1846 and the greater attention paid to the surveying and registering of lands and deeds which followed from lip service to Wakefield's theories, there was a progressive increase in the number of officially registered titles, and somewhat greater precision in the delimitation of private, public and officially unalienated Crown Lands. But while the value of legal title for at least a house-lot became more apparent, it did fix the method of conveyance in the European mould, or determine that ordinary farmers would restrict themselves to areas over which they had strictly legal tenure.

The predominant Out Island economy had become a shifting type of peasant farming. This depended very much upon the family unit, even within the Commonage areas. But the interdependence of all family members — females as much as males — the need for a shifting and seemingly casual form of farming, the prevailing vagueness about other persons' titles and boundaries, and, by and large, the general availability of unused land, reinforced the African traditions that all land was for common use according to need, that land belonged equally to the user group, and that this informal type of tenure existed within the family from generation to generation. This was the genesis of the concept of generational property; that even where official title resided in a single family member, he or she only held it in trust for the family at large, any member of which might be the actual user, and that even where wills might give priority to one descendant over another, all descendants retained a fundamental claim. Some wills and deeds, indeed, actually specified this method of transmission, naming the immediate tenant but reserving the rights in the land to all descendants, even in some cases those who were technically illegitimate.[35]

Generational land was common in all areas first developed and then deserted by Loyalist planters. Yet the loosest and most general of all generational customs were found, naturally, in those islands least developed before slavery ended. Such an island was Andros, scarcely touched by the Loyalists, which was, for the most part, first settled in the mid-nineteenth century by ex-slaves from nearby islands which had less free or unexhausted land, such as Exuma and Long Island. It was at Long Bay Cays, Andros, a century later, that Keith Otterbein found and analysed the extreme form of generational tenure and transmission that could allow on one tract of land 'not only the descendants of the ancestor, but also some of his sister's descendants, a niece of his son-in-law, and his grandson's mother-in-law'. This system Otterbein termed 'bilateral with unrestricted land-holding descent', in contrast to the more strictly 'ambilineal' Jamaican system of family land described by Edith Clarke, or the more formal and self-regulating Barbadian system described by Sidney Greenfield. He attributed the differences mainly to the comparative abundance of land in Andros, the fact that many of the ancestor's direct descendants were off in Nassau and thus not eager to exercise their rights, and the greater sophistication of the Barbadians in adapting the English legal concept of entail.[36]

As in Jamaica and other West Indian colonies with large areas of vacant land, very many ex-slaves in the Bahamas became technically squatters. This trend was anticipated as early as 1834, when an act empowered JPs to order the summary ejection of unauthorised persons from private land on the plea of the titleholder, though at the same time an important principle was established by making an exception for squatters who had enjoyed uninterrupted possession for 20 years.[37] In 1839, just after 'full freedom' was granted, the law was tightened to allow Stipendiary Magistrates to order the ejection of untitled persons from any land, including Crown Land, and to imprison at hard labour those who resisted the order — though again the law was mitigated to except from immediate dispossession those who had enjoyed 'quiet possession' for at least five years — that is, since before the first Emancipation Act.[38]

Forcible ejection of squatters, though, proved impracticable, especially from Crown Lands, and the savage eviction process enacted in 1839 was amended within a year to except those who had enjoyed quiet possession for at least a year.[39] The Crown simply insured itself against 'unlawful alienation' by decreeing that unauthorized settlers could only gain title by 'squatters' right' after 60 years of un- challenged occupation, rather than the 20 years which applied to private land.[40] In practice then, the ex-slaves found it relatively easy to gather wood, run sheep or goats, farm or even live on lands belonging to others or the Crown, but never easy to gain title for themselves by squatters' rights. Their access to free land by informal custom, moreover, was curtailed wherever resident landowners were able to enforce leasehold or sharecropping tenures, or during periods when the government was willing (and able) to encourage development by foreign investors.

Many ex-slaveowners attempted to sustain a return from their lands by binding their ex-slaves to sharecropping leases. A typical example applied to the Farquharson Estate on Watling's Island as late as 1865, though Charles Farquharson himself had long been dead and most of those working the land now lived at nearby Prospect Hill. In this case, the tenants were pledged to pay to Charles Wilson, the manager, one-third of their produce. They were allowed to keep one breeding sow free of rent or charge, but if they kept more they had to give up one pig from each litter.[41] In the more developed islands, with more resident planters and a shortage of Crown Lands, the terms could be even stiffer, especially during periods of relative farming prosperity. In Eleuthera towards the end of the pineapple boom of 1857–1902, for example, sharecroppers were subject to a variant of the notorious 'truck system', becoming hopelessly indebted to their landlords for advances made in the form of seedlings, fertiliser, tools and provisions.[42]

Elsewhere, sharecropping leases were very difficult to enforce, particularly where there was an abundance of Crown Land on which the peasants could squat. Crown Land itself came under government pressure when Governor Ambrose Shea (1887–1895) promoted the sisal industry, and a dynamic Colonial Secretary, Joseph Chamberlain (1895–1900), preached that Crown Lands throughout the Empire should be exploited. Ostensibly, Shea tried to aid 'poor settlers' by making ten acre grants at 5/– an acre, which would become freehold tenures if developed in sisal within ten years. But the failure of this scheme to transform traditional Out Island farming was guaranteed by the simultaneous encouragement of outside capitalists to lease huge acreages (the only means by which sisal could profitably be grown) for sisal plantations in Andros, Abaco, Inagua and even New Providence. Not coincidentally, the largest investor of all was Joseph Chamberlain, who sent his son Neville to develop a lease of 20,000 acres in northern Andros.[43]

Yet, after a brief boom during the Spanish-American War, sisal failed once the U.S.A. took over and developed Cuba and the Philippines, just as Bahamian pineapples slumped after the U.S. annexed Hawaii. Squatting resurged, not least on the Chamberlain estate. In 1903, the agent wrote to Neville to inform him that several Androsians had already encroached, building houses, growing crops and cutting sisal. One of them even had the temerity to ask, in vain, that the Chamberlains grant him title to the land on which he was squatting.[44]

Squatting remained the rule rather than the exception in much of the Bahamas for another generation, and squatters were secure in many islands for another 50 years. What brought the change, and provoked the ultimate crisis in the tension between informal custom and official legal tenures, was the wave of foreign investment, speculation and development which began in the 1920s, paused in the 1930s and 1940s, and climaxed in the period between World War Two and the achievement of Bahamian independence in 1973.

The modern problem: The Bowe Case in Exuma, 1961–2

By the twentieth century the condition of Bahamian land tenure was almost anarchic. Thanks to incomplete and inaccurate surveying, to incomplete registration and a bewildering range of documentary and customary claims, many of them conflicting and overlapping, those who wished to purchase and develop land were often faced with almost insuperable difficulties.[45] Conversely, those who occupied and worked land without incontrovertible title were often placed in conflict with those who could command stronger legal resources in Nassau or the support of government (including the assistance of a not always incorruptible Crown Lands Office).

Attempts by government to resolve the dilemma were largely frustrated. Compulsory surveying of Crown Lands was authorized by an act in 1882 but proceeded at a snail's pace, mainly because of cost. It was far from complete a century later. Even more visionary was the Land Roll Act of 1920, which made provisions for a complete cadastral survey, in order to collate occupancy and land use with legal title. This never came into effect at all.[46]

As to titles, government did initiate a system of 'quieting' or resolving unclear titles in the Acquisition of Lands Act (1913). But this applied exclusively to lands which government wished to appropriate for public purposes. Moreover, the incentive for resolving tenure conflicts lay almost entirely with the government, not surprisingly giving rise to the sentiments of ordinary islanders that any such legislation was against their interests. This feeling was reinforced by the tougher provisions of the Squatters and Trespassers Act of 1927, and was not quelled by the general Quieting of Titles Act, brought into effect in November 1959.[47] This act, which accompanied the greatest surge of foreign investment in land in Bahamian history, ostensibly aided both the buyers and sellers of land to remove encumbrances to title. But it was itself cumbrous, either revealing hopeless tangles and only enriching the lawyers involved, or, where resulting in decisions against sitting tenants, even regarded (by them) as 'a licence to steal'.

The modern dilemma over Bahamian land tenures, and much of the foregoing, can best be illustrated by litigation brought under the 1959 Act, of which the landmark case was that involving the Bowe estate of The Forest, Exuma, in 1961–2.[48] The case came forward because the documentary titleholder, a black Exumian called Maxwell Bowe, aged 71, petitioned the court to establish his undisputed freehold right to the land, in order to sell it to a Floridian real estate developer for a very large sum of money. The Quieting of Titles Act required a petitioner to advertize his intentions in the newspapers in order to give any adverse claimants opportunity to come forward to dispute his right. In the event, Bowe was confronted by no less than 28 adverse claimants, who contended that they had a generational right to the land in common, which in practise meant that they had to establish their rights as squatters.

The Forest Estate was a 3,763 acre tract of typical scrubby limestone in the centre of Great Exuma, adjacent to the Rolle commonages of Mount Thompson and Ramsey's. Identical in its boundaries to an old Loyalist slave plantation, it consisted of some 15 ramshackle 'fields', mainly covered in bush but intermittently used for farming and grazing. These fields totally surrounded a settlement, which in 1960 had a population of 200 in 37 households, two churches and a school. The Forest had been sold by the Adderley family (the original owners) to Max Bowe's father in 1903, bequeathed to Bowe and his three siblings in 1920 and devolved on Bowe alone in 1948. The Bowe family lived just outside the settlement, in a smallish house on the site of the old plantation great house, nicknamed the 'Slave House', destroyed in the hurricane of 1926.

The rights of the inhabitants to the settlement itself were not disputed by Bowe. As Judge Scarr noted, 'At one time the Settlement itself reputedly belonged to the Estate, but with the end of slavery it was given to the freed slaves, whose descendants are represented by the present inhabitants'. All of them referred to the settlement as 'generational property', and some of them applied the term to the Forest Estate as a whole. 'It was, however,' added Scarr (unintentionally showing his bias from the beginning) 'quite impossible to ascertain exactly what was meant by this expression except that in some way the property passed from parents to children.'[49]

Max Bowe claimed that his family had farmed the estate for at least 40 years, raising horses, sheep and poultry, and growing provisions, and that the residents of the settlement had 'merely provided labour on the Estate . . . occupying moveable small-holdings for which the rent consisted of annual thirds of the crops produced'. The adverse claimants, on the other hand, asserted that for well over 30 years they had used and enjoyed the whole of The Forest Estate 'at will, farming where they wanted, moving when they wanted, and keeping what they called their "creatures" (that is to say poultry, sheep, goats, pigs and so on) where they wanted'. They emphatically denied ever working for Bowe, paying him shares of their produce, or even asking his permission to work the land. They did acknowledge that Max Bowe and his father had lived in the Slave House and its successor, and that the Bowes had reared a lot of stock, including race-horses, on various parts of the estate, but claimed that the Bowes merely did this 'as a matter of sufferance on their part'. In obvious emulation of the Exuma Rolles, the inhabitants also claimed that the affairs of The Forest were 'watched over and supervised by a small self-elected body which they called the Committee', a practice which Judge Scarr admitted was 'fairly common throughout the Bahamas in places where there are settlements and common land'.[50]

Despite overwhelming evidence of customary usage over generations, the inhabitants had no chance at all against the resources of the law. As Judge Scarr pointed out, they had to prove that the owner had either abandoned the land or been dispossessed, that adverse possession had been taken by another (or others), and had been continued without interruption for 20 years. Quite apart from the impossibility of denying that Bowe had lived on and worked at least part of the land for 40 years, there was no evidence that any effort had been made to oust him. English precedents decreed that the 'smallest act would be sufficient to show him that there was no discontinuance', and Bowe had in fact provided innumerable proofs of his contribution towards The Forest Estate as a whole (including the maintenance of wells, walls and gates, and the donation of land for the churches and school). 'I would not go so far as to say that Mr Bowe ignored the residents completely in these matters,' wrote Scarr, 'or that the local committee was never involved, but what I do say is that all these things clearly and abundantly show that Mr Bowe regarded himself as the owner in possession and behaved as such and was by general repute such until at least 1960 when this trouble started between him and his tenants.'[51]

The very solidarity of the adverse claimants worked against their case. For an effective joint claim it would have to apply to the same piece of land, continuously occupied by the claimants in common; that is, acting as 'a unified body . . . as mutual agents the one for the other'. This was obviously impossible since it was clear that each separate family worked different parts of The Forest Estate, independently. Moreover, even if the claims had been made singly, it would have been impossible for any one family to prove continuous working of any area for the necessary 20 years. The poverty of the soil and the traditional system of slash-and-burn determined that no area could be farmed for more than 2–3 years, having to be left fallow for at least an equal period. Even the claim that animals grazed the fallow land was inadmissable, since 'the evidence that this was done continuously for 20 years in the case of any one single pasture on the estate is most unreliable (as well as being unlikely)'.[52]

In proof that the adverse claimants were in fact sharecropping tenants, Judge Scarr cited ten items from the voluminous evidence presented by both sides. Perhaps the most damaging evidence came from a case heard before the local magistrate the previous year, when three of the present adverse claimants had given evidence of sharecropping arrangements in order to upset a charge of trespass brought against them by Bowe — a melancholy example of the principle of 'Catch 22'. Despite remarking that Maxwell Bowe was a poor witness in his own defence, and that over the previous 25 years the general system had been 'run in a very loose and unbusinesslike manner', Judge Scarr concluded that 'whichever way one looks at it, and taking the most benevolent view of the Adverse Claimants' case, it is entirely devoid of merit and fails completely'.[53]

Accordingly, Bowe was granted clear freehold title, and in due course the land was sold to the American developer. Bulldozers crisscrossed the bush, hundreds of lots were sold to gullible foreigners, and The Forest settlement was left a landless enclave — a symbol of legal despoliation. Apart from the short-term benefit of earning wages from the developer, the only positive feature, ironically, arose from the fact that the development failed. As happened in other cases throughout the Bahamas, nearly all lots were speculatively bought by persons without the means or intention to build. Within 20 years, The

Forest Estate had reverted to bush, except for a dozen new homes and gardens, and the areas cleared and grazed by a whole new generation of squatters from the settlement.

Land tenures in an independent Black Nation, 1967–1985

The coming to power of a party representing the black majority in 1967 and, even more, the achievement of Bahamian independence in 1973, should have signalized a revolution in the structure of landholding in the Bahamas. But difficulties remained, not only disorder over titles and the tension between the desire to reserve land for the people and the need for development, but also basic confusion about the ideology of land tenure.

One of the most potent motivations for the emergent Progressive Liberal Party (P.L.P.) before 1967 was disgust at the way that under the previous regime foreign leaseholders had been able to hem in or squeeze out local settlements, discriminate against Bahamian blacks, or simply rape the landscape. P.L.P. platforms and the Independence constitution represented the land as the national patrimony. At the same time as international agencies were providing aid to map and survey the use and potential of the islands (which incidentally led to an upward revision of the land area from 4,375 to 5,358 square miles), the new government made plans to revise or even cancel the leases of such giant corporations as the Grand Bahama Port Authority or Owens-Illinois, to review the terms by which bases had been leased to the U.S.A. by the British imperial government, and to draft a comprehensive national Land Act.

An unwillingness to jeopardize foreign investment or to antagonize the U.S. government by arbitrary actions, though, led the Bahamas government to proceed with very great caution. Respect for the rule of law was, indeed, one of the strongest legacies of the old colonialism, reinforced by the fact that a very high proportion of the new politicians (on both sides of the House) were professional lawyers. Innate conservatism also played a part, as was epitomized by the general horror in Nassau at the proposal by the abortive Abaco separation movement in the 1970s that each adult Abaconian be given a share of the land, which, it was said, would guarantee an income for life of $15,000 a year.[54] Far from any land appropriation, no foreign leases were actually cancelled or shortened without compensation, and the U.S. bases were either renegotiated or quietly allowed to lapse by mutual consent. The amount of unalienated land belonging to the

Commonwealth of the Bahamas — still termed Crown Land — actually increased, and very little progress was made towards a cadastral survey or a comprehensive registry of titles.

The long debated land law which came into effect in 1983 was essentially moderate. Its purpose was 'to reserve certain categories of land for acquisition by Bahamians, to prevent the sale to foreigners of land adjacent to out island townships where it might inhibit urban expansion, to ensure that land is available to future generations of Bahamians, and to encourage the orderly development of land held by foreigners'. As Prime Minister Lynden Pindling said (in words that might have been used by any of his predecessors), 'The policy is not to make land unavailable, but rather to make it available to those who will use it beneficially'.[55]

That government land policy was not more draconian was no doubt also due to the continued drift of Bahamians away from the Out Islands towards Nassau and Freeport, and other forces which devalued customary methods of holding and transmitting land. The declining number of Out Islanders who depended upon traditional farming continued to favour a generous policy towards squatting tenures. But the fact that the majority of those actually squatting on vacant lands were now illegal Haitian immigrants definitely qualified the attitude of average Bahamians. Commonage tenure also no longer held all its former attractions. The area of common could not support more than a fraction of those eligible for it, and even those with only a level of subsistence regarded it as retrograde. Yet development that was possible on private lands — such as leases for large farming concerns or hotels — were inflexibly forbidden by the terms of the Commonage Act. Similarly, at least a minority of migrants from the Out Islands regarded the system of generational tenure — with its theoretically exponential number of qualified tenants virtually entailing the land — as blocking development along 'modern' lines.

Certainly, there was a growing realisation of the need for clarification and reform. Even lawyers, who traditionally flourish on complexity and delay, found the trouble and time involved in searching, proving, quieting and registering title as counterproductive. In the mid 1980s, a government select committee was set up, which was expected to recommend the acceleration of the cadastral survey, simpler methods of quieting title, and a more efficient system of documentary registration. Yet the thorniest problem remained the resolution of the status of lands held by customary tenures, particularly generational property. Since the appointed committee consists of lawyers and politicians, and the prevailing motive is to unlock lands for development, it is to be feared that the result might be a determination to eradicate all customary tenures, in favour of strictly legal and documentary titles, based upon the precedents and precepts of English Common Law and statutes. While this might bring benefits for a few, it would surely speed the alienation of the Bahamian majority from its native land and culture.

Several heartening tendencies, however, militate against this unfortunate outcome and suggest the possibility of at least a compromise 'Creole' solution.[56] Now that the shame and stain of slavery are overlaid by a proud black nationalism, and the effects of modernization are seen to have been overvalued, many of those living in overcrowded Nassau feel a sense of nostalgia for island roots, and for the structures of kinship and community which are fading or being lost. Such a feeling doubtless inspired the rechristening of the Bahamas Out Islands as the Family Islands in 1972. It was manifest in Cleveland Eneas's romantic reconstruction of a quasi-mythical Bain Town (1976), and in the national Archives' exhibition celebrating Fox Hill and other 'African' settlements in New Providence (1982).[57] More directly, it has resulted in the spontaneous creation of seemingly artificial sub-communities in Over-the-Hill Nassau, such as the curiously named Finmasbur Association, formed in 1983 to give a sense of identity to those persons who happen to live in the area bounded by Fort Fincastle, Mason's Addition and Burial Ground Corner. But most of all, it has led to a remarkable number of organisations for strengthening family and island connexions, such as the long-established Cat Island, Long Island and Southern Eleuthera Associations, or the much more recent Hanna-Heastie-Tynes extended family group, which arranged a temporary remigration to its own Family Island, Acklins, on Emancipation Day (August 1) in 1983.[58]

What all this restorationist activity clearly demonstrates is that a nationalistic negritude can as easily lead to a greater affinity to the land and customary ways on the part of the people as a whole, as to determination simply to exploit the land on behalf of a fortunate black minority. In such a healthier atmosphere, the value of African customs, as melded over generations in the crucible of Afro-Bahamian life — the ownership of land in common, its transmission through the kin from generation to generation, and the allocation of its use to families according to need — may well continue to prevail over a borrowed and expediential legalism that stems from the European Middle Ages and the subsequent era of bourgeois capitalism.

Notes

1 McPherson, C.B. *The Political Theory of Possessive Individualism: Hobbes to Locke*, Oxford, Oxford University Press, 1964.

2 Being, with the adjacent mainland, 'yet hitherto untild, neither inhabited by ours or the subjects of any other Christain king, Prince or state But in some parts of it inhabited by certaine Barbarous men who had not any knowledge of the Divine Deitye'. Calendar of State Papers, Colonial, 9:70–71, quoted in Craton, Michael, *A History of the Bahamas*, 2nd. ed. London, Collins, 1968:51.

3 Ibid:52–54,67–70. The distinctions between the two forms of quasi-feudal grant depended on the fact that Durham, being a borderland against the Scots, had almost autonomous privileges, and on the difference between ordinary socage and the freer kind found in Kent. The Palatinate of Durham was dissolved in the 1630s and the model thus became archaic. Socage in Kent related to the ancient system of *gavelkind*, unique to the county. Harris, Marshall, *Origin of the Land Tenure System of the United States*, Ames, Iowa, Iowa State College Press, 1953:29–39.

4 The very word *gavelkind* comes from the Saxon word *gafol*, meaning rent-paying. Kentish custom allowed 'socmen' to partition, sell and bequeath their land quite freely, and to sue for it in the King's court even against their lords. Unlike other forms of tenure, no fine was payable upon alienation. Besides, legal processes in Kent were more direct and less cumbersome than elsewhere, conditions for widows and heirs were easier, and lands could not be escheated for felony. Ibid.:37–38, quoting Sir William Holdsworth, *History of English Law*, 12 vols. London, Methuen, 1925, III:260–1.

5 Harris, *Land Tenure System*: 194–236. The headright system was inherent in the first instructions of the London Company of Virginia (1606), which specified that land-ownership was not to be confined to shareholders, and that everyone who emigrated to the colony or who brought or sent over another person was entitled to land. As the Virginia colony developed, though, a distinction emerged between the original (pre-1625) adventurers, who received land grants in fee simple, free of all feudal charges, and non-shareholders and later emigrants, who received land subject to annual quit rents. Ibid:199–201.

6 See below, page 12.

7 Craton, *Bahamas*: 100–103,172. Woodes Rogers became the first royal Governor in 1718, but the colony was also administered through a private company, which simply leased the right of collecting quit rents from the Lords Proprietor for 21 years, for a total of £2,450. Ibid:102.

8 3 Geo. II, c. 4; Nassau Public Record Office, MSS Laws, Vol. 1, 1729–1831, 5–6. Where title was proved against an occupier, any person who had been on the lands for two years or more was to be given a year to move and reimbursed for any improvements made, as assessed by a specially empanelled jury.

9 4 Geo. III, c. 1, Ibid:16–20.

10 Craton, *Bahamas*: 172; 29 Geo. III, c. 1, Nassau P.R.O. MSS Laws, I:26–28.

11 Acting Governor Powell made the first proclamation in September 1785,

and Governor Lord Dunmore the first actual grants in 1788, typically rewarding himself and his family with a lion's share of some 7,000 acres. The Loyalist grants were to be free of ground rents for the first 10 years, being liable thereafter to 2/- per year per 100 acres. London, P.R.O., C.O. 23/30:216–224, quoted in Riley, Sandra, *Homeward Bound: A History of the Bahama Islands to 1850, with a Definitive Study of Abaco in the Loyalist Plantation Period*, Miami, Island Research, 1983:181.

12 Figures for the numbers of Loyalist immigrants and lands alienated to them remain imprecise. Bethell (1914) listed 114 grants totalling 43,000 acres, but this was clearly incomplete. William Wylly (1789) listed 330 new white heads of household, who had cultivated a total of 13,000 acres in seven islands. Craton, *Bahamas*, 164–167; Saunders, D. Gail, *The Slave Population of the Bahamas, 1783–1834*, U.W.I. M.Phil. Thesis, 1978:48–54.

13 43 Geo. III, c. 1, Nassau P.R.O., MSS Laws, I:97–99.

14 46 Geo. III, c. 16, ibid:146–151.

15 9 Vic., c. 10, ibid.II: 170–175.

16 Peggs, A. Deans, *Farquharson's Journal or A Relic of Slavery*, Nassau, 1957; Saunders, Gail, *Bahamas Loyalists and their Slaves*, London, Macmillan Caribbean, 1983:27–32. The Farquharson Estate, originally 500 acres, was increased to 1,900 by a Crown grant. At the time of slave emancipation there were 52 slaves, only one African born. Most slaves lived in nuclear family households, in a small village of stone-built huts some 300 yards from the owner's house. During the Slave Registration period (1822–1834) there were two mulatto slaves, presumably Charles Farquharson's illegitimate children.

17 This was true in due case for the Farquharson Estate; see below, page 101. Another case was the larger Watling's Island estate of 2,600 acres formerly owned by Burton Williams (1769–1852), which was sold to Fr. Chrysostom Shreiner O.S.B. in 1916 for £100 by one Rawlings George Williams, a brown man who called himself 'Gentleman and heir-at-law of Burton Williams late of Watlings Island, Planter deceased'. Needless to say, Fr. Shreiner's title was hotly disputed or bluntly ignored by all those living on the constituent parts of the old Williams Estate, as well as by other alleged descendants of Burton Williams. Nassau, Registry, All: 304–308; Riley, *Homeward Bound*: 219–222. As is shown by his answers to an 1829 inquiry made in Trinidad (to which he had transferred most of his slaves) Burton Williams was a notable paternalist. A similar Bahamian planter was William Wylly, who wrote and published *Regulations for the Government of the Slaves at Clifton and Tusculum in New Providence*, Nassau, 1815, enclosed in Wylly-Munnings, August 31, 1818, C.O. 23/67:147.

18 Mintz, Sidney W., The Question of Caribbean Peasantries: a Comment, *Caribbean Studies,* I, 1961:31–34; also, *Caribbean Transformations,* Chicago, Aldine Press, 1974:146–156. Praedial slaves were the great majority who were designated agricultural workers, as distinct from domestic and town-dwelling slaves, called Non-Praedials.

19 Craton, Michael, Hobbesian or Panglossian? The Two Extremes of Slave Conditions in the British West Indies, *William & Mary Quarterly,* 3rd. ser. XXXV, April 1978:324–356; Changing Patterns of Slave Family in the British West Indies, *Journal of Interdisciplinary History,* X:1

(Summer 1979):1–35; 'We Shall Not Be Moved: Pompey's Slave Revolt in Exuma Island, 1830', *Nieuwe West Indische Gids*, 57, 1–2, 1983:19–35; Saunders, *Bahamian Loyalists*: 21–27; McDermott, Benson, 'Lord Rolle', *Bahamas Handbook and Businessman's Guide*, Nassau, 1981:14–32.

20 On his Devonshire and Florida estates alike, Denys Rolle had behaved very much like a feudal lord. He had originally built a grand house and settled 300 poor Cockneys on the St John's River. When this Oglethorpe-like settlement, originally called Charlotia, failed, it became a more orthodox plantation, called Rolleston. McDermott, 'Lord Rolle', 16.

21 Rolle to Bathurst, August 12, 1824, March 31, 1825, C.O. 23/73, 257; 74, 275–277. Woodford (Trinidad) to Bathurst, December 31, 1825, April 13, 1826, C.O. 295/67:219; 71:26–7. Rolle enclosed in Farquharson to Huskisson, October 12, 1828, C.O. 295/78:233–238. Rolle to Murray, August 22, 1829, C.O. 23/81:375–6.

22 Grant to Murray, December 8, 1828, C.O. 23/28:156–178.

23 Letters of Thomas Thompson, Overseer at Steventon, to Mr Taylor, Merchant in Nassau, dated early November 1828, and Lt. Thomas McPherson to Governor Grant, December 10, 1828, enclosed in ibid:159–60, 176–178. Governor Grant, who left Nassau shortly afterwards for a new post, wrote to the Colonial Office from H.M.S. *Barham* off Grand Bahama on December 27, recommending that if Rolle's slaves were to be shipped off to Trinidad, all 'Heads of families and leading characters' among them should be promised that no families would be split up, that all families would be allocated generous provision grounds and given a second day each week to work them, that females under 14 years of age would be instantly freed, and all slaves allowed to pay for their own manumission, at a rate of $360 each. Ibid:166–169.

24 Rolle to Murray, August 22, 1829, C.O. 23/81:375–6.

25 Craton, *Pompey's Slave Revolt*, 26–28. One slave told the magistrate sent down with 50 soldiers to restore order, that the refusal to move was 'in consequence of information received from George Clarke and William Neely, Free Black Men, that they were to be Free, and the land was to be divided among them' — a form of wish-fulfilment very common throughout the slave colonies on the eve of Emancipation. Report of John Grace to Carmichael Smyth, June 29, 1830, enclosed in Smyth to Murray, June 29, 1830, C.O. 23/82:355–367.

26 Rolle to Spring-Rice, August 11, 1834, C.O. 23/92, 497.

27 McDermott, 'Lord Rolle', 28.

28 Craton, *Pompey's Slave Revolt*, 28.

29 However, in 1840 when the Harbour Islanders petitioned for clear title in common for 6,000 acres they actually offered $1,000 for the land. It was said that they had worked the land for more than a hundred years, that is, for at least 40 years before Deveaux came on the scene. The Council had ordered in 1810 that these customary lands should not be sold to others, but did not give specific title to the Harbour Islanders. Extract of Report of Colonial Land and Emigration Commissioners to James Stephen, July 23, 1840, C.O. 23/100. See 'Resolution of Committee of Commoners, Harbour Island, February 6, 1963', cited in Saunders, D. Gail, *The Social History of the Bahamas, 1890–1953*, Ph.D. Thesis, University of Waterloo, 1985:66.

30 An Act to Provide for the More Beneficial Use of Lands Held in Common, 59 Vic., c. 14; *Statute Law of the Bahamas*, rev. ed. London, 1965, c. 123, 1855–1858. Lands held in common are defined as 'any lands which have been granted to more than twenty people and not partitioned'.

31 Williams, Patrice, *A Guide to African Villages in New Providence*, Nassau, Public Record Office, 1979:4–15,27–28; Department of Archives, *Settlements in New Providence*, Catalogue of Archives Exhibition, Nassau, 1982:22–36,44–52. Similar settlements were also projected, with limited success, at Williamstown and Victoria in the Berry Islands, Bennett's Harbour, Cat Island, The Bight and Great Harbour, Long Island, on Rum Cay and in the Ragged Islands. Craton, *Bahamas*: 207.

32 Ibid:209.

33 *Settlements in New Providence:* 37–43; Williams, *African Villages*: 21–26.

34 Ibid: 18–20; *Settlements in New Providence*: 53–56; Eneas, Cleveland W., *Bain Town*, Nassau, 1976.

35 The existence of such documents, of course, placed the law in an impossible dilemma, a reverence for the wishes of those making formal wills and deeds conflicting with a general preference for simple lineal inheritance and transmission. Such legislative attempts to cut the Gordian Knot as the 1830 Act to Amend the Law of Inheritance (3 Will. IV, c. 20), being based on English conditions, were almost nugatory in the Bahamas.

36 Otterbein, Keith F., A Comparison of the Land Tenure Systems of the Bahamas, Jamaica and Barbados: The Implications it has for the Study of Social Systems Shifting from Bilateral to Ambilineal Descent, *International Archives of Ethnography*, 50, 1964:31–42; *The Andros Islanders*, Lawrence, Kansas University Press, 1967. Clarke, Edith, Land Tenure and Family in Four Communities in Jamaica, *Social and Economic Studies*, I, 4, 1953:81–118; *My Mother Who Fathered Me*, London, Allen and Unwin, 1957; Greenfield, S.M., Land Tenure and Transmission in Rural Barbados, *Anthropological Quarterly*, 33, 1960:165–176. See also Smith, Raymond T., Land Tenure in Three Negro Villages in British Guiana, *Social and Economic Studies*, IV, 1955 (Supp.): 64–82; Smith, Michael G., The Transmission of Land Rights by Transmission in Carriacou, ibid. V, 1956:103–138. For Bahamian family, farming and tenure practices in various islands see, for example, La Flamme, Alan G., *Green Turtle Cay: A Bi-Racial Community in the Out Island Bahamas*, Ph.D. Thesis, University of New York, Buffalo, 1972; Rogers, William B., *The Wages of Change: An Anthropological Study of the Effects of Economic Development on Some Negro Communities in the Out Islands*, Ph.D. Thesis, Stanford University, 1965 (Abaco); Savashinsky, Joel S., (ed.) *Stranger No More: Anthropological Studies of Cat Island, the Bahamas*, Ithaca, Ithaca College, 1978.

37 Act to Provide Summary Remedy against the Occupation of Land by Persons Having no Title to the Same, 4 Will. IV, c. 37, March 20, 1834. In an ejection, all buildings and 'improvements' were to be dismantled, and all goods and chattels sold. Fifteen days grace were given before the lawful owners moved in.

38 2 Vic., c. 2, June 21, 1839.

39 3 Vic., c. 3, February 20, 1840.
40 This principle, which followed English precepts, came into effect in 1847, the year after the Commutation Act. Craton, *Bahamas*, 210.
41 'Memorandum of Agreement between Alexander Forsyth of Rum Cay, Attorney for William Marshall of Nassau, Merchant, and Undersigned persons and servants working on land of the Estate of the late Charles Farquharson, August 1865', Public Records Office, Nassau, O'Brien Family Collection, Box 1, March 21, 1801–1911, cited in Saunders, *Social History*: 21.
42 Ibid:31–34.
43 Craton, *Bahamas*, 250–1; Saunders, *Social History*, 17–20, 42–47; Dilks, David, *Neville Chamberlain*, Vol. 1, Cambridge, Cambridge University Press, 1984:54–77.
44 James P. Sands to Chamberlain, May 21, 1903; E.Y. Villiers Sutton to Sands, July 3, 1906, Birmingham University, Neville Chamberlain Papers, August 3, 1925, 42, cited in Saunders, *Social History*, 19–20.
45 An amusing example was Rosita Forbes, who described the generational system and her difficulties with it in Eleuthera (1939) in *Appointment with Destiny*, London, Cassell, 1946, 157:201–2.
46 Crown Lands Office Act, 1882, *Laws of the Bahamas*, 1957:280–282; Land Roll Act, 1920, ibid. Class XI, c. 187:1632–1637.
47 Acquisition of Lands Act, 1913, ibid. IV, c. 254:2341–2366; Squatters and Trespassers Act, 1927, ibid:934–936; Quieting of Titles Act, 1959, *Statute Law of the Bahamas*, 1965:1895–1906.
48 Judgement in the Case of the Petition of James Maxwell Mitchell Bowe under the Quieting of Titles Act, 1959, concerning The Forest Estate, Bahama Islands Supreme Court, Equity Division, No. 137 of 1961. Other interesting and precedential cases include the Price-Robinson claim for a strip of land from sea to sea across the middle of Paradise Island, which dragged on from 1960 to 1968; No. 171 of 1960, 391 of 1963, and the subsequent Appeal to the Privy Council, No. 40 of 1964. See also, Grand Bahama Port Authority vs. Albert Cox of Smith's Point, Grand Bahamas, 170/1961; Rodehn vs. ten Adverse Claimants (Harold Road, New Providence), 20/1965; Petition of Tracey Knowles (Morris's, Long Island), 24/1966; A.S. Nesbitt and Daisy Cox vs. Abaco Lumber Co. etc. (Riding Point, Grand Bahama), 70/1967; Harrisville Co. vs. three sets of Adverse Claimants (Hatchet Bay, Eleuthera), Nos. 5, 6/1970.
49 Bowe Judgement, April 11, 1962:2.
50 Ibid:3.
51 Ibid:8.
52 Ibid:9.
53 Ibid.
54 Dodge, Steve, *Abaco: The History of an Out Island and its Cays*, Miami, Tropic Isle, 1983:110–131. Each Abaconia was also promised a one-acre house-lot. See also, Abaco — The Past, *Bahamas Dateline*, 9:4, July 1984.
55 The Immovable Property Act, 1983. *Bahamas Dateline*, 7:10, January 1983. See also, ibid. 4:8, November 1979; 4:12, March 1980; 5:4, July 1980; 5:10, January 1981; 6:2, May 1981; 8:8, November 1983.
56 For a brief introduction to the problems involved in this, see Marshall, O.R., West Indian Land Law: Conspectus and Reform, *Social and*

Economic Studies, 20, I, 1971:1–14.

57   Eneas, *Bain Town*; Williams, *African Villages*; Department of Archives, *Settlements in New Providence*.

58   *Nassau Daily Tribune*, July 20, 1983.

Section B

The Impact of Structural Change on Attitudes to Land

CHAPTER 5

Ecology and politics in Barbudan land tenure

Riva Berleant-Schiller

Everywhere in the world today communal systems of land tenure are crumbling under the introduction of cash crops and other forms of development. These traditional systems of group-owned lands are usually associated with extensive land uses, such as shifting cultivation, open-range stock-keeping, and transhumance. They survive the longest in places where population densities remain low and where, for whatever reasons, conditions are uninviting to economic interests from beyond the community.

Barbuda was long such a place. Before 1981, when Barbuda struggled unsuccessfully for political self-determination, the island was little known and little heeded. Its thin soils and dry climate had thwarted the development of plantations in the eighteenth century, diverting Barbuda from the mainstream of colonial economy in the British Leewards. A curious form of colonial control had removed Barbuda from Leeward Islands politics as well: for two hundred years Barbuda was the private domain of a single family, the Codringtons, who leased the island from the Crown. When the Codringtons withdrew, other kinds of dependency followed. These conditions — dependency, the absence of plantations, and a meagre resource base — underlay the principal achievements of the Barbudan slave community, achievements that were well in place before emancipation and that survived until recently as the basis of a Barbudan peasant economy (Berleant-Schiller, 1977, 1978, 1983).

Although Barbuda is a spare land, the slaves who were brought there achieved an extraordinary measure of self-determination and a durable productive economy. Their adaptation was more than a complex of productive pursuits, although fishing, lobster-diving, charcoal-making, stock-keeping, and shifting cultivation were all essential elements. It was equally an organic set of values and practices that included an insistence on community control over community labour, on the ownership of the island by its inhabitants, and on common rights for all Barbudans to use the unparcelled lands outside the village for their productive activities. This organic system of land use, land tenure, and land ideology was the foundation for Barbudan social integration and community solidarity within dependency. In

1981 an unwilling Barbuda became part of the new independent state of Antigua-Barbuda. This chapter describes the values and practices attached to land before independence, and relates them to customary tenure elsewhere in the Caribbean. It examines some evidence for recent changes in land tenure and attitudes to land, and considers how such changes are related to Barbuda's altered political status.

Traditional land tenure and land use

By the word 'traditional' I mean the kinds of land use and customary tenure that prevailed before independence, and that still exist even in the midst of change. In the village, houses and yards are individually owned and may be sold and bequeathed, even though legal title deeds do not always exist. Outside the village, bush and beach lands are unparcelled and custom grants to all Barbudans equal rights to their use. Ideally, neither village house sites nor bush lands are alienable to outsiders.

With one exception, bush lands may not be individually owned and may not be bequeathed. All people of socially recognized Barbudan birth, parentage, or ancestry may exercise their use rights, even if they have been absent from Barbuda for a long time. The social recognition depends on the continuous involvement of absentees with relatives on the island, and can extend even to third and fourth generation descendants of emigrants.

The tradition of communal ownership of the bush has persisted in word and behaviour. It is bolstered by the Barbudan folk belief that the island was bequeathed to its inhabitants by the last of the Codringtons. This bequest has never been verified in fact and is most likely a mythical charter for customary practice. The Barbuda Ordinance of 1904 states that all Barbudans are tenants of the British Crown (Antigua 1962:v.2, p.968), but the ordinance has never affected Barbudan beliefs about the Barbudan commons.

As is usual where individuals have rights to the use of group commons, the sites of gardens, sheilings, and charcoal kilns outside the village belong to the person who made these improvements only for as long as he or she uses them. When the sites are abandoned, they become once more a part of the commons.

There is one exception to this rule in Barbuda: it is possible to establish long-term rights to a piece of bush land by planting a fruit tree. Once the tree has been planted, the tree, its fruit, and the land immediately surrounding the tree are recognized as belonging to the one who planted it. Although there is some disagreement among Barbudans about how much land goes with the tree, most will grant at least the area beneath its branches; others point out a radius of twenty feet or so around the trunk. If in practice the owner of a fruit tree wants to reserve a larger area, he or she must enclose the area in a circle of dagger plants (century plant; *Agave karatto*). The tree and its enclosed land are individually owned, and may be bequeathed and inherited.

Claims to land established by fruit tree planting are never contested. It is the tree and its fruit that appear to be important. The dagger circle is less for the purpose of establishing land rights than for establishing tree rights. One may not enclose another's tree into a swidden plot without permission. In practice, such an enclosure is unlikely to occur. Swidden land is abundant, and no one would wish to create confusion.

The ownership of trees is more recognized than respected. Everyone knows who owns any particular mango or cashew tree, but few are above enjoying the fruit. I once went to help an informant collect mangoes from the tree she had inherited from her mother, but we found the tree stripped despite its dagger fence. Often I saw fruit taken. When I asked if the tree belonged to anyone, I would be answered with some variation of 'Yes, but we don't mind about that just now.'

All other enclosures are temporary, though the period of time is variable. Most of them are for provision gardens. Swidden plots are used for a year or two. Some gardeners enclose larger plots for a longer, indefinite period, rotating the land inside them until yields begin to decline. Gardeners are supposed officially to register their plots, but not all do. Since there is far more land than is needed, quarrels over garden sites are nonexistent. A man or woman chooses the plot and marks its borders by intermittent brush heaps or by a cut line. A wire, brush, or woven withy fence can be put up later, mainly to keep wandering livestock out. Barbudans say often, and with some pride, 'No one needs to starve in Barbuda. Anyone at all can cut bush and make grounds.'

Enclosures for cattle are far fewer, since they are practicable only during years when there is enough rainfall to stimulate the continuous growth of fresh grass for the animals inside. I first went to Barbuda in 1971, during a long drought, and again in 1973, when the drought was ending. There were no individual paddocks then, although there was a large government paddock enclosed for communal use. Another visit in 1977 disclosed a number of individual small paddocks, and one large one. I was surprised at what I thought was an innovation, until I came to understand the relationship of enclosure to rainfall and the fact that paddocks may make sense when grass grows thick, whereas open-range husbandry is necessary during the ever-recurrent periods of drought. Then cattle forage widely for their own food and cost their owners nothing in either time or money. The commons system permits both alternatives.

Hundreds of sheep and goats also forage in the bush and come back unshepherded to village pens in the evening. Feral horses and donkeys range the bush continuously, but their owners know their haunts and bring them in for breaking when necessary. None of these animals could be kept in such numbers except on open range.

The bush is important economically to many Barbudans as a source of wood and timber. Although boat-building has just about disappeared from the island, Barbudans burn wood to make charcoal for home use, home sale, and export sale. Woodcutters may choose appropriate sites anywhere in the bush for their charcoal kilns.

The commons also offer important food resources: deer, doves and pigeons, wild pigs, edible tortoises, land crabs, and many fruits. The beach commons that ring the island yield sea grapes (*Coccoloba uvifera*), cocoplums (*Chrysobalanus icaco*), and tiny periwinkles (*Littorina* sp.) from which soup is made. The commons also supply necessary raw materials. Barbudans glean the beach for strands and fibres of rope, washed from the sea, that they replait into strong new lengths. The commons provide withies for making fences and fish trap frames, dagger stalks for making rafts (Berleant-Schiller, 1984:805–808), and many plants for medicines and tisanes. Not so long ago they supplied thatch for roofs and straw for fish traps, but these are now made of galvanized iron and chicken wire respectively. Also important are the many dug wells and modified sinkholes scattered in the bush, to which all Barbudans have rights and which supply water for laundry and livestock.

Clearly land tenure and land use are closely tied and mutually reinforcing in Barbuda, and both are linked to a physical environment that discouraged the development of a plantation economy. Yet Barbuda, despite some unique features, is part of a larger region, and it is proper to consider whether and how its folk tenure is related to folk tenure elsewhere in the Caribbean.

The Barbudan commons and Caribbean family land

Some scholars have suggested that Barbudan customary tenure might be a special or variant case of the family land tenure found throughout the Caribbean (Besson, 1984; Comitas, 1974). Family land tenure grants to all the children of the original owner the joint ownership of an undivided plot. The land is inalienable and indivisible, and is passed in turn to all the children's children. A cognatic descent group coalesces around the land, and its members have equal rights to the use of the land.

Jean Besson has reviewed the important literature concerning family land and argues, using her own research in Jamaica, that the institution of family land is an Afro-Caribbean adaptation, a creative response to a history of landless plantation slavery and a post-emancipation condition of continued plantation dominance. It cannot be explained as an African or European survival, nor can its pan-Caribbean distribution permit individual explanations for individual islands. I agree, and would add a corollary to the last methodological rule: we must consider local features in the light of Caribbean regional patterns, and be slow to claim uniqueness. It is important, therefore, to consider carefully whether the Barbudan commons are a variant of pan-Caribbean family land.

Barbudan communal tenure shares three basic features with family land. Tenure is customary rather than legal; undivided land is owned by a group whose members have use rights; group land is inalienable. These are important features, but not distinguishing features, as they fit many tenure systems in many kinds of societies. Family land is further qualified by the minuscule size of most plots, by its conversion from individually-owned land by means of customary legacy, and by its restriction to a cognatic descent group. These features distinguish family land from other forms of inalienable, impartible, group-owned lands.

The joint owners of family land all trace their ancestry to an original owner who bought or otherwise acquired the piece after emancipation, and as Jean Besson has shown, form a cognatic descent group (1979). Inmarrying spouses and their outside children are not included in this consanguine landholding group (although they might be members of another).

In Barbuda, rules much less restrictive grant rights to lands much more extensive. Individuals receive rights by parentage or filiation rather than by descent (Fortes, 1959), by birth in Barbuda regardless of parentage, by marriage to a resident Barbudan, and even by long residence in Barbuda regardless of birthplace, parentage, or marriage. Barbudans by birth or parentage who live elsewhere can keep their rights warm by keeping up their contacts on the island. Almost all Barbudans are related to each other, often in more than one way, but the community is not a descent group; it is a set of overlapping kindreds.

Nor are the Barbudan commons a minuscule plot originally

acquired by an individual and left to a sibling group; they include most of the island, an area of over 150 square kilometres, and were never owned by any Barbudan. The only tiny owned enclosures in the commons are lands around fruit trees, which are not bequeathed to a sibling group, but to an individual. Are these differences merely differences in scale, or are they differences in kind? A comparison of functions and origins will help to answer that question.

One of the major functions of all land ownership in the Caribbean is a cultural function: the ownership of a piece of land is significant far beyond its size or the uses to which it is put. Prestige and pride attach to land ownership, whether or not the land is productive. Family land allows many to enjoy prestige and pride, even though the plots are often too small to be an economic advantage to all their owners.

The Barbudan commons have the same cultural function for Barbudans that land ownership has for other Caribbean people. The commons evoke pride of ownership and identification with the community. But they have more than cultural significance. The Barbudan commons are an economic necessity for many Barbudans. They are a basis for social integration of the community, and a spur to community political action. I do not recall a case of family land bolstering community political action, but in Barbuda, cultural values and economic necessities together have repeatedly spurred active defence of the commons system (Berleant-Schiller, 1978).

Family land may be divisive of the kinship group as well as integrating (Wilson, 1974:67–68; Clarke, 1956:56). But in Barbuda, solidarity and integration rest on communal ownership of land so plentiful that no conflicts arise. Equal access to all the resources of the commons promotes a basic equality among Barbudans and debars land from becoming an agent of internal stratification.

Some writers have pointed out that family land may inhibit efficient land use (e.g. Finkel, 1964; Keur and Keur, 1960:72; Besson, 1984:73 summarizes). Barbudan commonlands do the opposite. They encourage the most efficient use of land by allowing pursuits that require undivided expanses and make the most of an arid environment with few endowments.

Finally, Barbudan customary land tenure is an integrated part of an entire ecological complex that includes culture, social organization, external relations, economy, land use, and physical environment. It performs social and economic functions for the entire community apart from the cultural value, prevalent throughout the Caribbean, of land ownership. The cultural and economic functions of family land can be performed equally well for individuals by individually-owned land; its special functions revolve around kinship, and around community status for those who dwell upon it.

In Barbuda, the cultural functions of land ownership could be satisfied by another form of tenure, but the ecological and economic functions are specific to the commons, and do not apply to other instances of family land in the Caribbean. That is, in family land tenure the idea of ownership may be more important than use, and use may be inhibited by ownership, but in Barbuda land use and communal rights are inseparable.

These functional differences, together with the formal characteristics that distinguish family land from Barbudan common tenure, are qualitative and profound. An entire community is not a descent group magnified, nor is an entire island commons a simple enlargement of a minuscule plot. Most important, however, is the integration of Barbudan land tenure with land use, where each is a *sine qua non* of the other. This fundamental quality does not belong to family land.

The argument that the differences between the Barbudan commons and Caribbean family land outweigh the similarities (which in any case belong to many forms of communal tenure in many places) is supported by the different origins of the two forms. Family land begins with land that was bought or otherwise acquired by an individual after emancipation. The roots of communal tenure in Barbuda reach at least to the eighteenth century.

As early as 1715, Barbudan slaves owned livestock and worked their own provision grounds. A letter from William Codrington to his manager in Barbuda names four slaves who were not to be 'molested or troubled in their grounds or provisions by anybody' (Codrington Mss. 1715). The same letter includes a list of the horses, cows, and sheep owned by slaves. There is some evidence that the slaves and European indentured servants had the run of the island at the time, hunting and poaching domestic, feral, and wild animals, and even trading surreptitiously on their own account. In 1717 William Codrington urged his manager to seize boats that were coming to Barbuda to trade, as they brought guns for killing sheep, game, and turtles (Codrington Mss. 1717). Since there were only about 118 people on the island at that time, of whom 93 were slaves and 24 indentured servants, we are probably safe in the inference that the slave community developed a feeling of rights to the island along with their use of the island for themselves (Codrington Mss. 1719).

The later eighteenth and early nineteenth centuries confirm this inference. The slaves appropriated and shot the Codrington livestock, grew provisions for themselves where soil was best and deepest, and generally ranged the bush at all hours for their own purposes (Tweedy, 1981:131,171–193). The garden land available to individuals was not limited. With only three or four overseers to four hundred slaves, the latter were able to enjoy free use of the island and even to earn an income by marketing their provisions, their livestock, and the products of their hunting, which they sent carriage-free to Antigua in Codrington boats (171–172). Punishment did not affect their poaching; they showed a remarkable attachment to their island and refused to be sent away; they died when removed by force to Codrington estates in Antigua (Lowenthal and Clarke, 1977; Tweedy, 1981:223–256).

Thus we have, at least from the latter part of the eighteenth century and possibly from its beginning, evidence for unrestricted lands available to a slave community whose members used it in ways that were suited to arid conditions and that called for unbroken tracts. After emancipation, the inhabitants continued to regard and use the land as their own (Berleant-Schiller, 1978). The Codringtons were still lessees from the Crown, so there is reason to consider that Barbudans were tenants-at-will, but we have seen that the views of the outer world on Barbudan land tenure did not affect either Barbudan belief or Barbudan practice.

Despite these differences in the function, morphology, and history of customary tenure, Barbudan land evokes the same sentiments that family land evokes. Barbudans regard their island as a common inheritance. The Barbudan folk belief that the last Codrington lessee bequeathed Barbuda to its inhabitants accords with the frequent origin of family land in a verbal bequest or customary, non-legal will that leaves the undivided property to all the children. And, like land everywhere in the Caribbean, its emotional and symbolic significance is great. Outside of ideology, the important similarity with family land lies in one other function — resistance to commercial agriculture after emancipation. On the whole, however, Barbudan tenure is distinct from family land in significant features of form, function, and origin, and this departure from the regional pattern must be explained.

Barbuda's customary land tenure deviates from the regional pattern because Barbuda's history, ecology, proprietorship, and slave community deviated from the common pattern of Caribbean sugar islands, and the post-emancipation adaptations answered different imperatives. The freed slaves were faced not with the challenge of finding land on which to make an autonomous living, but of hanging on to the land-use privileges they had already acquired.

Strangely enough, the spare physical environment favoured

them, as did another, more singular, condition of Barbudan life — the island's status as a private fief. The Codringtons surrendered their lease in 1870, and a string of different lessees followed. All of them tried to introduce commercial agriculture. All of them failed. But the Barbudans had learned how to use the dry island and to compensate for its natural deficiencies. No one else had learned this skill, nor did anyone think that former slaves might have something to teach. Thus Barbudan livelihood was assured no matter who nominally controlled the land. The very absence of fixed plots and paddocks constituted resistance to commercial lessees. Barbudans cultivated their scattered swiddens, poached the lessees' animals, grazed their own on open range, harvested the other offerings of their island, and refused to work for wages on projects that threatened their accustomed ways. If they did not claim individual plots, their ownership could not be gainsaid. Their common tenure reinforced and maintained solidarity of feeling and unity of action (Berleant-Schiller, 1978; 1983).

The leases were fruitless, and Barbuda was made a Crown Colony after 1899. The Barbuda Ordinance of 1904 declared that Barbuda was Crown Land and Barbudans Crown tenants. From this legal point of view, Barbudan lands were not commons at all, but squattage.

Now squatting on unclaimed and government land is common enough in the Caribbean, especially where there are mountainous interiors. But in Barbuda there is a significant discordance between the Barbudans' view of themselves as communal owners and their status as tenants, or, in the absence of rent, squatters. Before independence, this discordance was muffled in a working misunderstanding that was in no one's interest to clarify. It was part of the entire Barbudan adaptation that included land use, land tenure, physical environment, and political dependency. But the alteration of even one element in an ecological system may easily threaten the whole. In Barbuda, independence connotes more than an altered political status; independence harbours a new perception of Barbudan land as a resource, new plans for land use, and a potent interest on the part of a few in demolishing the old working misunderstanding. This new attitude towards land is not a home-grown Barbudan ideology. Its source is Antigua, and to understand its power over Barbuda we must understand the relationship of Barbuda to Antigua in the new independent state of Antigua-Barbuda.

Land tenure and Independence

Before emancipation, the connection between Antigua and Barbuda lay only in the fact that the Codringtons, lessees of Barbuda, used

Barbuda as a place to grow provisions for their sugar estates in Antigua. Some years after emancipation, Antiguan law was extended to Barbuda, and the two islands became firmly linked in the colonial perception, although their histories, economies, and interests were, and continued to be, divergent.

In 1969 Antigua became an Associated State of Great Britain, a political entity that included Barbuda. A Barbudan separatist movement developed as a consequence. In spite of a spirited, intelligent, and just struggle, Barbuda was condemned to independence as part of the state of Antigua-Barbuda, which came into existence on November 1, 1981. The issue of Barbudan land and its control was central to the Barbudan fight for autonomy and the Antiguan determination to hold Barbuda.

Rarely can communal land systems and extensive land use withstand economic change. The Barbudan system, a beneficiary of colonial neglect and restricted resources, successfully baffled the incursions of agricultural development for a century and a half (Berleant-Schiller, 1978). Now, however, the very qualities that made Barbuda an agricultural risk appeal to new entrepreneurs with quite different ideas about development. Hotel developers covet the unbroken miles of empty pink beaches; they relish the dry climate and hanker to transform the flat acres into golf courses and riding trails. Only one small-scale hotelier had ever persuaded Barbudans to alienate land, but pressure on Barbudan principles against alienation began to intensify even during associated statehood.

In 1969, for example, the Bradshaw group of Canada proposed that central government (i.e. the Antiguan government) should give them exclusive rights to Barbudan development. Bradshaw would provide roads, piped water, telephone and electric service, and a clinic in return for rights to build a marina, two or three hotels, and a golf course, all of which the group would finance by first selling building lots in Barbuda to foreigners.

The Barbudan representative to central government refused. He demanded an environmental impact study and offered a far smaller tract of land. His alternative plan required that a sixty-room hotel be built before any lots could be sold to foreigners. Central government attempted to overturn the Barbudan refusal (rumour held that government officials owned shares in the Bradshaw scheme), but the British Government Representative intervened, instructing central government not to promote projects on Barbudan land without the approval of the Barbudan representative (*Barbuda Voice* 1970:2(6), supplement; 2(5), 1–2). Another similar scheme was advanced during the same period, and also failed (*Barbuda Voice* 1971:3(21), 3).

Barbudans rightly saw the Bradshaw scheme as a crisis, and sent to Britain their first petition for separation from Antigua. According to McChesney George, a Barbudan lawyer and the representative to central government at the time, the West Indies Act of 1967 had divested the British government of Crown Lands. Legally, therefore, Barbudan lands came under the control of central government in Antigua in continuation of the Antigua-Barbuda association begun after emancipation (*Barbuda Voice* 1970:2(6), 2).

At the same time the Antiguan government devised a scheme for granting title deeds to Barbudans for new house sites outside the village. Attractive as the offer was, since settlement outside the village had long been prohibited by law and legal titles to house sites within the village were rare, Barbudans understood that the plan was a wedge to pry open the entire customary system of communal land tenure. They responded passionately:

Fellow Barbudans, please don't take any title deed for our land. The day you start having such a thing the island is finished... Whoever tells you about title is setting a trap to catch you and get things their way.

Never accept a title deed from any Government for land... People of my Island, such things are dangerous to our birthright. (*Barbuda Voice* 1973:5(44), 8–9)

This attitude of resistance to any alteration in the land tenure system continued through the 1970s and into the negotiations that preceded the inclusion of Barbuda in the independent state of Antigua-Barbuda. In 1976 the Local Government Act was passed. It established the first self-governing body in Barbuda, the Barbuda Council (Antigua, 1976), for which elections were held in Barbuda in January 1977.

In 1978 Barbudans again sought separation. Their petition to the British Government Representative in Barbados recounts a recent history of Antiguan attempts to dispose of Barbudan lands to outsiders. The Bradshaw scheme had not been the only one. In 1971 Claude Earle Francis, the new Barbuda representative to central government, complained that government officials plagued him to arrange for them the acquisition of beach lands in Barbuda (Petition of Barbudans,1978:8; Francis, 1973). In 1977 an organization called Antigua Agricultural Industries Ltd. was granted sixty acres by the Council for agricultural experiment. They were using only ten when they tried, through central government, to get 2000 acres rent-free. When the Council resisted pressure and demanded rent, the company departed. In 1977 I saw their mostly unused 60-acre plot and talked in Antigua to the project director, Thomas Army, an agronomist from the United States. He explained that maize and sorghum could be profitably grown in Barbuda, which might well be the case. Still, the Barbuda Council was right to insist that rent be paid, and quite possibly to suspect that other ideas about development were subsumed in Thomas Army's faith in maize and sorghum (Petition of Barbudans, 1978:9; Army, 1977).

In any event, central government repeatedly bypassed, harrassed and pressured the Barbuda representative and, after 1977, the Barbuda Council, in attempts to sell Barbudan lands for the benefit of Antigua. Barbudans understood very well that Antigua needs Barbudan lands. The 1978 petition argued that joint independence would give Antigua:

> ... sovereign rights over the lands and beaches of the Island and in the name of 'Development' make land deals with enterprising foreigners and use the money obtained to swell their bank balances in overseas secret accounts, reduce or pay off the huge debts that Antigua has incurred over the years, as well as assist in the numerous ambitious programmes they have for the development of Antigua (Petition of Barbudans, 1978:6).

The land issue was at the centre of Barbuda's struggle for separation. In 1980, a constitutional conference was held to discuss the issues surrounding independence. The Barbudan delegation was dedicated to achieving separate status (though not necessarily independence), the continuation of existing land law, both legal and customary, and the complete control by the Council and the Barbudan people over land leases to foreigners for development projects (Great Britain, 1981).

Central government responded in a way that leaves no doubt about their determination to gain dominion over Barbudan land. The Antiguan government delegation offered to grant Barbudans ownership of the lands on which they resided, and to allow the Council to request lands for housing and development. 'Upon the application to Cabinet and the presentation of feasibility studies and plans, the Government undertakes to respond as may be appropriate...' (42). The Antiguan delegation also said they would accept a plan by which alienation of Barbudan lands to outsiders would require the consent of both central government and the Barbuda Council, but only if it was also agreed that 'all citizens of the

State of Antigua and Barbuda would have equal rights to land use in Barbuda. . .' (12).

When the conference closed, on 16 December, 1980, the Barbudan delegation refused to sign on the grounds that no Barbudan concerns had been settled satisfactorily. Control of land and resources had not been secured to the Council, nor had Antiguan trespasses in the form of heavy-handed policing, failure to provide legally allocated funds, and contempt for Council decisions, been checked. In July 1981, Parliament passed the Antigua Termination of Association Act, closing the issue of separation and establishing the independent state of Antigua-Barbuda.

This new political status for Barbuda raises many questions. Has central government's authority over former Crown Lands altered local land use and productive economy? Has the political solidarity of the separation movement endured, or have the new possibilities for resource use and the loss of community control over them engendered factionalism? How have development projects affected wage labour, economy, community integration, internal politics, and internal social and economic differences? Will economic development by outsiders provide more wage opportunities for Barbudans? If so, how will migration patterns, income, and the standard of living be affected? Will economic changes induce changes in household economy and organization?

These important research questions follow from the changes in land policy that have taken place since independence. Here I will only summarize these changes and indicate their incipient effects on development, on land acquisition by foreigners, on Barbudan attitudes to land, and on community solidarity.

Less than a year after independence, central government legislated changes in Barbudan land law which permit Barbudans and their children to own land at the discretion of central government. Put differently, individual Barbudans may, by Antiguan leave, own a bit of their own land. This is the offensive against customary rights that Barbudans feared in 1973.

The response to this legislation revealed that profound change in Barbudan attitudes to land and Barbudan social solidarity had already begun. The popular outcries of 1973 were not repeated. The Barbudan representative to central government chose to ignore the resounding implications of the law and affirmed his satisfaction that central government had at last provided for a matter of great concern to Barbudans (*Caribbean Insight*, 1982:5(3), 3). As an elected representative he surely reflects the willingness of some Barbudans to trade communal ownership and group solidarity for other kinds of opportunity that private ownership and accommodation to the new state will bring.

The chairman of the Barbuda Council, also an elected official, responded quite differently. The bill, he rightly claimed, '... is a stepping stone to eventual privatization of the lands which have been held in common since emancipation and to date have not been sold or purchased by anybody. It erodes the traditional, customary and constitutional authority handed down to the Council' (*Caribbean Insight* 1982:5(3), 3). The disparity between the two responses is itself a manifestation of change: Barbudan solidarity has begun to crumble, and social unity founded on common lands has begun to give way to divergent interests founded on private property.

The elections of 1985 confirmed the trend implied by the representative's position of 1982. None of the candidates of the Barbuda People's Movement (BPM), the separatist party that supports traditional land policy, won Council seats, although the party had held the Council majority since 1979 (*Barbuda Voice,* 1985:16(172), 1–2). The representative to central government, who favours accommodation, was re-elected, defeating a tireless BPM supporter of separation, Council control, and common land rights. Both the representative and the newly-elected Council chairman are members of a new party, Organization for National Reconstruction. Although the new Council and the new party have pledged not to sell land to outsiders, it must yet be seen how far this pledge can be reconciled with their stated commercial development goals and clear sympathies with central government (*Barbuda Voice,* 1985:16(173), 3–5).

Private ownership and internal schism are not the only changes. As we might expect, commercial land use and foreign development projects have been the means adopted by central government for exploiting Barbudan lands. Much of what Barbudans feared and tried to forestall at the constitutional conference has been realized: corrupt or questionable investors, exploitation of Barbudan resources for Antiguan ends, disregard of the Council, and diversion of revenues to Antigua.

Although the Council has succeeded in stopping some questionable, even bizarre, schemes for establishing sovereign states on land leased from Antigua (*Barbuda Voice,* 1982:13(146), 3–6; 1985:16(173), 2–3), one doubtful investor (now being investigated by the United States Internal Revenue Service) has already gained a foothold in Barbuda (*Barbuda Voice,* 1984:16(167), 1–2; 1985:(172), 1–2). For several years a company known as Red Jacket Mines, and more recently as Sandco, has been taking sand from Barbuda (and doing irreparable environmental damage) while the Antigua Ministry of Finance collects the fees (*Barbuda Voice*, 1978:9(101), 1; 1985:16(171), 1-2). Most recently central government has created the Barbuda Industrial Development Agency, which supersedes the Council on development decisions. The Barbudans who sit on the Agency board are those who support accommodation and the new Organization for National Reconstruction.

What will become of the commons is not clear. Some development schemes, so far blocked by the Council, include plans for leasing enormous tracts (*Barbuda Voice*, 1985:16(173), 2-3). Other projects, controversial though they might be, would not necessarily interfere with the commons or the activities of those who wanted to use them. What is clear, however, is that the unity inspired by dependence and founded on equal access to communal lands has already given way to factionalism and conflicting interests. It is also clear that Barbudan economy and society have begun to change in ways that conform more closely with other Caribbean areas. With the advent of deeded property, it may even be that true family land will develop in Barbuda.

Acknowledgements

I thank Margaret Tweedy for allowing me to cite her thesis, *A History of Barbuda under the Codringtons, 1738-1833.*

References

Antigua. 1976. The Barbuda Local Government Act. Antigua, Government Printing Office.
  1962. Laws of Antigua. 2.v. (Rev. ed.) Lewis, P. Cecil, (ed.) St Johns, Antigua.
Army, Thomas. 1977. Personal communication.
Barbuda. 1978. *Petition of Barbudans.* Mimeo. Codrington, Barbuda.
Barbuda Voice. V. 1- ; 1968- . Bronx, New York, BUD Society.
Berleant-Schiller, Riva. 1977. Production and Division of Labor in a West Indian Peasant Community. *American Ethnologist*, 4:253-272.
  1978. The Failure of Agricultural Development in Post-Emancipation Barbuda: A Study of Social and Economic Continuity in a West Indian Community. *Boletín de Estudios Latinoamericanos y del Caribe*, No.25:21-35.
  1983. Grazing and Gardens in Barbuda. In *The Keeping of Animals.* R. Berleant-Schiller and E. Shanklin, (eds.) Totowa, New Jersey, Rowman and Allanheld:73-91.
  1984. Environment, Technology, and the Catch: Fishing and Lobster-Diving in Barbuda. In *The Fishing Culture of the World.* B. Gunda, (ed.) Budapest, Hungarian Academy of Sciences:803-817.

Besson, Jean. 1979. Symbolic Aspects of Land in the Caribbean: The Tenure and Transmission of Land Rights Among Caribbean Peasantries. In *Peasants, Plantations, and Rural Communities in the Caribbean.* M. Cross and A. Marks, (eds.) Guildford, Department of Sociology, University of Surrey, and Leiden, Department of Caribbean Studies, Royal Institute of Linguistics and Anthropology: 86–116.

   1984. Family Land and Caribbean Society: Toward an Ethnography of Afro-Caribbean Peasantries. In *Perspectives on Caribbean Regional Identity.* E. Thomas-Hope, (ed.) Liverpool, Centre for Latin American Studies, University of Liverpool: 57–83.

Caribbean Insight. V. 1– ; 1978– . London, Caribbean Chronicle Publ. Co.

Clarke, Edith. 1957. *My Mother Who Fathered Me.* London, George Allen & Unwin.

Codrington Manuscripts. 1715–1719. No. D1610/C2. William Codrington's Letters to His Managers. Universtiy of Texas General Libraries, on microfilm.

Comitas, Lambros. 1974. Personal communication.

Finkel. H.J. 1964. Patterns of Land Tenure in the Leeward and Windward Islands and Their Relevance to Problems of Agricultural Development in the West Indies. *Economic Geography* 40:163–172.

Fortes, Meyer. 1959. Descent, Filiation and Affinity: A Rejoinder to Dr Leach. 2 parts. *Man* 59:193–197, and 206–212.

Francis, Claude Earle. 1973. Personal communication.

Keur, John Y. and Dorothy L. Keur. 1960. *Windward Children.* Assen, Royal van Gorcum, Ltd.

Lowenthal, David and Colin G. Clarke. 1977. Slave-Breeding in Barbuda: The Past of a Negro Myth. *Annals of the New York Academy of Sciences* 292:510–535.

Great Britain. Secretary of State for Foreign and Commonwealth Affairs. 1981. *Report of the Antigua Constitutional Conference,* London, December 1980. London, Her Majesty's Stationery Office.

Tweedy, Margaret. 1981. *A History of Barbuda under the Codringtons, 1738–1833.* Unpublished M. Litt. thesis, University of Birmingham.

Wilson, Peter J. 1973. *Crab Antics: The Social Anthropology of the English-Speaking Negro Societies of the Caribbean.* New Haven, Yale University Press.

CHAPTER 6

Tourism and changing attitudes to land in Negril, Jamaica

Lesley McKay

Negril, formerly a small fishing village on the west coast of Jamaica, has in only the past twenty-five years become one of the island's fastest growing tourist resorts.[1] This development has been only partly as a result of official planning. When the authorities' large-scale plans for the area fell into disarray as a result of party politics, bureaucratic confusion, and fiscal difficulties, the middle-class and peasant entrepreneurs continued the initiative, both creating and catering to the demand for alternatives to the mainstream tourist facilities on the North Coast. This has made tourism in Negril atypical to that of the Caribbean as a whole in the degree of local participation in the industry. Of the Negrilians, however, generally only some of those migrants who returned from abroad have any major business interests in the industry. Those other Negrilians with more marginal businesses should be seen as responding to an imposed development rather than actively building a new tourist resort *per se*.

One response, in the course of the development, has involved a significant change in the Negrilians' attitudes to their land and adaptive strategies as regards its tenure. Initially many took advantage of the inflation in land prices and official confusion over lack of land titles to sell their land to raise the money to invest or migrate. Their decision to sell was precipitated further in that, at the time, not only was the land held to be of little financial value, but it was even seen as being metaphorically 'dirty' after the palm trees in the area had been struck by a lethal disease. More recently as land values have escalated and the area changed beyond all recognition, the Negrilians have sought to protect their claim to the remaining land through leasing rather than selling it, and by creating 'family land'.

That the appropriation of land should be seen as a major issue by Negrilians is not surprising. Wilson in his study of Providencia notes '... knowledge that he owns a piece of land on Providencia is perhaps the single most important factor in the preservation of a man's identity' (Wilson 1973:46). This is an attitude which he feels is general to the Caribbean as a whole. More recently Besson (1979) has argued that the institution of family land throughout the region has to be seen as the outcome of such sentiments. As the inalienable property of the

132

family rather than any individual member, family land has a symbolic value quite independent of any agrarian use (cf. Clarke, 1971). It would appear that the new tourist industry, by creating such a demand for land, has given further impetus to Negrilians to conserve their land. The modern adaptive strategies, leasing and family land, differ from the folk systems of the past in that they are legal in the eyes of the wider society. Rather than oral tradition or non-legal wills, lawyers are now used in the transmission and creation of family land. Land lease systems allow land held by an individual or family to be used by others outside the kin group without the original owners losing ultimate control of the property. As such this is an extension of the family land system, where the ultimate control of land lies not with the user but with the family group thus, theoretically, ensuring that the latter has access to land in perpetuity.

In Negril, however, there has also been a change in the actual sentiments felt and professed by the locals towards the land. The primary meaning attached to the land continues to be that of belonging, but the secondary, economic, level of meaning has changed: it is now of commercial rather than agrarian importance, as recent land disputes show. The tourist development has, in fact, heightened those paradoxical aspects of Caribbean land tenure in folk custom (see Chapter 1). For the central symbolic importance of land to identity and belonging as exemplified in family land is incompatible with simultaneous co-residence and land use by all the landholders. So that which is intended to be most expressive of family unity, the land, can in practice be very divisive — and all the more so where, as in Negril, land has become so valuable in commercial terms.

In this chapter I will first give a general overview of tourism in Jamaica, placing the Jamaican case in its wider Caribbean context. I will then show how Negril's tourist industry differs from that found in the island as a whole. After detailing those factors which contributed to this particular development, I will go on to describe the contemporary patterns of landholding and usage, and attitudes towards land which I found during my stay in Negril. In conclusion I compare and contrast these with examples described in other Caribbean ethnographies and works on peasant land tenure.

Tourism in the Caribbean and Jamaica

In recent years the Caribbean has become synonymous with tourism. Although North America and Europe dominate the world market in terms of tourism arrivals, sharing over 80 per cent of the tourist traffic

between them (WTO), the Caribbean is certainly one of the largest
Third World destinations. In 1983 there were an estimated 7.5 million
visitors to the area (CTRC). Of all the islands, Jamaica's tourist
industry is one of the largest, with 843,774 visitors in 1984 (JTB).
With the exceptions of the election years of the mid and late 1970s, the
growth of tourism in Jamaica has been fairly steady. The island's
tourist figures have shown few of the fluctuations suffered by the
smaller islands following the decline of one metropolitan market.
Jamaica has benefited from having a well established tourist industry
to build on. Although, as on the other islands, the tourist industry was
only to be consolidated with the advent of mass tourism over the past
twenty years, Taylor (1975) has identified the emergence of tourism
on the island as a 19th century phenomenon. Originally orientated
towards the rich, white tourists of the West, the Jamaican tourist
industry has now adapted to the less affluent, American package
tourist. This change has not, however, affected the structure of the
tourist industry itself; the tourists remain racially, economically,
and spatially distinct from the Jamaican population, whilst the
management and control of the industry generally remains outside
Jamaican control. If there was an apparent lessening of direct foreign
control in the 1970s this was largely due to a situation forced on the
government by the near collapse of the tourist industry at the time,
following the widespread Western media coverage of the social unrest
on the island. The current leasing and franchise arrangements
(cf. Ohiorhenuan, 1979) are actually a more insidious form of foreign
control with the Jamaican government assuming responsibility for the
building and potential losses of hotels and facilities.

There is some question as to the efficacy of tourism as a means
of development (cf. Bryden, 1973; Talbot, 1974–5; Matthews, 1977;
Kaufman, 1985; Momsen, 1985). Economic issues apart, such as the
lack of multiplier effects, or leakage of the tourist dollar, there would
appear to be a general consensus of opinion among sociologists as to
the adverse social effects of the industry (Perez, 1973–4, 1975; cf. Turner
and Ash, 1975). Those writing specifically about Jamaica have been
the least temperate in their criticisms (Floyd, 1973–4; Goffe, 1975;
Taylor, 1975; Norton, 1979). Throughout their work the twin themes
of racial subordination, whether economic, social, or cultural, and
appropriation of land through lease, franchise, inflation, or usage, are
reiterated. The parallels of this situation to that of the old colonial
society have been highlighted. Taylor (1975) argues effectively that the
whole of Jamaica's tourist industry emerged from a system intended
to rejuvenate the social, economic and cultural hegemony of the
whites on the island.

Negril

Negril (Map 4) is, so far at least, an exception to the rule of foreign control and local exclusion from the tourist trade; although with foreign and government interest in the area this could soon change. The Urban Development Corporation (UDC), for example, has drawn up plans for large scale projects in the surrounding areas. These include a 240 room hotel, and 151 apartments at Rutland Point, and 300 hotel and 392 apartment rooms at Ireland Penn. To date though, as many hoteliers and locals are keen to point out, Negril's development is generally despite, rather than because of, government and tourist board action. The first hotel was built in 1962, but the area has come into its own as a major resort only in the past ten or fifteen years. Today there are still only four hotels in the area with more than 60 rooms. None of these are foreign owned (though significantly none of them are owned by Negrilians either). The form of tourism is also reflected in the Jamaican Tourist Board's figures of cottage to hotel rooms — and this feature becomes even more striking when the number of unregistered rooms is considered.[2] The foreign ownership of Jamaica's past has also been given a new face in those businesses recently established in Negril. Several of these are actually owned by past visitors. They differ in that even if, arguably, the profits will eventually 'leak' back to the West, they are small scale, and run in the main as much for the owners' satisfaction or interest as pure profit. One cottage owner, for example, frankly admitted that she could not afford to live on the money from her rooms alone, but depended on her husband's salary as well.

Physically too, although signs and tourist related 'businesses' line the main road through and as far as five or six miles outside the town, Negril is still relatively undeveloped in appearance. Larger hotels are mainly confined to the beach area, which has itself been subjected to an Urban Development Corporation order limiting, for example, the height of hotels ('no higher than the height of the tallest palm tree' is the rule of thumb), and room density (fifteen rooms per acre). In other areas of Negril the buildings are still small, often run down, and there is only one narrow, roughly surfaced road through the town.

Geographically, and to some extent socially, Negril can be divided into three distinct areas: the beach, the West End and Red Ground (Map 4). These social divisions pre-date tourism in the area. In the past, although there was little economic difference between the residents of these divisions, families were definitely associated with one specific area. Tourist development in Negril may have had the paradoxical effect of both exacerbating the original differences

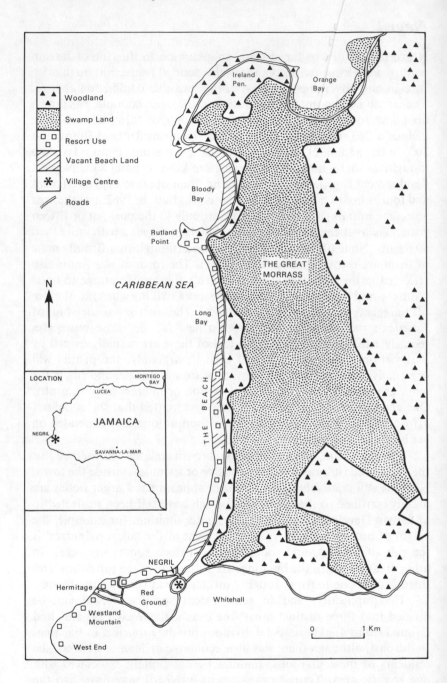

Map 4   Land use of Negril, Jamaica

between beach families and other Negrilians, as the value of beachland rose, and detracting from the original social differences as
Negrilians as a whole assert a community solidarity against the influx
of newcomers, tourists and developers. The beach is the most
developed area in terms of expensive new buildings. Only three of the
more impressive buildings are owned by Negrilians — all three of
whom are returned migrants.

On the whole Negrilian owned enterprises are 'rootsier' than
those of the other, Jamaican or foreign, investors on the beach. That
is they are of lower initial capital investment, and cater for the younger
or less affluent tourists. Red Ground is so called for the different red
colour of its soil. This is the most crowded and uncommercial area of
Negril. Apparently always the most densely populated, Red Ground
has become an increasingly difficult place to live in since the advent of
tourism. As land prices have always been lower here, this area received
first those Negrilians who had sold their beach land, followed by
hotel employees and their families, then the squatters, hustlers, and
prostitutes. South of Red Ground are the Hermitage and Westland
Mountain areas. As in the West End, these areas are a mix of old and
new, local and tourist accommodation, and Jamaican and foreign
owned businesses, large and small.

The development of Negril

Negril can be seen as developing on two interacting levels: the formal
and the informal, or large scale as opposed to small scale. The former
group includes government bodies and larger private investors; the
latter the people from the surrounding areas, poorer Jamaicans from
other parts of the island, and the Negrilians themselves.

Initially it would appear that tourism was envisaged as being
developed along similar lines to that of Montego Bay, or that of Ocho
Rios in recent years, with Jamaican government bodies acting to
attract large amounts of foreign investment to the area. It was to this
end that the Negril Area Land Authority (NALA) was set up in 1957
to open up this area, which had hitherto been a purely local tourist
spot due primarily to its inacessability. NALA was to provide the
infrastructure necessary to attract foreign investment for tourist
development. Electricity, water, and a sewage system were brought to
the area, the swamp behind the beach was drained, and a road built
to connect Negril directly to the North Coast tourist centres and the
airport. These measures have raised the living standards of the

villagers, and have ensured support to this day for the People's National Party (PNP) under whose administration the project was initiated.

The same year that the road was completed, however, saw the election of the previous opposition party, the Jamaican Labour Party (JLP). From this time the development of Negril, which was seen as a PNP project, was to all intents and purposes shelved at the official level. The story of the following years was one of official obstruction: for example, long periods of delay for planning permission or funding of projects, but most especially confusion over the role of NALA. In 1966, for example, its powers to approve or reject applications for development projects were revoked, and transferred to the town planning offices. The situation was further complicated, rather than resolved, with the creation of the Urban Development Corporation in 1968, so much so that one senator for the area called for a government statement to clarify the issues. In 1981 NALA was, in fact, finally disbanded. Its planning function already given to the Town and Country Planning Department, its lands were now given to the UDC and further responsibilities allocated to the two parish councils responsible for the village.

The UDC was responsible for many major projects around Negril, for example the beach club, now known as Hedonism II, the airfield, and craft markets at Negril village and Rutland Point; developments which helped establish Negril as a resort, and which in turn attracted further private investment. Confusion continued, however, as to the official responsibility for the area, not least as regards planning and enforcement of planning regulations. This situation was compounded by the continuing fiscal difficulties of Jamaica as a whole. The UDC, for example, is only responsible for its own lands. Since these lie outside the village boundaries, this means that the UDC has very little interest in the development of Negril village itself; whilst its being based in Kingston means that it remains out of touch with the day to day running of its projects, and the activities of its employees. The Town and Country Planning Department is also located outside Negril, hence there has been little action taken on the influx of squatters into the area. Other problems such as garbage disposal, sanitation, roads and crime, which are now the concern of the parish councils, also remain largely unresolved for a number of reasons. Firstly, Negril actually falls between two parish councils, Westmoreland and Hanover. Secondly, at this time the parish councils are in disarray as the JLP attempts to restructure local government. Thirdly, partly as a result of this restructuring, financial resources are being denied to local government, and some sectors are unsure from one month to the next whether they will even be able to meet their wages bills.[3]

It is the continuing confusion at official level more than anything else which allowed the 'little people', as many style themselves, to participate in Negril's tourist industry. However, here a distinction should be made between Negrilians and 'outsiders' or the poorer Jamaicans who have moved into Negril in recent years to capitalize on the tourism there. Firstly, because many of the older Negrilians especially are antagonistic towards 'the outsiders'. Secondly, since the official confusion has benefited each group differently according to their relationship, or access to land. The outsiders have benefited from the lack of official action on squatting, taking the opportunity to 'capture' land on which to build their stalls, shops and houses. The Negrilians, as landholders, benefited initially from absence of legal land titles, later from land ownership itself. As such, it is they who are the focus of this discussion.

Tourist development and the Negrilians

Before the late 1950s, I was told, land was 'of little account'. Since both the swamp behind the beach, and the rocks of the West End were of little use agriculturally, this is likely in financial terms — although, as I hope to show below, Negrilian sentiments about their land go beyond its economic value alone. The majority of Negrilians derived their main livelihood from fishing, subsistence production and, to a lesser extent, cash from casual labour. As such, although there has been some controversy over the precise meaning of the term 'peasantry' (cf. Philpott, 1973:85–89; Harrison, 1979:54–58; Mintz, 1973–4; 1984:40), the Negrilians of the past can be defined as such if the interpretation given by Dalton (1967) is adopted. Dalton's definition undercuts such claims as Comitas', '. . . that no viable peasant subculture exists in Jamaica' (1973:162) by taking that feature which Comitas sees as contrary to a peasant economy, that is the sale of labour, as integral to his definition (cf. Besson, 1984a:75–6). Dalton's further characterization of a peasantry as generally lacking modern technology, and maintaining traditional social and cultural practices, can also be seen to be applicable to the Negril of the past. Land-ownership followed the usual pattern of 'bought land', or, more commonly, 'inherited' and 'family land' (cf. Clarke, 1971; Davenport, 1961; Besson, 1984a:58–60; 1984b). There was no outside interest in the land or its monetary value, therefore land-ownership was not a major issue. One older man joked, 'You couldn't give it away. Try and pay debts with it and they'd laugh at you'. Land-ownership could even be seen as problematical, as the story of the Whitehall estates shows. Under Jamaican law, those landowners whose lands border swampland are accorded the usage of the swamp too. This was the case with the largest landowner of the past. When the Betterment Tax, a tax levied on lands owned, was introduced, the owner refused to pay it on the swamplands. This was a decision he was later to regret when, after the property boom, his claim to these lands was denied on the grounds of non-payment of taxes. In any case in 1962, when the last full scale survey map of the area was drawn up, few held land titles in the area. For administrative purposes ownership was designated by officials according to heads of family.

If there was little interest in the legal ownership, however, this is not to imply a lack of interest in the land itself on the part of the Negrilians. Very many of those families who have since re-located in the area still identify strongly with 'their' bit of beachland:[4] land they, and family members had been born on, planted on, 'courted on' and been buried on. Initially beachland, when it came to be sought after by property speculators and developers, was not easily parted with. This despite the fact, as many landowners and Negrilians today concede, that the money offered for land was especially good for the time. In three cases known to me sale was hindered only by the land being family land. In many other cases, however, it was a combination of sentiment and fear of, or lack of knowledge of, alternative ways of life which made the Negrilians reluctant to part with land. An older man recalls how his father was 'mocked', first when he sold his land, then when he relocated his family on ten acres on the rocks: 'How you going to plant on rocks? they said'. This man is now, however, held up as one of the few who has succeeded in the new tourist industry in Negril. The money he gained from his land sale he later put to use in the building of hotels. His family now controls three different hotels and cottages between them. This, however, does not stop his son from feeling 'guilty' at the sale of the family's beachland: 'If it was left to me I'd have kept a little piece, not for the money, but just to have, and for my sons to know'.

Despite that man's brave gamble, it is unlikely that many others would have sold their land had it not been for the lethal palm disease, Yellow Leaf, which struck the trees in the area in the late 1950s. Before this time the beach families had derived extra income from the oil the women made from the coconuts. The disease had two effects: it impoverished the peasants still further, and made them 'disgusted' with their land. These feelings persisted even after the introduction of the Malaysian Dwarf tree to replace the old. The land was still felt to be 'dirty'. Moreover the new tree could not replace the old in terms of palm oil production, as yields of oil per nut are estimated to be only half the yield of the old trees.

The palm disease of the 1950s coincided with another 'push' factor in persuading the Negrilians to sell: that of the tradition of migration common to Jamaica as a whole and the Caribbean region (Foner, 1979; Philpott, 1973; Thomas-Hope, 1980). This is a pattern of young people leaving to find work in Kingston, USA or Britain; whether from choice to escape the limited opportunities open to them at home, or sent to relieve pressure on scarce resources and/or to improve their families' life chances through the addition of migrant remittances. Again the timing of foreign interest in Negril land was significant, coinciding as it did with the rush to migrate. For as Britain was indicating her intentions of limiting migrant numbers, her need for migrant labour at an end (Hiro, 1971; Rose, 1969), West Indians were hurrying to try and beat the impending legislation. Money offered for the land was seen as a preferable alternative to loans from the banks, or from friends and family already 'in foreign'. As a source of migrant money the sale of the land, be it family land itself, or other bequeathed yet undivided property, could therefore be further justified as benefiting the family as a whole, or at least several of the members of it. Further, the absence of so many family members also facilitated the sale of land itself, with co-heirs not being present to contest it.

So the land, while of deep sentimental value, was seen as financially useless and metaphorically dirty, and therefore sold for rational reasons. Given the decision to sell, the Negrilians can be seen to have used the subsequent lack of titles to their benefit — there are many tales of land being sold at least twice by the original Negrilian holder. However, I found only two who had done so successfully, and one man who had fought unsuccessfully to reclaim ownership of land he had sold; his claim being based on residence rights after the sale. Those who sold land either moved away, or relocated in the area. Many families, for example, sold only part of their land — generally that closest to the beach — and built a new home on the rest, at least until the prohibition on subdivision of beach lands was imposed. Not all land sales were to the benefit of the inhabitants however. In some cases land was sold on the understanding that Negrilians would continue to live on it since the new foreign owners did not want to build on it or use it for the most part of the year, but wanted just to have it, a sentiment well understood by Negrilians. When the pieces of land were re-sold, often in the USA, the Negrilian families involved found themselves squatters on land they had formerly believed to be theirs.

Confusion extended to families too. When some family members took advantage of the absence of others to sell, the technical difference between family land, and land held by family became only too apparent.[5] Whatever the motivation in its sale, by the 1970s landholding and land-ownership had been transformed. Whilst formerly an inward looking and close community, Negrilians were now outnumbered in terms of land-ownership by non-Negrilians. That many of these people were Jamaicans is irrelevant to the general effect. Whereas before land-ownership had been synonymous with Negrilian community membership, and membership conversely synonymous with access to some land in Negril, now land-ownership did not necessarily imply interest or involvement within the community as Negrilians understood it.[6] Even more problematically, a Negrilian, especially a returning migrant, many of whom only 'went to come back' (cf. Thomas-Hope 1980), could find himself with no land rights at all in the area.

That many Negrilians benefited initially from bureaucratic confusion is, however, undoubted. A further important feature is how little of this money was invested in tourist businesses, at least at that time. There are many valid and, in retrospect, unsurprising reasons for this. On the most elementary level there was very little tourism in Negril until the late 1960s. There was little reason therefore for a Negrilian fisherman to try his hand in an unfamiliar and uncertain business. Even now, for example, it is recognised that, compared to Montego Bay, Jamaica's 'tourist capital', Negril has a very short tourist season with a peak period of approximately four months. Money, therefore, was invested elsewhere, and tourist enterprise was small scale and often unsolicited. For instance, the Negrilians took the hippies of the late 1960s, into their yards. This solution suited the Negrilians for a variety of reasons. Firstly, by accommodating tourists in their own homes, they escaped taxes on income and business ventures, and also the initial outlay on new buildings. Secondly, it gave those Negrilians of other areas — Red Ground and West End — a chance to 'get some of the tourist dollar', previously more difficult for them because they held less desirable land. For example, two of the most successful landladies in Negril are on Red Ground and the West End. Thirdly, it gave the peasants a gradual training in an unfamiliar business, and in dealing with the, until then, unfamiliar 'white man'; this latter feature being especially important in a country riven by colour and class boundaries.

There were, however, drawbacks in this early start — for reasons specifically Jamaican. The type of tourist arriving in Negril in the late 1960s and early 1970s were the 'non-institutionalised tourists' of Cohen's typology,[7] in this case specifically draft dodgers and hippies. Although many were undoubtedly of good character and intentions (many, for example, now have their own businesses in Negril), and contributed extensively to tourist development in the area, very many also came to Negril because, to quote one, 'I can do things here I can't at home'. This included nude sunbathing, smoking ganja or taking other drugs, or finding alternative lifestyles living with Rastafarians or dreadlocked black men. All of which, if not unheard of in Jamaica today, were certainly at variance with Negrilian mores and standards of the time. That it was the 'white man' himself who was behaving in this way was even more shocking. Because of this, though some viewed the hippies with amusement, they were generally termed 'dirty', or most telling of all 'not real tourists'. This 'dirtiness' is possibly one reason for the other significant feature of early tourist accommodation in Negril homes, that of the tourist's exclusion from the home itself. In the majority of cases it was stressed that they slept across the yard, or even on the porch. While this coincides with the peasant precept of a separate residence for each cohabiting couple (Davenport, 1961; Mintz, 1984:238–40), the reason seems to go beyond this, not least since obviously not all tourists travelled in mixed couples.

The peasants were aware of the difference between the usual middle-class, white tourist to Jamaica, and 'their' tourists who were often literally those whom the larger hotels refused to accept on account of their clothes, hair or behaviour. This in turn only compounded those other specifically Jamaican barriers to working with tourists, that is the abhorrence of anything with the taint of slavery — domestic labour being an archetypal example of such work. Those who could afford to — the majority of the families who sold land on the beach for example — therefore did not start up tourist businesses.

This, in turn, accounts for the disproportionate number of Negrilian owned businesses, in terms of original numbers of inhabitants to each area, being located in the Red Ground and West End areas. As land was never in such demand here, the inhabitants had to find alternative means of getting at the tourist dollar. Later they had the means to do so, i.e. land to build on. The fact that prices were lower in these areas also meant that a few relocating beach families and returning migrants could afford to buy land to develop here.

More than any other group in Negril, it was the returning migrants who in fact took up tourist development in a big way.

Although the emergent tourist industry was never the sole or main motivating factor in their return, their participation does come from their having advantages and motivating factors absent from Negrilians as a whole. Having lived amongst them for perhaps ten or twenty years, they had lost much of the respect for the white man. In addition, they brought greater knowledge of business, or knowledge of those Western mores and tastes that were so often incomprehensible to the Negrilian at home, for example vegetarianism. They came home too with an expectation of status in the community, or an experience of a higher standard of living, which in turn resulted in a greater drive to succeed. Given that as from the late 1960s they were no longer 'big fish in a little pond', with status automatically conferred on them from their time spent abroad, they were more likely, as some did, to take advantage of the increased opportunities that tourism brought, especially as it was closer to their previous work experience abroad than, say, farming or fishing. Some migrants, too, had accumulated useful business contacts abroad. A partner to distribute ganja for a half profit, or sell time-sharing, or even recommend guests, is an invaluable help.

There was a second smaller group of returning migrants, who were also to be influential in the development of tourism in the area. These were the women whose marriages broke up whilst they, or their husband alone, were 'in foreign'. Given the centrality of domestic labour, i.e. that labour usually designated as 'women's work', to tourism in the catering and accomodation sectors, it was inevitable that women would play a key role in the development of the industry. These women, however, while having the motivation and experience of the above group, were, in many cases, penniless. One woman in fact, had to be 'rescued' by her mother who raised her fare home after her marriage 'mashed up'. It was these women who, having no alternative, made the greatest use of family land on which to build their businesses. In this they differed sharply from their male counterparts who, on returning, settled on land to which they had title, whether inherited or bought. The reasons for this are obvious, and seem too to highlight the central paradoxes of family land (cf. Chapter 1). Put simply, not all those with rights to the land can use it, the acreage involved is usually too small. It is, therefore, morally encumbent for a returnee, whether from other parts of the island or abroad, to settle elsewhere if at all possible. This moral pressure is not the only disincentive to settling on or developing family land. The constant risk of 'fuss' with other family members is a strong deterrent too.

Land and tourism

That Negril is now a tourist area has exacerbated these problems. As land prices have become inflated beyond belief — beach land is now sold by the square foot, for example — it has become more difficult for even wealthier returning migrants to find land to settle on. Further, although development seems to have no effect on any migrant's initial decision to return, it has attracted Jamaicans previously living in other parts of the island. Family land is therefore more likely to be in demand by many more family members. A further problem is that it is much more difficult for tourist enterprises to coexist on a given area than agricultural ones. Firstly, a building, even in the case of the thatched bars or portable chalet rooms, involves much more commitment in terms of money invested, and permanency of land utilization. Secondly, businesses can be mutually exclusive — so a tourist dollar earned by one family member is at the direct expense of another, given the close proximity of businesses on the land. One case illustrates these points.

Mr A, 44, returned from Britain eight years ago, after being made redundant. Although he found work at the UDC airfield, he also built up a bar on family land on the beach. This bar, with its central beach location, lower prices and live music in season, came to be especially popular with the younger tourists. Yet Mr A was still reluctant to commit himself fully to the business, trying for four years instead to balance his work at the airfield with barwork at night. The main reason for this, he told me, was family 'interference' with the bar. Though other family members were willing to let him take risks in, for example, taking out loans to develop his business, they wanted an ever increasing say in its running and the development of their land. Nor were they willing to sell any to him. One major dispute involved a cousin building his bar directly opposite Mr A's. Not only was this bar given a very similar name to Mr A's, but was also directly opposite, equidistant from its outdoor stage, and so similar in appearance it could easily pass for being part of the same establishment.

Throughout this example there is a further underlying theme, that of the retention of land by Negrilians at the present time. Whilst earlier many were willing to sell land, now there seems to be the opposite desire, to retain land. Several Negrilians I spoke to talked of their 'making the land for family'; that is, formally establishing family land from land they themselves had bought or inherited. Their reasons for this were often given as keeping a stake in the land: 'something to come back to'. Ironically this sentiment, apparently altruistic and ostensibly applicable to all, is not as impartial as it would at first appear. The same woman, for example, who stated that her land is for all, also expressed her horror when questioned on returning family members: 'They can't come back! There's no room!'

Nor does the establishment of family land mean a renunciation of interest in the land or pure philanthropy on the part of the donor. Mr B is a case in point. Having declared this intention of 'turning his land over', and gone as far as seeing lawyers about it, he has however firm ideas as to whom he wants to occupy the land, and what he wants them to do with it. At the moment Mr B has, amongst other holdings, two acres inherited from his father. On returning from Britain two years ago he found some of this land already occupied by family. Daughters of the brother who had been guarding the land for him had put a couple of shops on it. After some 'fuss' he let them stay there on the understanding that they pay rent. Now other family members have expressed interest in developing his land. Mr B, although he wants the land to be developed, also wants his son to know Negril, and the business to be for closer family. In this he has a problem in that he has six children by six different mothers, not all of whom know of each other's existence, and his son's mother will not let him travel to Jamaica. In turning the land over Mr B is avoiding the problem of direct legacy — 'Let them fight it out' — and the possibility of the land being neglected by an uncaring legatee, and taken over by squatters from outside. He believes this will also give his son's mother further incentive to send her son over to Negril to make his claim known. His decision, however, is not a totally voluntary one. Mr B has, in fact been manoeuvred into it by other relatives building on his land and pressing him for further access to the land.

A further striking feature of such talk of the land is, at least in many cases, the essential stress firstly on belonging, and secondly on economic entrepreneurship, rather than agrarian or subsistence value.[8] Nor is family land the only means of ensuring belonging. A larger number of land plots are being leased rather than sold. One man explained his system. The lease lasts for five years. At the end of this time the rent can be altered, or the tenant evicted. Thus not only does he have a guaranteed income, but in a sense he can have what the white man wants, i.e. his land. His tenant's repeated attempts to buy only increase his satisfaction in this. The Negrilian with experience of 'development' in the past decade or so can therefore be seen as having evolved another coping strategy, that of leasing, in addition to the traditional one of family land.

In the Negril experience the greatest losers now, it would seem, are the beach people. If once their income from palm oil and money from land sales gave them status, it is those people of Red Ground and

West End, and the few relocated beach families who invested early in tourism who are smug. 'Anyone who says he don't regret selling is a fool', I was told. The most important thing here, however, is not what these people may or may not have lost economically, but what they lost in sentiment. One man whose father sold their family's land on the beach told me, 'It was my father who sold. If it'd been me now I'd have kept some back, not for the money but just to have'. That man who, when asked how he felt about foreigners on his bit of beachland, answered 'Guilty', underlines every point above.

Conclusion

The symbolic importance of land to the rural peoples of the Caribbean, as mentioned earlier, are to be found in many key works in Caribbean studies. Mintz states quite unequivocally that, 'the symbolic significance of land for Caribbean rural folk ... far exceeds any obvious economic considerations' (1984:155). This statement is in turn a direct echo of Clarke's earlier reference in connection with family land, that 'The possession of an interest in family land or a family house produces a sense of security out of all proportion to the actual economic security, which at best is slight' (1971:238). Similar references can be found in Wilson (1973), Horowitz (1967), Lowenthal (1961), Besson (1979, 1984a, 1984b), and Philpott (1973).

The Jamaicans emerged from a variant of slavery which, from its pivotal role in a capitalist mode of production, was particularly harsh. In this society, to quote Braithwaite, the slaves were '... regarded legally and to a large extent socially, as things, human machines ...' (1978:151). Given this, the need to establish the self as an individual, or as part of an alternative, human, community can be seen to be tantamount. Some writers such as Beckford (1983) point to the high value on land as coming from the continued competition between the peasantries and plantations for land. This competition undoubtedly exists, and was a key factor in the development of Caribbean peasantries. Mintz, for example, argues that the history and sociology of 'Caribbean peasantries represent *a mode of response* to the plantation system and its connotations, and *a mode of resistance* to imposed styles of life.' (1984:132-3). However sentiments to land, as can be inferred from Mintz's statement, transcend a purely socio-economic context. Wilson (1973) provides a particularly empathic depiction of the significance of land in his study of Providencia. He argues, 'Living on and owning part of Providencia is what makes a person different from everyone else and at the same time identifies those who are like oneself' (1973:45). As argued previously, family land has to be seen as the logical outcome of such attitudes. Clarke notes that it '... may be regarded from the functional point of view as a conservative force, directed to ensure that the inheritance is kept intact and contributing also to family cohesion and solidarity.' (1971:237–8; cf. Besson, 1984a).

I found attitudes in Negril to fit the attitudes above exactly. Throughout fieldwork Negrilians expressed deep attachment to their land — as expressed, for example, in their guilt at its sale. The deep disgust with which they viewed the diseased land is further evidence of this. The importance of land to community is shown in the Negrilians being identified according to which area they came from: Red Ground, West End or Beach. That families could be classified as such reflects on the continuity of land-ownership, where different parts of land came to be associated with various families through time. With the advent of tourism in the area, and an influx of 'outsiders', this system has been 'mashed up', with land falling out of local Negrilian hands. But if land-ownership no longer denotes membership of the Negrilian community, the establishment of family land or the leasing rather than the sale of land, can be seen to be two means of ensuring that native Negrilians will continue to have access to land in Negril.

With respect to Clarke (1971), in Negril family land is in no way 'unproductive' or 'neglected'. This in turn leads to another contrast between the use of Negrilian family land in commercial ventures, and that in agricultural production. The contrast is this: if family land evolved as a means of existing independently of a dominant colonial system, that of plantation agriculture (Besson, 1984a; cf. Chapter 1), then the use of family land here can be seen as a means of competing with, or maintaining an interest in a new, export-orientated, foreign-dominated industry. This adds a new dimension to Mintz's theme of 'response' and 'resistance' (1984:132–3). As Mintz shows, past local West Indian reactions to such export-industries, as exemplified by the plantation system, was to struggle to exist independently, on other marginal land, or serving other local markets. Given that in Negril the industry has still been imposed, and that the villagers are catering for an 'alternative' tourist, that is a younger or less affluent one, they are still participating in, and more importantly helping to build Jamaica's tourist industry.

Such developments do, however, correlate with findings on the paradoxical aspects of landholding in the Caribbean (see Chapter 1), where that which is most expressive of equality, identity, and solidarity is also the most potentially divisive. As Wilson puts it, '... if ... land is a primary basis of social identity and of belonging to the island, then owning more of the island is indicative of a greater sense of belonging and ownership — a sign of wealth, power, status, and prestige.' (1973:58). Conflict over land is again a recurrent theme in the ethnographies referred to above. Tourist development would appear to have heightened this paradox.

Notes

1   This chapter is part of an M. Litt. thesis, 'The effects of tourism on a Caribbean rural community', in preparation for the Department of Sociology, University of Aberdeen. A grant from Aberdeen University enabled me to live in Negril for five months, from April to August 1985, as part of a field study for this degree. I am grateful to Dr Jean Besson, my thesis supervisor, for comments on earlier drafts of this essay. I also wish to thank the Department of Sociology, University of the West Indies, Kingston, Jamaica, and especially Miss June Dolly-Besson for assistance in the field.

2   The JTB, for example, shows Negril as having seven hotels and 472 cottage rooms with 30 guest-houses. This is the highest cottage to hotel room ratio in Jamaica. The ratio in Montego Bay is 35 hotels to 299 cottages, and only one guest-house. Rooms in private homes not included in the JTB figures for Negril, I would estimate as being as high as 45.

3   A *Daily Gleaner* front page report of 9th August, 1985, for example, states:

> The Ministry of Local Government has directed all Parish Councils to make all employees in cemeteries, parks and gardens and life guards at public beaches redundant with immediate effect as no money will be available to pay them as of today, . . .

4   It should be stressed that it is the land adjacent to the beach, and not the beach itself, with which these people identify. One great change following from tourism was the change in conception of the beach. Previously the beach was 'for everyone': a public walkway, and site for church outings and picnics on national holidays. Now not only has the beach itself become a particular focus of attention, but many parts are reserved for specific hotels and cottages.

5   Briefly, family land is that to which, theoretically, all descendants have equal rights of access; and which cannot be sold, partitioned nor subdivided without the consent of all family members. Although, having said this, as mentioned above, in Negril family land had, in practice, sometimes been sold without such total consent. The inflation of land prices following tourist development encouraged some Negrilians to take advantage of the absence of some family members and sell the land; a pattern of events similar to that described elsewhere (cf. Olwig 1977). The malleability of land tenure systems in Caribbean folk custom is explored in Chapter 3. Confusingly, in Negril 'family land' was also sometimes used to refer to land to which an individual may have had access through his kin ties with the owner, or which was to be partitioned at a later date. My use of the term in the text is that as standardized by Clarke (1971) and Besson (1984a).

6   However, some early businessmen were involved in community matters. One of the earliest investors was a church minister from a neighbouring area. The Negril Chamber of Commerce today, in addition to organising projects of general use to the community as a whole, is also involved in, for example, a school feeding and building programme, and charity work.

7   Cohen (1972) has evolved a typology of different types of tourist according to the varying combinations of novelty to familiarity in their tourist experience. The four types, namely, of mass organised tourist, individual organised tourist, explorer, and drifter, fall into two main categories of institutionalized and non-institutionalized respectively. The degree of guest to host interaction and empathy is greatest in the latter, while that of environmental impact is greatest in the former.

8   It is entirely possible that this impression of mine derives from the fact that my fullest discussions on land were with former migrants, that is those people whose past worklife had been in industry, rather than those who had continued to plant and fish in Negril. However, in such talk of land as I had with the latter, the theme of belonging was again uppermost. The poorer of Red Ground especially worried that 'there's no room' although this sentiment was also voiced by a woman whose elder children were all in paid employment.

References

Beckford, George L. 1983. *Persistent poverty: underdevelopment in plantation economies of the third World*. London, Zed Books.

Besson, Jean. 1979. Symbolic aspects of land in the Caribbean: the tenure and transmission of land rights among Caribbean peasantries. In Cross, Malcolm and Marks, Arnaud (eds.). *Peasants, plantations and rural communities in the Caribbean*. Guildford, University of Surrey and Leiden, Royal Institute of Linguistics and Anthropology.

1984a. Family land and Caribbean society: toward an ethnography of Afro-Caribbean peasantries. In Thomas-Hope, Elizabeth M. (ed.). *Perspectives on Caribbean regional identity*. Liverpool, Liverpool University Press.

1984b. Land tenure in the free villages of Trelawny, Jamaica: a case study in the Caribbean peasant response to emancipation, *Slavery and Abolition*, 5(1):3–23.

Braithwaite, Edward. 1978. *The development of creole society in Jamaica, 1779–1820*. Oxford, Clarendon Press.

Bryden, John M. 1973. *Tourism and development: a case study of the Commonwealth Caribbean*. Cambridge, CUP.

Clarke, Edith. (1953) 1971. Land tenure and the family in four selected communities in Jamaica. In Horowitz, Michael M. (ed.). *People and cultures of the Caribbean*. New York, Natural History Press.

Cohen, Erik. 1972. Toward a sociology of international tourism, *Social Research*, 39(1):164–182.

Comitas, Lambros. (1964) 1973. Occupational multiplicity in rural Jamaica. In Comitas, Lambros and Lowenthal, David (eds.). *Work and family life: West Indian perspectives.* Garden City, New York, Anchor Press/Doubleday.

Caribbean Tourism Research and Development Centre. 1984. *Statistical News.*

Daily Gleaner. 9 August 1984.

Davenport, William. 1961. The family system of Jamaica, *Social and Economic Studies,* 10(4):467–53.

Dalton, George. 1967. Primitive money. In Dalton, George (ed.). *Tribal and peasant economies: readings in economic anthropology.* Garden City, New York, Natural History Press.

Floyd, Barry. 1973–4. The two faces of Jamaica, *The Geographical Magazine,* 46:425–431.

Foner, Nancy. 1973. *Status and power in rural Jamaica: a study of educational and political change.* New York, Teacher College Press, Columbia University.

1979a. *Jamaica farewell: Jamaican migrants in London.* London, Routledge and Kegan Paul Ltd.

1979b. The Jamaicans: cultural and social change among migrants in Britain. In Watson, James L. (ed.). *Between two cultures: migrants and minorities in Britain.* London, Basil Blackwell.

Goffe, Peter. 1975. Development potential of international tourism. *Cornell Hotel and Restaurant Administration Quarterly,* 16:24–31.

Harrison, David. 1979. The changing fortunes of a Trinidad peasantry. In Cross, Malcolm and Marks, Arnaud (eds.). *Peasants, plantations and rural communities in the Caribbean.* Guildford, University of Surrey and Leiden, Royal Institute of Linguistics and Anthropology.

Hiro, Philip. 1973. *Black British, White British.* New York, Monthly Review Press.

Horowitz, Michael M. 1967. *Morne-Paysan: peasant village in Martinique.* New York, Holt, Rinehart and Winston Inc.

Jamaican Tourist Board. 1984. Travel Statistics.

Kaufman, Michael. 1985. *Jamaica Under Manley: dilemmas of socialism and democracy.* London, Zed Books.

Lowenthal, David. 1961. Caribbean views of Caribbean land, *The Canadian Geographer,* 5(2):1–10.

Mathieson, Alister and Wall, Geoffrey. 1982. *Tourism: economic, physical and social impacts.* New York, Longman Group Ltd.

Matthews, Harry G. 1977. Radicals and Third World Tourism: A Caribbean Focus, *Annals of Tourism Research,* 5:20–29.

Mintz, Sidney W. 1973–4. A note on the definition of peasantries. *Journal of Peasant Studies,* 1(1):91–106.

1984. *Caribbean transformations.* Baltimore, Johns Hopkin's University Press.

Momsen, Janet Henshall. 1985. Tourism and development in the Caribbean. *Mainzer Geographische Studien,* 26:25–36.

Norton, Graham. 1977. Tourism, can the patient recover? *West Indian Chronicle News,* 90:53–55.

Ohiorhenuan, M. John F.E. 1979. The social and economic implications of technology transformation in Jamaican tourism. *UN conference on trade and development.*

Olwig, Karen Fog P. 1977. *Households, exchange and social reproduction: the development of a Caribbean society.* PhD thesis, University of Minnesota.

Perez, Louis A. Jnr. 1973–4. Aspects of underdevelopment: tourism in the West Indies. *Science and Society*, 37:473–481.
     1975. Tourism in the West Indies. *Journal of Communication*, Spring 136–143.
Philpott, Stuart B. 1973. *West Indian migration: the Montserrat case.* London, Athlone Press.
     1979. The Montserrations: migration dependency and the maintenance of island ties in England. In Watson, James L (ed.). *Between two cultures: migrants and minorities in Britain.* London, Basil Blackwell.
Rose, E.J.B. et al. 1969. *Colour and Citizenship: a report on British race relations.* London, Oxford University Press.
Talbot, Neil. 1974–5. A note on tourism in the West Indies. *Science and Society*, 38:347–349.
Taylor, Frank. 1975. *Jamaica — the welcoming society: myths and reality.* Institute of Social and Economic Research, working paper No 8, University of the West Indies, Jamaica.
Thomas-Hope, Elizabeth. 1980. Hopes and reality in the West Indian migration to Britain. *Oral History*, 8:35–42.
Turner, L. and Ash, S. 1975. *The golden hordes: international tourism and the pleasure periphery.* London, Constable.
Watson, James L. (ed.). 1979. *Between two cultures: migrants and minorities in Britain.* London, Basil Blackwell Ltd.
Wilson, Peter J. 1973. *Crab antics: the social anthropology of English-speaking negro communities in the Caribbean.* London, Yale University Press.
World Tourist Organization. 1983. *Regional Economic Statistics.*

CHAPTER 7

Children's attitudes to the island community
The aftermath of out-migration on Nevis

Karen Fog Olwig

It is generally assumed today that an important basis for the existence of a nation lies in a certain innate attachment to the native land, particularly in agricultural areas. This idea, as will be seen, clearly lies behind the efforts of some local governments and international aid organizations to plan for independent nationhood in the Caribbean. This chapter questions the broad applicability of this assumption and, by extension, the developmental strategy towards nationhood being undertaken in some areas of the Caribbean.

Since the 1950s, the West Indian islands have been exposed to mass out-migration on the part of people looking for employment opportunities abroad. As a result, islands have become dependent upon the remittances which are received from émigré relatives, and local social relations have been redirected towards these expatriots (Manners, 1965; Frucht, 1968, 1972; Philpott, 1968, 1973). At the same time as some island societies have become submerged in extra-local relationships of a global dimension they have been in the process of being transformed from the status of colonies to that of independent nation states. This has occurred as part of the post-Second World War decolonization efforts. For these new nations, independence has involved not merely the constitution of self-government over already existing colonial entities, but attempts at creating local social and economic systems out of the fragments which are left in the wake of emigration. Independent nation states thereby have attempted to establish themselves in the face of the over-whelming presence of global networks of ties, which for all practical purposes constitute the real framework of existence of most people living in these island states.

I shall here explore some of the problems connected with creating an independent, local, social and economic system on one island, Nevis, where large-scale emigration has created a dependent, frag-mented society.[1] Nevis, an island of 36 square miles, is one of the two islands constituting the West Indian state of St Kitts-Nevis, which obtained independence from the United Kingdom in September 1983. In this discussion I focus on the role of children's attitudes towards this new island nation held just prior to independence by the children who were to become the citizens of this state.

An externally-oriented society

Since the 1950s, Nevisians have moved to Great Britain, North America and other West Indian islands in large numbers. During the decade from 1955 to 1965, almost 15,000 migrants emigrated to Great Britain from the then associated state of St Kitts-Nevis-Anguilla (Richardson, 1983:151–152), and between 1968 and 1976 a further 15,000 moved to the American Virgin Islands (Annual Report, Immigration and Naturalization Service, 1968–1976). A considerable number of migrants went to Canada (St Kitts-Nevis-Anguilla, Annual Report of the Department of Labour, 1971:5), and most recently Nevisians have migrated to the nearby Dutch island of St Martin as well as to the British Virgin Islands. At least one-third of the emigrants from St Kitts-Nevis were Nevisians, and with a local population of less than 9,500 in 1980, it can be estimated that more than half of all Nevisians presently live and work outside their native island.

This emigration has naturally had a great impact on the island. When it began in the early 1950s, Nevis was an agricultural island, producing cotton and sugar for export as well as a number of root crops largely for home consumption. Much of this agriculture was in the hands of smallholders who were also engaged in animal husbandry (Finkel, 1964:168). With the out-migration of most of the able-bodied segment of the population, however, sugar and later cotton production ceased entirely, and the remaining small farmers, most of them ageing parents of émigré offspring, converted entirely to animal production, keeping herds of goats, sheep and cattle which could be maintained with the help of the small children who stayed behind (Richardson, 1983; Barker, 1981). As production declined, households became dependent on remittances from the emigrants to purchase those provisions which formerly were grown by every small-holder. The departure of most of the working population also resulted in the partial break-down of local community activities, such as formal social gatherings, and co-operative labour organizations (Abrahams, 1968; Frucht, 1968; Richardson, 1983). Analyses of households carried out by Richard Frucht in the early 1960s indicated that the island was becoming a society of old people and children left permanently or temporarily by the intermediate parental generation (Frucht, 1972).

The last few years have seen a number of attempts on the part of the government of St Kitts-Nevis to overcome the increasing dependence of Nevisians on overseas economies. This has occurred in the light of the declaration of independence and because of a growing awareness that it will be more and more difficult for the local population to find migration destinations. With unemployment problems in the Western industrialized countries, further immigration to the United Kingdom and North America has been severely curtailed. The efforts of the local government have focused on rehabilitating agricultural production on the island and developing wage employment. Various types of local co-operatives, including a credit union providing inexpensive loans and local farming co-operatives, have been organized with the aid of the island government. Agriculture is a mandatory subject in the schools, which are supposed to provide theoretical as well as practical instruction. The supply of electricity is being expanded in order to enable foreign industries to establish plants on the island, and investments in tourism are being encouraged. The local government also attempts to recreate local community activity and spirit through officers who help organize social clubs throughout the island. Here young people are encouraged to participate and work for the good of the local community.

The efforts at nation building on the part of the local government have been supported by various international aid organizations. Grants and loans have been extended to the newly independent nation to develop the infrastructure so as to attract foreign investors to the island. Several agricultural programmes, including an irrigation project and communal pastures, have been funded largely by international agencies such as the British Development Division and the United States AID. They have also sent agricultural extension officers to help farmers improve their techniques. Volunteers from the American Peace Corps are engaged in helping Nevisians utilize local materials for craftwork and are also involved in the organization of 4-H clubs to improve local attitudes towards farming and create a greater awareness of the importance of community activities among the young.

In so far as the Nevisians can see an immediate benefit from these activities they have reacted to them in a positive way. Thus the credit union has attained a membership of about 1,100 since 1972, when it was reorganized, and has assets totalling more than $750,000 (Cashbox, 1984:5), and those co-operatives which offer cheap supplies and other services to their members have grown. However, it is difficult to ascertain any major changes in the local economy and the pattern of dependency on emigration. According to a 1980 survey of a sample of 120 farmers on the island 86 per cent of the farmers were over 40 years of age, with almost 64 per cent being over 55 years of age (Lowery and Lauckner, 1984:Table 2). The wage employment that has been created on the island has offered primarily low-paid jobs that have difficulty competing with the wages being offered outside the island. The organization of community clubs has met with limited success, and several local areas have not managed to sustain functioning clubs despite several years of organizing effort.

Children's attitudes

In a questionnaire survey of five school classes, involving a total of 157 students, I examined the attitude of the children towards their island community, the socio-economic network in which they live, and the impact of emigration on their lives. Finally, their career goals were ascertained. The sample included two sixth grades with students 11–12 years old, representing the senior group in two rural primary schools. There were also two fifth forms and the one sixth form, which were the senior classes in the two secondary schools on the island. The students in these grades were 16–19 years old. The three-page questionnaire contained a total of 25 questions.[2]

The importance of extra-island ties to the children was apparent in the replies to the first question concerning who lived in their household and the follow-up question asking the children to specify the residence of their parents, if they were not living in the household (see Table 4). One-third of the children had at least one parent living outside Nevis: with 15 per cent having both parents living abroad, while 6 per cent had their mother and 12 per cent their father off the island. The percentage was the highest among the youngest children. Here no less than 46 per cent of the students had at least one parent abroad and 22 per cent had both parents off the island.[3]

The children seemed to be very much oriented towards a field of social and economic relationships with their émigré relatives, rather than to the local community of Nevis. This was brought out in an unexpected way. I had expected the children to answer the questions concerning household membership in a few minutes and then to spend more time on the questions concerning their knowledge of relatives abroad. After about half of the time allotted for the questionnaire had passed, however, I noted that quite a few of the students were still struggling with the household question on the first page of the questionnaire. The idea of delineating a firm household group seemed foreign to some, and they quite simply were not able to decide who

Table 4: The residence of the parents*

Age and location of children	Both parents lived outside Nevis		Only the mother lived outside Nevis		Only the father lived outside Nevis		Total number with parent(s) outside Nevis		No parent lived outside Nevis	
	No	%	No	%	No	%	No	%	No	%
11–12 years Prospect	6	25	3	13	3	13	12	50	12	50
11–12 years Gingerland	6	20	1	3	6	20	13	43	17	57
16–18 years Gingerland	7	15	1	2	4	9	12	26	35	74
16–18 years Charlestown	2	7	1	3	3	10	6	20	24	80
17–19 years Charlestown	2	8	3	12	2	8	7	28	18	72
All children	23	15	9	6	18	12	50	32	106	68

* One questionnaire was not used in this table, as the replies were too unclear.

Source: Fieldwork.

lived in the household, particularly as some relatives lived part time in the household, having seasonal employment abroad. With all the coming and going it was unclear who to include in the domestic unit. Another problem was that some relatives, though living and working abroad, contributed so much to the upkeep of the household that their presence was felt to the extent that they seemed to be part of the household, even though they did not live there. Thus, several children listed parents as members of the household, even though these same parents were listed as living abroad in the following question directed explicitly to the residence of émigré parents. Finally, a few of the children did not live permanently in one household, and therefore were uncertain in which household to place themselves. For the children the functions of the household as well as the actual residence of people were so fluid that a domestic unit did not seem to be of overwhelming importance.

The young children did not have any difficulty listing relatives living abroad (see Table 5). Some 93 per cent of the younger children knew a number of family members living outside Nevis and were able to list their country of residence. The scattered residence of these relatives is indicated in these examples from the questionnaire: 1) mother in St Martin, father in Trinidad, aunt in Puerto Rico, aunt in Dominica and uncle in England; 2) mother in Canada, father on St John, the Virgin Islands, aunt in Trinidad and uncle in England; 3) sister in the United States, sister in Barbados, brother in St Martin, uncle and aunt in England. The children in the senior classes had little difficulty delineating household membership and added many notes concerning, for example, temporary or seasonal residence. The importance of relatives abroad was quite significant here also, however, and 98 per cent of these children were able to list such relatives, several of them extending the list to the back of the page of the questionnaire. One student listed no less than 22 relatives living in St Thomas, Tortola, St Croix, St Kitts, St Martin, Florida, New York, Texas and England.

It is understandable that the children placed so much emphasis on these relatives, because most of them had received letters, money and packages from them. Among the younger children, 75 per cent had received something during the year of 1980, whereas 96 per cent of the older students had received something during this period. While a few of the older students managed to earn a little money on Nevis, working in shops or selling handicrafts or agricultural produce, for most of the students the only source of income was the money which was sent from abroad. In reply to a question whether they made any money, several students, in fact, wrote 'yes, from relatives abroad'.

Table 5: The importance of the extra-local relationships

Age and location of children	Family living overseas				Received gifts from outside Nevis				Would like to remain living on Nevis						Thinks he/she will move away from Nevis to live						Total	
	yes		no		yes		no		yes		no		uncertain		yes		no		uncertain			
	No	%	No	%	No	%	No	%	No	%	No	%	No	%	No	%	No	%	No	%	No	%
11–12 years Prospect	23	96	1	4	19	79	5	21	4	17	19	79	1	4	12	50	11	46	1	4	24	15
11–12 years Gingerland	28	90	3	10	22	71	2	7	8	28	20	69	1	3	14	48	13	45	2	7	31	20
16–18 years Gingerland	45	96	–	–	45	96	2	4	13	28	34	72	–	–	30	64	13	28	4	9	47	30
16–18 years Charlestown	30	100	–	–	29	97	1	3	14	47	14	47	2	7	16	53	12	40	2	7	30	19
17–19 years Charlestown	25	100	–	–	24	96	1	4	6	24	12	48	7	28	12	48	7	28	6	24	25	16
All children	151	96	6	4	139	89	18	11	45	29	99	64	11	7	84	54	56	36	15	10	157	100

Source: Fieldwork 1981.

Though few of the children earned any money on Nevis, this did not mean that they did not work. Most of the children helped in crop cultivation and caring for the livestock (see Table 6). Among the younger children 78 per cent helped cultivate the soil and 95 per cent helped care for the animals, whereas the corresponding figures for the older students were 84 per cent and 78 per cent.

The children received presents and money from relatives abroad, without having worked for these goods, whereas they received no immediate remuneration from working in agriculture on the island and this situation may have resulted in the children acquiring a rather negative impression of the relative economic value of local agriculture as opposed to migratory work. This negative attitude, generated from practical experience, was strongly reinforced by the low social prestige given to agriculture by Nevisians. Thus parents wasted no time inculcating the children with the importance of gaining a good education so that they could qualify for a white collar job and in this way avoid agricultural work as adults.

This attitude is evident in the replies which the children gave to questions concerning their career goals and plans for future residence. Of all students, only three per cent declared agriculture as their preferred profession. When asked explicitly whether they would like to be farmers, 38 per cent replied yes, but most qualified this statement by making clear that this was only as a side line to supply the home with fresh produce, or to save money on the grocery bill. Very few had positive feelings about becoming full time farmers, even though this is one of the chief occupational opportunities presented to young Nevisians today, and there was little interest in the other types of manual work offered on the island. Among the younger children, where the students knew little about the occupational possibilities available, almost half wished to become either a teacher or a nurse (see Table 7). The students in the senior classes displayed a greater range of interests, although nursing and accountancy were the most popular choices.

The students who had advanced to the higher grades and therefore were fairly certain that white collar jobs might be within their reach, felt the most positive about staying on Nevis. The younger children, many of whom were uncertain about succeeding in the secondary school and thus acquiring such jobs, were the least positive about staying. In response to the question whether they would like to remain living on Nevis, 71 per cent of the younger children replied no, whereas 59 per cent of the older children answered in the negative with 4 per cent of the younger children and 9 per cent of the older ones expressing uncertainty. The older children emphasized here that their

Table 6: Children's attitudes to farming

Age and location of children	Assists in cultivation				Assists in care of livestock				States farming as an occupational preference	
	yes		no		yes		no			
	No	%	No	%	No	%	No	%	No	%
11 – 12 years Prospect	17	71	7	29	21	88	3	13	1	4
11 – 12 years Gingerland	26	84	5	16	31	100	–	–	1	3
16 – 18 years Gingerland	46	98	1	2	38	81	9	19	3	6
16 – 18 years Charlestown	22	73	8	27	25	83	5	17	–	–
17 – 19 years Charlestown	18	72	7	28	17	68	8	32	–	–
All children	129	82	28	18	132	84	25	16	5	3

Source: Fieldwork.

remaining on the island depended on whether they received adequate examination success to obtain the good jobs (see Table 7).

While a total of 64 per cent of all students would like to emigrate from the island, and 7 per cent were undecided (see Table 5), only 54 per cent actually thought that they were going to be able to leave. The students were aware that it is becoming increasingly difficult to obtain visas for residence abroad, and many children mentioned this as a reason why they would not be able to emigrate. Others mentioned lack of money. As expected, the most common reason noted for wanting to leave was the desire to find satisfactory employment or pursue a chosen career. Many students also expressed a wish to join relatives abroad and to see more of the world. One youngster explained 'I want to see somewhere', another stated 'I've seen everything down here in Nevis'. Some of the students, however, expressed regret at having to leave Nevis for economic reasons, emphasizing that they liked the island. For most of the young children, however, emigration did not

Table 7: Career Goals *

Professional	11 – 12 years Prospect	Gingerland	16 – 18 years Gingerland	Charlestown	17 – 19 years Charlestown
Teacher	4	12	1	3	5
Nurse	7	3	5	6	1
Lawyer	1	–	–	1	3
Doctor	2	2	5	2	4
Minister	–	1	–	–	–
Psychologist	–	–	–	–	1
Meteorologist	–	–	–	–	1
Actress	–	–	2	–	–
Musician	–	–	2	–	–
Veterinarian	–	–	–	1	–
Accountant	–	–	9	4	–
Economist	–	–	1	–	–
Nutritionist	–	–	1	–	–
Engineer	–	–	–	2	1
Agricultural economist	–	–	–	–	1
Linguist	–	–	–	–	1
Sub-total	14	18	26	19	18

*Total career goals exceed total number of children because some children stated more than one career goal.

	11–12 years		16–18 years		17–19 years	
Tourism and Travel						
Airport control officer	—	—	—	—	1	
Immigration officer	—	—	2	—	—	
Airline clerk	—	—	—	1	—	
Travel agent manager	—	—	—	1	—	
Hotel receptionist	—	—	—	1	—	
Air hostess	1	—	2	1	—	
Driver	1	—	—	—	—	
Sailor	1	1	—			
Pilot	1	—	2	—	2	
Mechanic	3	—	1	—	—	
Sub-total	7	1	7	4	3	

	11–12 years		16–18 years		17–19 years	
Agriculture and Fishing						
Farmer	1	1	2	—	—	
Fisherman	1	—	—	—	—	
Work in agriculture department	—	—	1	—	1	
Sub-total	2	1	3	—	1	

	11–12 years		16–18 years		17–19 years	
Government service						
Policeman	1	1	5	—	—	
Postman	—	1	—	—	—	
Sanitary officer	—	—	1	—	—	
Sub-total	1	2	6	—	—	

	11–12 years		16–18 years		17–19 years
Services					
Carpenter	1	—	—	1	—
Shop assistant	1	—	—	—	—
Hairdresser	—	—	2	—	1
Radio work	—	—	—	1	1
Lab. technician	—	—	2	2	1
Business manager	—	—	—	1	—
Banking	—	2	1	—	—
Office work	—	3	5	3	—
Work in restaurant	—	1	—	—	—
Sub-total	2	6	10	8	3
Other	1	—	2	2	3
Don't know	2	4	1	—	1

require an explanation, but was something to be taken for granted. When asked why they desired to emigrate, one student replied 'I do not born here', implying that with foreign citizenship and no visa problems emigration was natural. Another child simply explained 'because my mother told me so'.

Whereas the children were rather realistic to the point of being negative in their evaluation of their possibilities on Nevis, they were quite unrealistic in their optimism about their future overseas. For example, almost 10 per cent of the children expected to receive education abroad which would enable them to become medical doctors, and several had already chosen such specialized fields as cardiologist, pathologist or gynaecologist.[4] Two students wanted to become actresses, and two wanted careers in music, one as a singer in Switzerland. The high expectations and ambitions which the students professed reflected a feeling that the possibilities were unlimited at the migration destinations, rather than any knowledge about actual conditions. This is quite apparent, for example, in the reply by one fifth form student who said he wanted to work in a car factory in the British Virgin Islands. The general lack of knowledge of the countries in which they wished to live and work corresponds to the small number of children who had experienced this outer world. Half the students had never travelled outside the state of St Kitts-Nevis, and most of those who had, had only visited nearby West Indian islands (see Table 8). With few newspapers, magazines or other forms of current literature on foreign countries available on Nevis, the children derived their information largely from radio and television shows as well as from migrant relatives on visits to Nevis. Popular television programmes do not show the most representative aspects of life overseas, just as emigrants, keen to make a favourable impression on their homeland, do not paint the most realistic picture of the emigrant life.

The general conclusion that can be drawn from this survey of the five classes is that most of the children did not see much future in staying on the island. If they had a choice, two thirds of all students would like to leave, and three fourths of the younger students wished to emigrate. Staying on Nevis was contingent upon the obtainment of white collar jobs which carried both high status and relatively good pay. Lacking this opportunity, virtually all wished to emigrate. The older students were not untouched by the fact that local social and economic development was necessary, if the newly independent state of St Kitts-Nevis was to succeed as an autonomous country. A large number of students did express a desire to contribute to building up their country. They did not want to do this as manual labourers, helping to increase production, however, but saw their role as technicians, advisers or administrative staff supervising the work of others. The oldest school-children living in the main city of Charlestown were most likely to expect to enter a profession (Table 7). The youngest students, not far enough along in their studies to see these roles for themselves and knowing only the hard physical labour of tilling the soil and caring for the animals, wanted to leave the island at the first opportunity. This leads to the conclusion that only those who could aspire to the upper class status of being civil servants were interested in the emerging nation state, seeing more opportunities in local government. Those who might expect to have a future in farming, industry or tourism, in other words the productive basis of the country, wanted no part of life on the island and wished to emigrate. To a great extent, this attitude can be explained by the fact that work in these economic sectors is poorly paid, in fact so much so that it is virtually impossible to support a family. The weekly salary of $50–60 EC to be earned from most manual work is just enough, for example, to purchase a decent pair of shoes.[5] One Nevisian, who received regular economic support from his father in England, remarked sarcastically that he had a job, not for the money it

Table 8: Travel experience abroad*

Age and location of children	Travel experience outside St Kitts-Nevis						Travel destinations						
	yes		no		unclear		Virgin Islands	St Martin	Antigua	Other WI islands	USA	Canada	England
	No	%	No	%	No	%							
11 – 12 years Prospect	12	50	10	42	2	8	5	2	1	4	1	2	1
11 – 12 years Gingerland	6	19	23	74	2	7	3	5	2	–	–	–	–
16 – 18 years Gingerland	25	53	22	47	–	–	13	9	5	8	4	1	–
16 – 18 years Charlestown	16	53	14	47	–	–	8	7	1	12	3	1	–
17 – 19 years Charlestown	15	60	9	36	1	4	5	5	5	7	1	1	–
All children	74	47	78	50	5	3	34	28	14	31	9	5	1

* The travel experience of the 6th grade children at Prospect may include some imagined trips.

provided, but for the entertainment value it offered! Many Nevisians quite clearly could not obtain even the most basic necessities of life, if they had to depend only on the money earned on Nevis.

The migration tradition

While present economic conditions go a long way towards explaining the Nevisian propensity towards emigration, historical factors of a socio-cultural as well as economic nature also play a role. The mass migration which has characterized Nevis along with other West Indian islands during the last 30 years thus can be seen as merely the peak of developments beginning during the colonial era. In the colonial period, the Afro-Caribbean population on most islands had limited economic opportunities and was discouraged from developing its own culture. The result was that the colonial era, to a large measure, alienated the West Indians from their native islands, and after Emancipation from slavery during the 19th century, an increasing number of West Indians chose emigration as a means of searching for a more satisfactory life. A whole migration tradition emerged throughout the West Indies during the post-Emancipation period, permeating virtually all aspects of life (Patterson, 1978; Thomas-Hope, 1978).

In many ways Nevis exemplifies some of the most severe effects of the social and economic deprivation which West Indians experienced after Emancipation. Unlike several of the neighbouring islands, Nevis saw no emergence of free villages after Emancipation, the freed being forced to live on the plantations. Furthermore, no peasant farming developed during the years following Emancipation, rather the old plantocracy held on to sugar production by introducing crop-sharing, whereby the workers were expected to work for no wages against receiving part of the crop at the time of harvest (Hall, 1971:49,114; Frucht, 1966:57; 1967:297). The Nevisians reacted by emigrating in large numbers from the island, when there was opportunity to find paid work abroad. As early as the years immediately following Emancipation, from 1839 to 1846, more than 2,500 Nevisians left for Trinidad (Hall, 1971:41,49). This was followed by later migratory movements to distant destinations such as Venezuela, Panama, Cuba, the Dominican Republic, the United States, Aruba and Curacao (Frucht, 1968, 1972; Richardson, 1983). Apparently this emigration was dominated by those who were relatively well-off, the very poorest not being able to afford the passage.

When most of the sugar plantations were abandoned by the old planter families during the 1930s, as the conditions for sugar production deteriorated further, the British Crown acquired the land and began staking out small plots to be purchased by the former sugar workers in order to create a stable peasant class of small farmers. Though a sort of 'proto-peasantry' might have existed during slavery in the form of slaves cultivating provision grounds, a free peasantry had not been able to establish itself due to the stronghold of the plantocracy on the cultivatable land (Frucht, 1967:300). The Nevisians were *not* rural peasants displaying 'that love of the soil Redfield was so fond of apothesizing' (Frucht, 1966:108). This attitude to the land was also probably affected by the economic realities of the situation as described by the geographer Gordon Merrill during the 1950s, 'The purchase by the peasants of wornout land on the lowland of Nevis is as recent in time as it is questionable in opportunity. The end result is a peasant agriculture which has little to recommend it' (Merrill, 1958:112).

The parcelling out of the old estate land did not present the Nevisians with the long awaited economic opportunity on the home island. At the most it provided the Nevisians with lots on which to place their houses away from the plantations and some land on which to cultivate crops to supplement their income. The land settlement schemes hardly led to an increase in small farming, but rather contributed towards enabling a greater number of Nevisians to emigrate, when new migration destinations appeared during the 1950s. A great number of Nevisians financed the expensive passage to the United Kingdom for their children by using land as security to obtain loans in the newly formed Nevis Co-operative Bank (Frucht, 1968:201). Rather than establishing a local population of small farmers, the distribution of land among the rural poor therefore helped set off an unprecedented mass movement of emigration.

Conclusion

The history of Nevis indicates that the wish to emigrate is not just dictated by present economic problems, but also by a migration tradition which has evolved gradually during the colonial period. The independence of St Kitts-Nevis may create an economic and social niche for an emerging middle class of professionals and semi-professionals. It will not, however, create a home country for the many who see no way but to follow the long-established tradition of emigration. For those who will not be able to emigrate, the extra-local field of social and economic relations will probably continue to be a more relevant framework for life than a nation state, which has formal political independence, but no economic or social autonomy.

Notes

1   The paper is based on fieldwork on Nevis in January 1981, January 1982, February–August 1984; among Nevisian migrants on St John in December 1977–April 1978 and December 1979–January 1980; and research at the Institute of Commonwealth Studies, London, October–November 1979. The paper refers to the situation on Nevis in 1984. I wish to thank the many persons who aided me in this research, and the University of Copenhagen and the Danish Research Council for their financial support.
2   The schools involved were Prospect School, Gingerland Primary School, Gingerland High School and Charlestown Secondary School. I wish to thank the Ministry of Education for permitting this survey to take place and the teachers and students for helping me carry it out. It took place in January 1981, while negotiations for independence were on the way.
3   Several reasons may be offered to explain the difference in the parental situation of the 6th grade students and the 5th and 6th form students. The young children may join their absent parents as they become established abroad, and this would increase the proportion of children with parents present on the island in the upper grades. The upper grades, furthermore, may be dominated by more 'middle class' families, where both parents are present and working in civil service type jobs on Nevis, whereas the lower grades contain all children, including those who will drop out of school early to help support the family.
4   The very high educational expectations expressed by the children parallel the findings of Rubin and Zavalloni on Trinidad (1969).
5   One EC dollar equals approximately 0.40 US dollar. In 1984 the minimum wage had increased to c. 80 EC dollars a week.

References

Abrahams, Roger D. 1968. Public Drama and Common Values in Two Caribbean Islands. *Offprint Series of the Institute of Latin American Studies*, no. 82. The University of Texas, Austin.
Annual Report, Immigration and Naturalization Service 1968–1976. *Report of the Commissioner of Immigration and Naturalization*. Washington, D.C. Government Printing.
Barker, G.H., comp. 1981. St Kitts-Nevis. An Agricultural Profile. Caribbean Agricultural Research and Development Institute. *Agricultural Profile Series*. Small Farm Multiple Cropping Systems Research Project.
Cashbox 1984. The newsletter of the Nevis Co-operative Credit Union. Issue # –25.
Finkel, Herman J. 1964. Patterns of Land Tenure in the Leeward and Windward Islands and Their Relevance to Problems of Agricultural

Development in the West Indies. *Economic Geography,* 40(2):163–172.

Frucht, Richard 1966. *Community and Context in a Colonial Society: Social and Economic Change in Nevis: British West Indies.* Brandeis University, Ph.D. dissertation, Ann Arbor, University Microfilms.

   1967. A Caribbean Social Type: Neither 'Peasant' Nor 'Proletarian'. *Social and Economic Studies,* 16:296–300.

   1968. Emigration, Remittances and Social Change: Aspects of the Social Field of Nevis, West Indies. *Anthropological n.s.* 10(2):193–208.

   1972. Migration and the Receipt of Remittances. In *Resource Development in the Caribbean.* Montreal, Centre for Developing-Area Studies: 275–314.

Hall, Douglas 1971. *Five of the Leewards 1834–1870.* Barbados, Caribbean Universities Press.

Lowery, J. and Lauckner, F.B. 1984. *A Profile of Small Farming in Nevis.* Caribbean Agricultural Research and Development Institute.

Manners, Robert A. 1965. Remittances and the Unit of Analysis in Anthropological Research. *Southwestern Journal of Anthropology,* 21(3):179–195.

Merrill, Gordon G. 1958. The Historical Geography of St Kitts and Nevis, the West Indies. *Instituto Pan Americano De Geografia e Historia,* Mexico. No. 232.

Patterson, Orlando 1978. Migration in Caribbean Societies: Socioeconomic and Symbolic Resource. In *Human Migration. Patterns and Policies.* Wm. H. McNeill and Ruth S. Adams, (Eds.) Bloomington, Indiana University Press: 106-145.

Philpott, Stuart B. 1968. Remittance Obligations, Social Networks and Choice among Montserratian Migrants in Britain. *Man,* n.s. 3(3):465–476.

   1973. *West Indian Migration: The Montserrat Case.* London, The Athlone Press.

Richardson, Bonham C. 1983. *Caribbean Migrants.* Knoxville, University of Tennessee Press.

Rubin, Vera and Marisa Zavalloni 1969. *We Wish to be Looked Upon. A Study of Youth in a Developing Society.* New York, Teachers College Press.

St Kitts-Nevis-Anguilla 1971. *Annual Report on the Department of Labor for the Year 1971.*

Thomas-Hope, Elizabeth M. 1978. The Establishment of a Migration Tradition: British West Indian Movements to the Hispanic Caribbean in the Century after Emancipation. In *Caribbean Social Relations,* (Ed.) C.G. Clarke. Centre for Latin-American Studies, The University of Liverpool, Monograph Series No. 8:66–81.

Section C

Land as a Development Constraint

CHAPTER 8

The Guyanese rice industry and development planning
The wrong solution for the wrong problem?

Eric Hanley

Guyana, formerly British Guiana, sits perched on the north-east shoulder of South America, an anomalous English-speaking 'sugar island' marooned on the mainland of South America. The site of Raleigh's dream of Eldorado, it was settled in the seventeenth century by the Dutch, captured by the French and finally ceded to the British at the beginning of the nineteenth century. However, the abolition of slavery in 1834 and the prospect of a disastrous labour shortage led, in turn, to the importation of East Indian labourers from the British Indian possessions. The majority of these remained, so that their descendants now constitute more then half of the total population of approximately 800,000.

For the past forty years successive governments, both colonial and independent, have been struggling with this problem as they sought to devise an effective development strategy which would 'feed, house and clothe' the rapidly growing population. Agriculture, especially the rice industry, has been at the heart of these attempts at development planning and continues to play a central role. Yet agriculture in general, and particularly the rice industry, represents some of the most dismal failures of this planning process.

This chapter examines these attempts and sees a 'rice bias' in official thinking in the past. The legacy of this can be seen today, as the Government and international aid agencies continue to invest large sums of money in drainage and irrigation schemes for the expansion of rice production, despite abundant evidence that rice cultivation is strikingly unprofitable for small farmers. Why does this 'rice bias' persist? This discussion offers four suggestions for its continued domination of official thinking: infrastructure, the plantation society, ethnicity and ideology.

Guyanese agriculture

The territory was long dominated by 'king sugar' but gradually developed two other major export industries, bauxite mining and rice cultivation. Sugar was always controlled by expatriate interests until nationalized in the 1970s, and continues to be very significant in terms of the number of people employed, amount of land occupied, and infrastructural investment devoted to it, and contributes approximately 15 per cent of GDP. The rice industry, by contrast, is entirely locally owned and characterized by peasant family cultivation, something not encouraged by the sugar industry until very recently. Rice is the smallest of the three main export industries, contributing only some 4 per cent to GDP, but is extremely important in terms of its wide distribution and ease of participation. Agriculture as a whole contributes approximately 25 per cent of GDP, whilst bauxite mining makes the largest single industrial contribution at 16 per cent.

A major problem for Guyana, as for many Third World countries, is that of rural poverty, as was amply demonstrated by the results of the Rural Farm Household Survey carried out in 1979 (Nathan, 1980). This revealed that two-thirds of rural households have total incomes below the US target level for aid assistance of G$600 (US$270) per capita. As far as rice farmers were concerned, three-quarters of them fell into this category. In the case of the official Guyanese Government target income of G$900 per capita, we find that four fifths of rural households failed to reach this level.

It is possible that the year to which the income figures refer (1978) was a particularly bad one; indeed one almost hopes so, for they present a depressing picture, with more than a quarter of all farms indicating a net loss on their farming activities. This situation was not caused by diseconomies of scale on smallholdings, since losses were reported across many sizes of farm. It was not one of outdated methods, since the techniques of cultivation, including the use of fertilizer and machines, were found to be 'highly uniform', especially in the rice industry. It was not a case of isolation, since all cultivation took place on the coast. It was not a problem of education, for almost all farmers are literate in English. What, then, was the cause of the problem? Since only one in 16 farms were able to make the target income which took them out of poverty from farming alone, could it be the agricultural enterprise itself?

Traditionally sugar in Guyana has been produced on large estates using hired labour. Food crop production is mainly oriented towards subsistence and the local market. Rice is the only peasant export crop (Smith, 1964), with 56 per cent of all farms planting rice in 1978 (Nathan, 1980). It is therefore not surprising that rice has featured in almost all thinking about the development of Guyanese agriculture, both by farmers and planners.

The emergence of rice bias

After the slaves were freed the sugar industry in Guyana came to depend on East Indian indentured labourers for its workforce. During the great sugar depression of the last decades of the nineteenth century the planters became increasingly willing to allow Indians to grow rice on unused estate land, so as to keep these workers near the estates and available for when the industry expanded again. The rice industry dates from this period and by 1918 the country had become self-sufficient. There had been a boom in exports to the West Indian islands during the First World War, but this was abandoned with the resumption of supplies from Asia. The Second World War was, however, a more permanent stimulus to the industry as the colonial government strove to increase output at all costs; a decision which involved mechanized cultivation for the first time. After the War it was decided as a matter of policy that Guyana should be the principal supplier of rice for the British West Indian colonies. This captive market meant that the industry not only sustained its high wartime output but even had to increase it further. Consequently in the 1950s the acreage and the output of rice doubled, and the price paid to farmers showed an even greater increase.

However the environmental constraints on cultivation on the Guyanese coastal plain necessitate a strong sea wall. The cultivated area is also under constant threat of inundation from the accumulated rain waters to the rear, which entails more earthworks. Finally the whole cultivation area has to be irrigated from the flood waters to the rear and drained into the sea through the sea wall, all of which makes cultivation both expensive and technically demanding.

Traditionally rice cultivation had been an enterprise involving family labour on small plots with only oxen to assist. Now the expansion of the industry was to be based on mechanized cultivation. The implementation of this development received a good deal of government assistance, from the large-scale drainage and irrigation schemes that added 80,000 acres during the 1950s, to the guaranteeing of loans to farmers to buy machines and the provision of duty-free fuel. However the expansion was poorly co-ordinated and hardly supervised at all, which in turn led to the familiar tale of excessive numbers of inappropriate machines being utilized uneconomically. However, as if these pressures were not enough, there were technical difficulties too. Black Bush Polder, the largest of the development schemes with 27,000 acres, was originally designed by the British colonial regime, though it finally became fully operational during the People's Progressive Party (PPP) administration, and as such reflected older ideas about production. It was thus designed with animal power in mind and the cultivation of only one main crop of traditional varieties per year without the use of fertilizers. It therefore did not adapt well to the move to mechanized cultivation.

The older cultivation areas did not necessarily fare much better, for in many cases the movement to mechanization frequently meant merely substituting tractors for bulls within the existing landholding and cultivation practices. Although rice was grown by peasant farmers over large areas, individual farmers cultivated only 5.5 acres on average, and even this was often owned or leased in several small blocks. Thus the possibility of an integrated regime of extensive mechanized cultivation was not realized in the peasant farming communities, with no attempt to modify land-holding patterns or form co-operatives. Many farmers confirmed to me that such changes would have been very unpopular at the time and would have resulted in political pressure for them to be discontinued.

Not all farmers had access to the degree of water control offered by the new schemes or to the best land, so that in the rush to expand production more marginal land that had been used for cattle grazing was brought under rice cultivation, especially in West Coast Berbice. This cultivation was dependent on rain for water supplies and was thus unreliable. Furthermore, with poor water control there was a serious infestation of red rice, a wild variant which shatters and discolours during milling, reducing the overall quality of the crop. It also tends to choke out the more desirable varieties, which results in lower yields. These fell by something like 30 per cent during the 1960s throughout the country as a whole. Thus by the end of the decade there was a real need for a drastic re-examination of the objectives, organization and performance of the rice industry. USAID set out to do just this.

AID strategies

Traditionally Guyana had been a producer of 'brown' or parboiled rice, though not of a very high quality. Rising living standards in the post-war period had led to changes in Caribbean dietary patterns, including a switch to high prestige white rice in a number of islands, particularly Jamaica. Guyanese rice growers had tried to break into this much more profitable market, but without much success. Thus in 1967 USAID put up an aid package that was designed to move the industry much more towards this capability. Firstly, the industry was to switch, where possible, to new varieties that were more suitable for the production of white rice. Secondly, six new storage complexes were to be constructed throughout the rice growing areas to buy padi, dry it to the correct moisture content, blend it where necessary and store it until it could be milled in new mills attached to the silos. This would enable the rice to be shipped to markets in peak condition. Finally, a new rice breeding station was to be established to continue the work of improving the quality of the industry's product. This whole package was to cost US$17 million.

In 1978 another USAID mission came to the country to evaluate the effects of the first project, Rice I, and to see if further improvements were needed. In general they found that 'the majority of the technical objectives of the project had been achieved'. They thus went on to propose a further one, Rice II. This was to consist of more storage facilities like the ones originally constructed, to extend the area served to almost all parts of the rice growing areas. Associated with these silos were to be additional mills and a set of new handling facilities at the Guyana Rice Board's headquarters in Georgetown, the capital, where the exports are processed and packaged. In addition there was to be a series of technical training programmes for operatives and managerial personnel. This package was to cost US$22 million.

From the standpoint of the official development approach the rice industry can be presented as a great success story. The industry is very export-oriented, planting 225,000 acres, and exporting 70,000 tons of rice annually. It is estimated that the industry will soon be producing more than the West Indian market can consume and so there will be a need to break into newer and more demanding markets, for which the new handling facilities will be invaluable. The industry is manned by a well educated peasantry that is highly motivated to innovate technically, both with equipment such as tractors and combines, and with new techniques such as the use of chemical fertilizers and pesticides. They are also used to responding to stimuli from prices and other incentives to increase their investment and their output. Thus the new infrastructural investment would allow them to cope with the higher demands of more profitable markets, whilst at the same time being more effectively planned and regulated than the original move to mechanized cultivation in the 1950s and 1960s.

It is on the basis of arguments such as these that the government, and the growing number of aid agencies with whom they have dealings, have in recent years started more rice schemes, including an extension to both Black Bush Polder in Berbice and the Tapakuma scheme in Essequibo, whilst work has also started on the potentially huge Abary scheme, all of which could eventually affect 450,000 acres (Map 5).

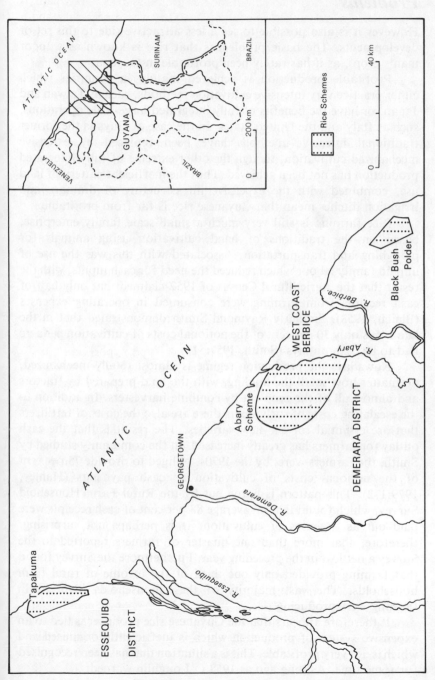

Map 5   Guyana drainage schemes

Problems

However it is also possible to see a less attractive side to this set of developments. The basic problem is that rice is known as a 'poor man's crop', as it has rarely been profitable in Guyana.

Profitable production is achieved mainly in countries which either practice very intensive cultivation methods, such as Taiwan and Japan, or have the benefits of fully integrated large-scale operations, such as Italy and the United States. In the case of Guyana the former traditional intensive methods have been replaced by extensive mechanized cultivation, though the other extreme of fully integrated production has not been achieved. Thus the inefficient pattern of land use, combined with the expensive infrastructure of drainage and irrigation ditches mean that Guyanese rice is far from profitable.

Rice farming is still very much a small-scale family enterprise, based on the traditions of hand cultivation using animals for ploughing and transportation. Associated with this was the use of unpaid family labour which reduced the need for cash inputs, with the result that the Agricultural Census of 1952 claimed that only half of cash receipts from farming were consumed in operating expenses (Blaich, 1953). Similarly Raymond Smith demonstrated that in the late 1950s only 30 per cent of the notional costs of cultivation per acre had to be cash outlays (Smith, 1957:512).

Nowadays the production regime is almost totally mechanized, no matter how small the holding, with the land prepared by tractors and almost all of the crop cut by combine harvesters. In addition to the escalating costs of such inputs there are also the costs of fertilizers that are essential for the new varieties. The result is that the cash outlay for farmers has greatly increased. In the community studied by Smith, the farmers were, by the 1970s, obliged to provide 75 per cent of the notional costs of cultivation as cash payments (Hanley, 1979:172). This pattern is borne out by the Rural Farm Household Survey, which found that on average 88 per cent of cash receipts were paid out as expenses of cultivation. It is perhaps not surprising, therefore, that more than one quarter of farmers reported to the Survey a net loss in the preceding year. Furthermore the Survey found that farming provided only one third of the income of rural farm households. The vast majority of these households involved in farming were producing rice.

It therefore appears that the Guyanese rice producer is tied to an expensive system of production which is inefficiently organised and which is not very profitable. This is a situation that has been recognised for some time. As long ago as 1958 O'Loughlin warned:

The share of the rice industry is thus approximately 5 per cent of the Gross Domestic Product. That is a very small part of the national income and indicates that in view of the large numbers employed in rice at some time or other, the earnings are shared out very thinly over those involved. (O'Loughlin, 1958:125).

Even Kenneth Berrill, the Government's Economic Advisor back in the 1950s admitted:

The swing away from rice has got to come, and the sooner the better. Few people in British Guiana need converting to the view that without diversification small farm agriculture will remain poor, or doubt the dangers of producing more and more rice for export. (Berrill, 1961:3).

Yet it would seem that many people, at least in Government, did need converting, for as late as 1968 K.F.S. King was arguing that:

Rice offers little scope for export expansion, little opportunity for absorbing surplus labour, and contributes little to the economic well-being of its growers. In addition it utilises a great deal of capital in hidden subsidies. No expansion in area is therefore recommended. (King, 1968:107).

King later became an appointed 'technocrat' Minister, but his strictures seem not to have been heeded, for the expansion of rice acreage continued.

The persistence of rice bias

It can reasonably by asked why the Government and the aid agencies persisted in the expansion and development of the rice industry in the face of such evidence against this course. In the post-war era there did appear to be advantages in this approach and incomes were rising rapidly. In the 1950s there was a slightly different problem, in that the sugar industry, the main employer in the country, was undergoing a process of mechanization that in the end displaced a considerable amount of labour onto the general labour market. At the same time the effects of the post-war population boom following the control of malaria was increasing the labour force too. In this situation the expansion of the rice industry offered the best prospects for absorbing this surplus labour and formed one of the basic reasons for government assistance (Hanley, 1975). Back in the colonial days

Berrill was very explicit about the constraints that operated on the Development Programme devised at the end of the 1950s (Berrill, 1961): the colonial government said there simply was no more money available and so he had to plan with what resources were to hand — the option of industrialization simply was not available and so the emphasis had to be on agriculture.

In the 1970s, however, the problems of the rapid and uncontrolled expansion of the industry had become very apparent to all, and had been analysed on numerous occasions. Why then did the expansion of the industry continue? The impetus seems to come from four sources. There are: 1) the existing infrastructural investment in land, equipment and facilities; 2) the legacy of the plantation society seen in habits of thought and practice; 3) ethnicity and associated attitudes to land; 4) political and economic ideology.

1 Infrastructure

As has been mentioned the Guyanese coastland is heavily and expensively networked with drainage and irrigation ditches, dams and sluices which are necessary if agriculture is to be at all possible. Thus it is very difficult to change crop systems and land use without a major upheaval and reorganisation. This means it is not possible to mix rice and sugar cane production, though these can be accommodated on separate blocks of village land. Even so, despite these environmental constraints, there is still the problem of why government continues to plan for new drainage and irrigation schemes to be devoted to rice.

In part this is explained by another dimension of infrastructure, that of organization. Since the time of the Second World War the rice industry has been heavily controlled from the centre, with the Guyana Rice Board (GRB) being the sole purchaser of all rice and the sole exporter. This arrangement has always been the instrument by which government was able to exercise control over the rice industry, through the manipulation of prices paid to farmers and the level of subsidies. The system is highly integrated and well organised. Since all paddy has to be milled, the rice mills are registered and farmers are paid through the miller who ships their rice to the Board, less any deductions for loans, advances and the miller's charges.

In recent years the People's National Congress (PNC) government that has ruled Guyana since 1964 has taken deliberate steps to increase their control of the 'commanding heights' of the economy through the expansion of central government control in the guise of 'co-operative socialism' (Thomas, 1984). For the rice industry this has been handled by the Guyana Rice Corporation, which is responsible for the operation of the government machinery hire pools, mills and a very large cultivation area. This in turn has entailed a substantial investment in centralized machinery pools of tractors and combine harvesters, with a consequent restriction on the sale of machines for private ownership. The inefficiency and corruption associated with the government machine pools are legendary throughout the country.

Finally the rice growing area has a network of Rice Action Committees which are local bodies charged with implementing the GRB's policy and improving practices at the local level. These committees have the power to regulate farmers' access to subsidized fertilizer, loans and the hire of equipment such as sprays and pumps. The fact that they are also closely allied, in most cases, with the ruling political party greatly increases their importance in the lives of farmers.

All these structures, therefore, constitute a powerful set of institutional pressures for farmers to operate within an established system of procedures, stimuli and values. This overt and official system is complemented by an informal system operating at the level of villages and face to face contact. At the end of the day it is normal for farmers to gather on street corners and other convenient meeting places to discuss the events of the day. At such times, and at other gatherings, both formal and informal, the talk invariably comes round to rice, the current crop and what their plans are. It is through this process that information, news and views are disseminated and judgements formed.

The result is that a consensus emerges as to what are currently the best times to sow and reap, the amount of fertilizer to be added and how best to cope with the problems of weeds, pests and diseases etc. By such means farmers minimize the risks which are inherent in cash crop farming by not only seeking out the best advice, but also ensuring that they are no different to others. Being in the crowd may not be a formula for economic success, but it at least ensures that one is no worse off than anyone else. Such a 'minimax' strategy is a common feature of peasant farming strategies (Heath, 1976). In such a situation it requires a considerable entrepreneurial effort for a farmer to break out of the formal and informal mould of rice cultivation. It is therefore common to hear farmers assert that they 'know rice' as their approach to farming, and given the scale of the supporting structures it is an accurate description of their situation.

2 The plantation society

An impressive case can be made for the view that the experience of
chattel slavery and the aftermath of this in the form of the continued
dominance of sugar plantations throughout this part of the New
World has had the most profound effects on the nature of the societies
concerned (Beckford, 1972, Mandle, 1973). In the case of Guyana this
has meant not only an unbalanced economy dominated by sugar and
bauxite mining, with an infrastructure heavily weighted to the needs
of the expatriate companies but also a very restricted role for
indigenous enterprise. The effects of the plantation society are to
be found also in the attitudes of the population to agriculture. The
orientation is instinctively to exports, which has led to the situation
where many of the food needs of the country were met by imports,
whilst investment and effort went into growing tropical products for
export.

In an attempt to reverse this situation the government banned the
importation of over one hundred food items in the early 1970s, a move
which continues to be bitterly resented by many, since it meant the loss
of treasured items such as potatoes and salt fish. The continuing
financial crises of the 1970s and 1980s led the government to restrict
food imports further. This in turn has reduced the success of the much
vaunted 'Feed, Clothe and House' campaign which was intended
to spearhead the government's programme of self sufficiency
(Thomas, 1984:35). There have also been worrying signs of declining
nutritional standards in the country as a whole (Standing, 1979:44)
and it is part of the development thrust of the government and the aid
agencies to remedy this.

This concern with exports, even though of low value and often
offset by alternative imports, is reflected in the case of the cattle
industry. Guyana has been unable to sustain a reasonable milk supply
for the coastal areas because there has not been enough raw milk for
the pasteurisation plant in Georgetown to process, so that it was
reduced to producing reconstituted milk from imported milk powder.
Many people continue to rely on imported tinned milk. Yet the coast
has many cattle. However, they are kept by farmers for domestic
consumption and do not produce milk for sale to the processing plant.
This situation was commented on by Rene Dumont when he reported
to the government in 1963:

> Guiana's peasant is first and foremost a crop grower, not a
> livestock farmer. Thus, as soon as a piece of land is suf-
> ficiently drained, he would never dream of establishing an

improved pasture, but will immediately turn it into a paddy field. In doing so, he is only carrying on in a way the sugar plantation tradition, where the approach was in terms of exports and not of cattle for domestic consumption. (Dumont, 1963:15).

Similarly this restricted perception of what is suitable agricultural activity is also reflected in the narrow range of areas in which farmers are in fact willing to innovate. For despite the appearance of being very 'modern' in their attitudes, the farmers have shown a marked reluctance to move into crops other than rice, even though it can be shown that they are more profitable.

The one crop that peasant farmers have shown any willingness to move into in substantial numbers is sugar. Traditionally the sugar industry in Guyana did not encourage peasant cultivation, preferring to concentrate production on large estates. However, for some time government has been encouraging the expansion of this section of the sugar industry and the Rural Farm Household Survey found this to be significantly more profitable for farmers than growing rice. It seems likely that one of the attractions of this move is the degree of institutional support which the industry offers, with loans to farmers, subsidized inputs, hire of equipment and the use of transport facilities. Thus once again the farmers are willing to move only into a crop which has the same all-embracing and paternalistic infrastructure as the rice industry.

There are, however, alternatives. For some time it has been apparent that the production of food crops for the internal market is far more profitable than the production of rice, a fact that was confirmed again by the 1979 Rural Farm Survey. Yet still many farmers are reluctant to become involved in this kind of agriculture, despite the fact that it is a form of cultivation with which they are familiar. All rural households cultivate food for domestic consumption, and indeed the 1979 Survey found that subsistance production accounted for a substantial part of the notional income of all households. At the same time there is an established system of distribution and marketing of food crops both within the rural areas and the towns, for which farmers have produced specifically. Indeed, one of the most repeated stories is of how farmers at Black Bush Polder found it more profitable to produce cabbages for the Georgetown market than to produce rice, which the Guyana Rice Corporation subsequently forced them to stop doing.

Although food crop production exists, it is very differently organised from that of rice or sugar. It grew up to meet the need of the internal market and so is informally structured, with none of the bureaucratic trappings of the export industries. One arm of the government's attempt to control the economy is the Guyana Marketing Corporation (GMC), which will purchase food crops, but only at basic prices. It offers no inputs to the production process and has tended to serve as a last resort of farmers who cannot get better prices elsewhere. The vast bulk of the industry's activities are carried out entirely in an open market environment, where it is possible to make great profits if successful, but also to incur losses. This is precisely why it is so unattractive to farmers used to the relative security of the institutionalized rice and sugar industries. The government has expressed its concern about the unreliability of this industry and there have been several reports on the subject, culminating in a Foodcrop Programme which is to include marketing centres and improved credit facilties. Whilst this is a start it is nowhere near the level of support offered to the export industries.

3 Ethnicity and attitudes to land

The pattern of perception of what constitutes appropriate agriculture is in part dictated by another aspect of the plantation society, the shaping of the ethnicity of the population. The 'core' cultural characteristics of the African and Indian sections of the population have been heavily modified by the processes of the plantation society, with the result that they represent only an attenuated form of the original. Nevertheless ethnicity has a considerable force in Guyana, since it is not only associated with racial and physical differences, but also specialized economic and ecological roles (Despres, 1969).

Over the years there emerged a spatial distribution of the two main ethnic groups as they moved into different areas of economic activity. Thus the Indians remained predominantly rural and were largely involved in the sugar and rice industries, whereas Africans formed the majority of the urban population and dominated the Civil Service. This pattern has led Despres to take the notion of 'ecological niche' as one of the bases of ethnicity and apply it to the Guyanese situation (Despres, 1969, 1975). In this analysis certain areas of economic activity and patterns of resource allocation become bound up with perceptions of ethnic identity and the assumed interests of the ethnic section, which have to be protected and if possible advanced.

Land and access to it is thus of central importance. The traditional view is that Africans have a range of attachments to a particular community, whereas Indians do not:

The Negro village tends to be regarded as the physical base, the birthplace, the place where one's 'navel string is buried', from which individuals venture forth to make a living knowing that they can always return to its security and the warmth of its human relationships in time of trouble. The Indian village by contrast is primarily the place where one has a rice farm. (Smith, 1964:316).

The African pattern is seen as arising from the development of the peasantry which emerged in the mid-nineteenth century following the abolition of slavery. Some villages were 'proprietary', in which individual owners had legal title to their own piece of cultivation land and possibly a separate houselot, though most were of the 'communal' form, in which members were collective owners of the village and in which they all had a share (Young, 1958:10–13). The potential for uncertainty in communal villages was made worse by the operation of the notion of 'children's property', whereby rights in the property of those dying legally intestate were inherited equally by all offspring. This in turn meant that in each generation the numbers of people who had an interest in the land of a communal village could increase considerably. These rights to an unspecified degree of interest in the property could not be alienated unless all living participants agreed to this, which has proved very difficult to implement.

The problems of inheritance of a share in a property in this way were also compounded by the system of kinship and marriage which emerged among the Afro-Caribbean section of the population. As in other parts of the Caribbean this system was characterized by a series of non-legal unions and possibly a legal marriage as well (Smith, 1956). The children of the non-legal unions were entitled to validate claims to a share in the property of their parents, which in turn represented a share in the main property. The result of this process was to make the legal control of a village property enormously complex as the numbers of valid claims expanded. The practical problems were compounded by movement out of the community and the difficulty of locating interested parties when changes were to be made.

The migrants may retain a hope of returning to their home community in later life to pass their last years in the warmth and tranquility that they missed in London or New York, as Smith described above. The practical outcome of this situation is that land in African villages can become very poorly utilized as control and ownership remain unclear (Smith, 1964:311). This is demonstrated very dramatically from the air where, for instance, the one wholly

African village in West Demerara stands out as a tangle of largely uncultivated land in the midst of thousands of acres of sugar estates and rice cultivation in Indian villages.

The conventional model sees Indians as having none of these problems, since they have a tradition of stable marriages and clear patterns of inheritance. This situation has encouraged Despres to conclude that Indians had a distinct adaptive advantage as far as the move to peasant cultivation was concerned (1969:36). This is also reflected in Smith's comment quoted above that for Indians the village is 'the place where one has a rice farm' (1964:316).

Historical events have also aided the establishment of Indian peasant communities, for even the earliest movement of Indians off the plantations at the end of the last century was in very different circumstances from that of the Africans a generation earlier. The ex-slaves were distancing themselves from the world of slavery and received little help from the plantocracy. The Indians, on the other hand, were encouraged to cultivate rice land near plantations as a way of reducing direct costs at the time of the great sugar depression at the end of the century (Adamson, 1972). There were also attempts at this time to create a permanent peasantry by encouraging Indians out of their indenture to remain in the country. Although these were of mixed fortunes they did establish a pattern which was repeated in the twentieth century (Nath, 1970).

However, such generalizations have to be used with caution, for as Smith says:

> In British Guiana people often speak as though each ethnic group possessed distinctive characteristics and as though each was a separate entity specialising in some form of economic activity. This idea sometimes finds its way into popular accounts of the country when Indians are spoken of as sugar workers and rice farmers, Portuguese as shopkeepers, Negroes as urban workers, and so on. In fact, of course, the situation is much more fluid than such abbreviated descriptions suggest. (Smith, 1964:325).

Thus the frequently perceived tendency for African villagers to cultivate subsistence root crops and look for employment elsewhere is just that: a tendency. There are plenty of African rice farmers for example. Similarly it would be quite wrong to portray Indians as taking a purely investment orientation to land. It is true that there are many cases of Indians who have perceived an economic advantage in moving to land elsewhere — in the West Demerara area in which I worked there were numerous examples of farmers who had gone to places like Black Bush Polder in the 1950s, as well as the famous case of the local man who took a gamble on a large run-down estate on the rather remote coastland of Essequibo and who became a millionaire as a result. At the same time there are many other values and sentiments tied up with ideas about land.

It is felt that ownership of land offers some form of security against the uncertainty of other economic enterprises. Thus it is common for Indian shopkeepers, taxi owners and small businessmen also to have plots of rice or cane land. This is often talked of as a way of supplementing their income, but as many eventually admit the amount of money raised by their relatively small acreages is not great. Nevertheless I have often been told how Indians 'like land' and how entrepreneurs felt they 'ought' to own land. This point was vehemently made to me by a businessman toiling in the hot sun on his one acre rice plot on a Sunday afternoon — he felt that he could make more money improving his stall in Georgetown market, but his wife felt that as Indians they 'ought' to have some land and that he should work it!

In recent years the mechanization of rice production has displaced a considerable amount of labour from the fields, which has increased the demand for full time employment elsewhere, a pattern brought out in the Rural Farm Household Survey. It is also very difficult to make a living solely from rice farming because of the costs of mechanized cultivation. Farmers who are obliged to seek supplementary income in off-farm employment usually retain possession of their rice land. Mechanization has now made it feasible for people to be 'absentee farmers' only needing to visit their fields occasionally, so part-time farming is possible. At the same time the rice land offers some form of security in the face of the uncertainty of employment. A villager who lost his job as a railway porter was able to tide himself over until he could find another non-farming job, by a combination of income from his rice land and earnings from an impromptu business collecting broken rice from the mills and selling it in nearby sugar estate markets as fowl feed.

For a growing number of young men mechanization has ended the possibility of employment in rice farming. Today they are most likely to aspire to regular employment outside agriculture for their primary income but nevertheless hope to acquire land in future, both as a source of supplementary income and as a valued resource. This continued attachment to land and agriculture reaches its most extreme form in the case of well educated young men who have secure employment in the Civil Service. They are relatively well paid and are unlikely to lose their jobs, so they do not need the economic support of farming to the same extent. Nevertheless they demonstrate an interest in agriculture which almost parallels that of the urban bourgeoisie of western societies — in one community a co-operative formed to convert to cane and root crop cultivation a tract of former pasture unsuitable for rice growing was almost entirely dominated by such 'weekend farmers'. All professed that it made them feel good to be part of the cycle of cultivation and harvesting with which they grew up. It was also striking that existing rice farmers did not take this opportunity to diversify into the cultivation of other crops but were happy to leave it to the amateurs.

Although Smith has rightly cautioned about the necessity to avoid simplistic ethnic labelling (see quote from 1964:325 above), it is nevertheless true that for some people participation in the agricultural system is a way of demonstrating their ethnic identity. This was particularly true of the established Civil Servants in my research community who, by engaging in the labour of cultivation, were not only demonstrating their Indian-ness but also their solidarity with the rural community in which they lived, in contrast to the city in which they worked. Thus 'knowing rice' is in some ways one of the ethnic characteristics of Indians, as is the feeling that it is appropriate for them to lease or own some agricultural land and to be involved in cash crop farming, no matter what their main economic activity is. Similarly the 'ground provisions' that represent the more profitable food crops are perceived as being 'African' crops, so that although many Indian villages grow these for domestic consumption it is on a small scale and generally not taken seriously as an economic proposition in many cases.

The conclusion of Despres' analysis is that the survival of ethnic sections in a plural society like that of Guyana was based on the ability of each ethnic group to exploit its own ecological/economic niche without interfering in the preserve of the other. This may describe the situation that pertained from the latter part of the last century until independence, but it does not characterize the present. For the penetration of one ethnic group into the preserve of the other is perceived as constituting a threat, and much of the racial and ethnic tension that has characterized Guyana over the past two decades can largely be attributed to the way in which Africans felt their economic base was being eroded by the penetration of Indians (Cross, 1978; Despres, 1975). Thus the extension of such perceptions into agriculture should not surprise us.

4 Ideology

The long-term social organization of agriculture that the Government and the aid agencies are aiming for seems to be very unclear. The one apparent thread that runs through this area is that of an unarticulated commitment to peasant family farming.

During the latter part of the nineteenth century the creation of a stable peasantry in the interests of national stability emerged as a government objective, supported by the Colonial Office. Since the first post-war rice schemes were originally designed during colonial times it is not surprising that they reflect this philosophy. This can clearly be seen in the case of Black Bush Polder, where the land was allocated to families in 15 acre blocks for rice, with some additional land for vegetables. The model here is obviously that of peasant family farming. However, as Dumont pointed out in his 1963 report it was illogical to plan a scheme which has 27,000 acres devoted to rice cultivation yet have the land worked in such small and uneconomic units.

The same kind of focus on the peasant household producer was evident throughout the expansion period of the 1950s and 1960s. Thus there was no attempt to implement any form of land rationalization and farmers were encouraged to expand on the basis of existing and often scattered holdings. The same kind of approach was applied to the import and sale of machines, which were allowed to replace oxen as a source of power without changing the existing family farming structure.

This orientation to the individual producer is something which continues to characterize the national rice administration. Thus the talk in the Rice Corporation is of the need to make the farmer a 'professional' producer, committed to high standards and modern methods. It is this orientation that lies behind the flow of advice, pamphlets and field days aimed at farmers. Similarly the administration is continually working out cost of production calculations to determine what is the minimum amount of land and equipment that a farmer needs to be able either to support his family or to achieve the level of income that satisfies national and international norms.

Yet with nearly two-thirds of the country's rice farmers working less than ten acres there is no possibility of them achieving this degree of 'professional' full-time farming. Rice simply does not provide adequate returns from such small acreages to support a family. This was brought out clearly in the Rural Farm Household Survey, which reported that only one-third of the income of rural farm households came from their own farms (Nathan, 1980:3–4). More than a quarter of all farm households reported a loss from farming with their major cash crop being rice (ibid).

Similarly the official attitude to family labour is confused, in that traditionally the land was worked by the members of the family, and there is much evidence to suggest that it was precisely this unpaid labour that made rice farming profitable (Smith, 1957; Hanley, 1979). However, with the move to mechanized cultivation in the 1950s and 1960s the need for this labour was effectively removed. Even the USAID's own report showed that only those planting less than five acres (almost a 'garden' type of cultivation) utilized family labour. The rest relied on machines and hired labour if necessary.

The question of alternative occupations for the workers no longer needed in agriculture is important. Married women who can now spend more time in the house have turned to dressmaking to supplement family income. The USAID report states that 'the present trend seems to be towards livelihood diversification', and claims 'parents are increasingly apprenticing their teenaged sons to craftsmen to learn a trade and bring in needed cash to the household' (Checchi, 1979:27). However, it says nothing about where these jobs come from or where they are to be found, nor, more importantly, how common they are.

The Rural Farm Household Survey demonstrated with dazzling clarity that it is in fact the income which a family obtains from its non-farming activity which is crucial for its economic survival. Furthermore, it is the income from non-agricultural employment which offers rural households the most effective path out of poverty: for them agriculture simply does not have the ability to generate sufficient income quickly enough to make an impact on their condition.

Yet the government and the international aid system continues to stress rice cultivation as the key to the attack on rural poverty. This dynamic has received further impetus from the fact that it is now supported by the United Nations International Fund for Agricultural Development (IFAD), which is specifically committed to directing aid to the very poorest sector of the population. Not surprisingly, perhaps, IFAD is connected with a scheme to improve rice cultivation on 58,000 acres in front of Black Bush Polder. One of the potential benefits of the IFAD approach is that a proportion of the finance for the scheme has to be devoted to an evaluation of the extent to which their benefits did indeed reach the poorest sections.

However, the government of Guyana is developing a depressing record of inability to fulfill its commitments to the welfare of its citizens (Thomas, 1984) and there are signs that the same could happen to these schemes too. There are disturbing reports of a shortage of trained personnel for the monitoring exercise, agricultural extension and other ancilliary services needed to ensure that poor people benefit from the new opportunities. In a worsening financial situation there are great pressures to trim the non-engineering aspects of schemes, and this could well be happening here. The result would be a core of improved drainage facilities from which only the wealthier and more efficient farmers would be able to benefit. This was not what the overall development strategy was supposed to achieve.

Thus it would seem that the Guyana Government, in association with the international aid agencies, is engaged on a programme which entails the expansion of rice cultivation and a sustained role for the rice industry in the economy of the country, without seriously examining the social implications of this programme.

Conclusion

The seeming inevitability of using the rice industry as a vehicle for agricultural development in Guyana poses some important questions about the planning goals of both the government of Guyana and the assisting agencies.

The first of these refers to the pattern of farming which is being aimed for. As we have seen there is a long history of implicit assumptions about peasant family farming which seem to have underpinned much development planning in this area. During colonial times this was an explicit goal which suited the interests of the metropolitan power and the planters; but does it represent the best interests of the people of an independent Guyana? Extreme doubt must be cast on this in view of the evidence of the growth of mechanized cultivation, rural under-employment and the evidence of the Rural Farm Household Survey.

Associated with this is the question of the scale of rice cultivation which is to be encouraged. The tradition of family farming is associated with small acreages which require intensive cultivation to make them profitable. Yet the Guyanese rice industry is highly mechanized and based on expensive imported inputs such as fuel and fertilizer; a pattern which is normally associated with extensive cultivation, as in neighbouring Surinam, rather than small peasant farming. Some of the current drainage schemes, such as the Black Bush Polder front lands, are oriented towards small farmers, whereas others, such as the Mahaicony/Abary scheme are concerned with land held in large blocks which could be extensively cultivated (Map 5).

However, such a policy in turn raises awkward questions about who would benefit from a system of extensive cultivation; small farmers certainly could not afford to buy land which had suddenly become much more valuable. Some jobs will be created on the big farms, but is it the aim of the development planners to create a rural proletariat in the rice industry?

The matter of rural employment is nevertheless crucial. For the clear message that comes out of the Rural Farm Household Survey is that farming, especially rice farming, is unable to support the majority of families adequately. Indeed, only one family in 16 managed to reach the target income which would lift them out of poverty by farming alone. The key to increased income for all areas was paid employment, preferably out of agriculture. The obvious implication of this is the need for a policy of rural job creation in non-agricultural sectors, which is sadly not in evidence.

Even sadder is the impression that the issues at stake here are precisely the same ones that were debated so heatedly almost twenty five years ago, concerning the viability of a development strategy based on the expansion of rice cultivation as opposed to one which went for industrial growth (Berrill, 1961; Newman, 1960, 1961). Then, Berrill made it clear that the People's Progressive Party (PPP) government of the time had very little choice in the light of the financial restrictions of the colonial power and the dominance of other international commercial interests. Is the government of Guyana any better off today? The continued reliance on rice as the engine for agricultural development would seem to indicate that it is not.

Acknowledgement

Much of the research on which this paper is based was carried out during 1972/73 as part of a project funded by the Social Science Research Council. Shorter visits were made in 1976 and 1981, which were financed by the University of Edinburgh and the Carnegie Trust. I should like to express my thanks to all of these organisations for their support.

Bibliography

Adamson A.H. 1972. *Sugar Without Slaves*. New Haven, Yale UP.
Beckford G. 1972. *Persistent Poverty*. London.
Berrill K. 1961. Comments on 'The Economic Future of British Guiana' by P. Newman. *Social & Economic Studies*, Volume 10.

Blaich O.P. 1953. *Agriculture in British Guiana: Census 1952*. Georgetown, Department of Agriculture.

Checchi & Co. 1979. *Rice II: Second Guyana Rice Modernisation Project, Feasibility Study and Report*. Washington D.C.

Cross M. 1978. Colonialism and Ethnicity: a theory and comparative case study. *Ethnic and Racial Studies*, Volume 1.

Despres L.A. 1969. Differential Adaptation and Micro-Cultural Evolution in Guyana. *South Western Journal of Anthropology*, Volume 25.

1975. Ethnicity and Resource Competition in Guyanese Society. In L.A. Despres (ed.) *Ethnicity and Resource Competition in Plural Societies*, The Hague, Mouton.

Dumont R. 1963. *Report to the Government of British Guiana on Planning Agricultural Development*. Rome, FAO.

Hanley E.R. 1975. Rice, Politics and Development in Guyana. In I. Oxaal et al (eds.) *Beyond the Sociology of Development*. London, Routledge.

1979. Mechanised Rice Cultivation: the Experience of an East Indian Community in Guyana. In M. Cross & A. Marks (eds.) *Peasants Plantations & Rural Communities in the Caribbean*. Leiden & Surrey.

Heath A. 1976. *Rational choice and social exchange*. London, Cambridge UP.

King K.F.S. 1968. *Land and People in Guyana*. Oxford, Commonwealth Forestry Institute.

Mandle J.R. 1973. *The Plantation Economy*. Philadelphia, Temple UP.

Nath D. 1970. *A History of Indians in Guyana*. London.

Nathan R.R. et al. 1980. *The Income and Production of Guyana Rural Farm Households*. Washington D.C.

Newman P. 1960. The Economic Future of British Guiana. *Social & Economic Studies*, Volume 9.

1961 Epilogue on British Guiana. *Social & Economic Studies*, Volume 10

O'Loughlin C. 1958. The Rice Sector in the Economy of British Guiana. *Social & Economic Studies*, Volume 7.

Smith R.T. 1956. *The Negro Family in British Guiana*. London, Routledge.

1957. Economic Aspects of Rice Production in an East Indian Community in British Guiana. *Social & Economic Studies*, Volume 6.

1964. Ethnic Difference and Peasant Economy in British Guiana. In R. Firth & B.S. Yamey (eds.) *Capital Saving & Credit in Peasant Societies*. London, Allen & Unwin.

Standing G. & Szal R. 1979. *Poverty and Basic Needs*. Geneva, ILO.

Thomas C.Y. 1984. Guyana: the Rise and Fall of Co-operative Socialism. In A. Payne & P. Sutton (eds.) *Dependency Under Challenge*. Manchester UP.

Young A. 1958. *The approaches to local self government in British Guiana*. London, Longmans.

CHAPTER 9

Land fragmentation and land-use patterns in Grenada

John S Brierley

Although land is a resource of fundamental economic importance on the densely populated islands of the Caribbean, its utilization has long been characterized by inefficiency. On some of these islands more than one-third of their potentially arable land lies in an idle state, while an even greater area may often be producing below optimum capability owing to inadequate inputs of labour and/or capital and inappropriate cropping practices. Concurrently, and paradoxically, many of these island nations rely increasingly on imported food to provide their populations with sustenance. Thus, the issue of agricultural development, which concomitantly implies the more effective use of land, is a pressing concern if these nations are to exhibit a higher level of economic independence than has been formerly the case. In this chapter consideration is given to the topic of land fragmentation and its impact on land utilization as present on small-scale agricultural holdings in Grenada; a nation which exemplifies many of the economic woes currently afflicting small nations within the Caribbean.

As elsewhere in the world, fragmentation of farms in the Caribbean is a topic that has largely been neglected. At best, reference is made to the number of parcels comprising agricultural holdings of specific sizes, and comments made about the desirability for land consolidation. The fact that detailed studies have generally eluded researchers is one noted as being 'peculiar' (King and Burton, 1983:475). Even Harwood (1979) in his book on small-farm development in the tropics provides no discussion of the subject. Nevertheless, the consensus in Third World Studies is to consider fragmentation as a 'major spatial impediment to production and agricultural improvements, especially to the economic use of labour and the introduction of such modern inputs as tractors' (Morgan, 1978:250). In view of the inexorable increases in man:land ratios, particularly in many of the world's developing countries, there is a growing need to reduce such impediments and thereby expedite development in farming. That stated, there are, nevertheless, some advantages to be derived from a limited degree of fragmentation. Farmer (1960) deemed that the fragmentation of Sri Lankan paddy fields provided security and reduced the problem of underemployment. Within the Caribbean, Wood (1963) has noted that Haitian farmers benefit from working discrete parcels of land in areas of different rainfall regimes and soil quality, because by so doing they can obtain either a greater range of crops or the same crops throughout much of the year. In addition, the spatial discontinuity of land in a holding gives some assurance that if crops on one parcel are damaged by disease, pests, rain or wind, then the farmer can reasonably hope his other parcels will not be similarly affected, so that he and his dependents will have some food supply. However, in the final analysis, as noted by Edwards (1960:121) in his detailed study of small farmers in Jamaica, the advantages that accrue from fragmentation are outweighed by their disadvantages.

Background to the study

The following analysis of fragmentation stems from a survey conducted in Grenada during 1982; a time when the People's Revolutionary Government (PRG) was actively pursuing policies intended to reduce waste of human and physical resources. Indicative of their concern in this regard was the policy by which 'idle hands marry idle lands'. Despite their emphasis on increasing land-use efficiency throughout the island, the specific topic of fragmented holdings, as a contributing factor to the presence of idle and inefficiently worked land, was not singled out for special consideration. Such an omission is symptomatic of the lack of attention given to the problem of fragmentation throughout most of the Caribbean.[1] While there are more pressing and readily identifiable problems confronting small farmers, the actual degree to which parcellization of farms affects land-use practices and productivity remains uncertain, owing to the lack of detailed analysis of the subject. This study attempts a partial assessment of the issue.

   In this survey a small farmer is defined as one who, at the time of the interview, occupied at least 0.4 ha, but not more than 6.0 ha of land. The nature of tenure had no bearing on the occupancy. Consequently, in addition to the more usual forms of tenure, ownership and renting, inclusion was also made of that which was undivided family land, that being caretaken for a friend or family member who was ill or unable to maintain his/her property and that which was sharecropped, because the farmer in question was responsible for overseeing and/or maintaining it. A random sample of 186 farmers throughout the island of Grenada was obtained and

Table 9: Farms by number of fragments

Number of fragments per farm	Number of farmers	Percentage of total number
1	28	15.1
2	61	32.8
3	47	25.3
4	35	18.8
5	11	5.9
6	3	1.6
7	0	—
8	1	0.5
Total	186	100.0

represents slightly more than five per cent of all small holdings, as recorded in the 1981 Agricultural Census of Grenada.[2]

Basic characteristics of small holdings

Farms in the survey occupied an average area of 2.02 hectares that was divided into an average 2.75 fragments of land. Consequently, the mean fragment size is 0.73 ha. In a nation where non-metric units of measurement have prevailed, areas of land are usually fractions or whole numbers of acres. Hence, individual parcels ranged in area from an eighth of an acre (0.05 ha) to twelve acres (4.9 ha). The most frequently noted fragment sizes were those between half and two acres (0.1 and 0.8 ha). Table 9 reveals that over three-quarters of the farms surveyed contained two, three or four pieces of land, eight per cent had five or more separate pieces and only 15 per cent of farms studied were unfragmented.

For the purpose of standardizing this analysis of fragmentation, the set of fragments which constitute a holding were numbered according to their respective distance from the farmer's place of residence. In most cases this residence occupied a piece of land on which fruit and vegetable crops were cultivated. This piece of ground, commonly referred to as the kitchen garden, was designated as fragment one (F_1). In settlements where either poverty and/or crowding preclude the presence of a kitchen garden, a minority of small farmers (33, or 18 per cent of the sample) occupied only a house spot, an area little larger than that of the house itself on which no food crops were produced. In these cases, then, that piece of land closest to the house spot and maintained by members of the household was designated as F_1. Consequently, the highest number was assigned to fragments located furthest from the farmer's home. As farmers were requested to consider each fragment independently and in sequence of their fragment number, it is presumed that an element of perceptual distance is incorporated in the analysis; a consideration that is deemed perhaps to influence a farmer's decision-making process in regard to the established land-use patterns more then the actual distance. Certainly, the physical distance *per se* does not take into account the concept of friction of distance, which can be considerable in situations where the terrain is especially rugged and slopes become treacherous during the rainy season.

In general, there is an identifiable pattern associated with the dispersal of fragments. Where rural settlement is largely confined to coastal areas and valleys that penetrate into the island's interior, then the fragments most distant from their farmer's domicile tend to be found on steeper slopes, at higher altitudes and heavier types of soils.[3] These factors jointly reduce the agricultural possibilities of many higher numbered fragments, i.e. F_3 and above. In spite of these parcels of land having limited opportunities and assorted problems for farming, some farmers considered them to be a meaningful, if not economical, investment of capital and time. For one thing, in rural circles the level of social status accorded an individual is often based upon the areal extent of land occupied and not on its productive capabilities. For another, to occupy land in the mountains provides the means of gaining a respite from the oppressive conditions of working soil in the heat associated with sheltered valleys or coastal plains, and possibly from any social pressures that may be experienced in village living. Several farmers indicated that they regard their regular, usually weekly, visits to property in the mountainous interior as a kind of pilgrimage, where in the cooler climes, they would spend the night, tend to a few chores on the land and return refreshed with what produce was available and readily portable. This illustration underlines a rationale for fragmentation that lacks an intrinsic economic basis. For these individuals their 'mountain lands' have an important therapeutic value, both physically and mentally. Because such fragments are often remotely located and have limited agricultural value, they can be purchased or rented cheaply. Owing to the relative abundance of land in mountainous areas, farmers wishing to occupy such land usually have a choice of location. On the other hand, land possessing more favourable locations and of better overall quality has traditionally been in short supply, so that farmers have little option but to purchase whatever piece is available, when they have the necessary capital at hand. Preferably, the land will be within an acceptable daily-walking distance (about 5 km) if the plot is to be tended regularly.[4]

When land is inherited from the estate of a deceased relative, there is no choice with respect to its location. As is frequently the case in Grenada, where the practice of joint inheritance is pursued, then, in the absence of any written will, the subdivision of the deceased's land becomes a contentious issue among heirs. The result can be undivided family land, a state of affairs that often leaves land being worked on an *ad hoc* arrangement or even abandoned should disputes between heirs exist (see Chapters 1 and 3). Solutions to such family disputes over land can exacerbate fragmentation for it is conceivable that each heir will receive an equal fraction of each of the deceased's individual pieces of land. Thus, this system of inheritance adds to the discontinuity of farm holdings.

Study of the 512 parcels of land monitored in the survey was undertaken by collectively examining fragments according to their fragment number. A summary of the basic findings is provided by Table 10, which reveals some notable trends with respect to land utilization and tenure. Despite its having the smallest average size, 0.56 ha, F_1 is the most intensively worked parcel of land. For the majority of farmers this fragment contains their home, hence all surrounding cultivated land is considered to be their kitchen garden. In addition the fragment has the highest incidence of ownership, 70.7 per cent. Consequently, for its size, it receives proportionally a greater investment of time and scrutiny than other parcels; a point reflected by its possessing the least amount of idle or unproductive land, 16.7 per cent.

In terms of collective area, F_2, the second most accessible fragment, is significant because it accounts for the largest share of the total area occupied by small-holders, 34.1 per cent. Thus, its areal extent is almost 60 per cent greater than F_1. On average its location is within ten to fifteen minutes walking time of the farmer's house. Not only is F_2 larger than F_1, but it is also more likely to be rented or sharecropped land.[5] As these latter types of tenure generally lack security, farmers have little or no incentive to undertake long-term investments in land, such as erecting wind breaks, digging drainage ditches or undertaking soil-conservation measures. Hence, land which is rented or sharecropped is neither as effectively utilized nor maintained as that which is owned. Normally F_2 will be regularly tended by the small holder, nevertheless, more than one-quarter of its area lies unproductive, with 47.5 per cent of parcels having this fragment number containing some idle land (Table 10). Although the explanation for the existence of idle land incorporates a variety of factors, both the degree of fragmentation and the intervening distance between parcels comprising a holding contribute to its presence.[6] Substantiation of this fact is borne out by fragment numbers F_3 and F_4 which reveal a continuation in the degrees and incidence of idle land (Table 10); a finding which accords with some of the basic tenets of fragmentation (Bowler, 1983:48). With the average age of farmers in the survey being 56.8 years, many individuals are no longer capable of effectively tending crops on scattered fragments. The fact that many fragments are accessible by narrow poorly kept tracks only aggravates the situation because the energy expended in reaching the fragment detracts from the work that can be performed on it. Furthermore, many older farmers are either reluctant or indifferent to employing hired hands to assist them in their farming tasks. The reasons being that they do not wish to acknowledge their infirmity, cannot afford the wages demanded by such workers, and are unable to secure and to keep good workers because they are in demand and invariably are lured away by more attractive offers. Another factor deterring farmers from investing time on outlying pieces of land was the incidence of praedial larceny, i.e. the petty theft of agricultural produce. This problem was identified in the 1981 Agricultural Census as the most common one confronting Grenadian farmers, and was acknowledged by the PRG as being a serious handicap to agricultural development. In certain areas its prevalence and magnitude were of sufficiently dire consequences that they warranted the abandonment of specific fragments. Farmers most vulnerable to this problem were those who made only infrequent visits to their land, and/or whose fragments were in isolated locations where neighbouring farmers could not provide the necessary surveillance that might deter would-be thieves. Thus, praedial larceny is an inherent problem of fragmentation, one whose incidence would appear to increase during periods of social unrest and economic hardship, such as those which have characterized Grenada's recent history.

Fragments F_5 to F_8 are insufficiently represented in the survey for any generalizations to be made. Even the making of inferences is curtailed as no distinct trends are apparent other than the sustained increase in the proportion of rented land through to F_6 (Table 10).

Table 10: Basic characteristics of small-farm structure

Characteristics	Fragment number							
	1	2	3	4	5	6	7	8
Number of farms with fragment	186	158	97	50	14	4	1	1
Mean distance from farmer's home (km)	0.21	1.38	1.92	2.69	4.99	3.31	3.62	4.00
Mean size (ha)	0.56	0.89	0.94	0.89	0.56	0.58	0.91	2.02
Total area of all fragments (ha)	103.9	128.1	86.3	44.3	7.9	2.3	0.9	2.0
Tenure (% of area)								
i) Owned	70.7	50.7	65.5	48.9	56.3	34.8	–	–
ii) Family or Rent Free	27.0	27.4	17.0	34.4	9.0	26.0	–	100.0
iii) Rented	2.3	16.5	16.0	16.7	34.7	39.2	100.0	–
iv) Sharecropped	–	5.4	1.5	–	–	–	–	–
% land in idle condition of total fragment	16.7	27.0	57.7	58.9	36.1	61.0	0.0	50.0
% of fragments on which idle land is found	29.6	47.5	70.1	78.0	64.0	100.00	0.0	100.0

Land use and fragment number

Through an examination of the occurrence of tree and vegetable crops by fragment number, the impact of fragmentation on land utilization becomes more apparent. In general, the results provide an endorsement of von Thünenian concepts, since the intensity of land use declines with increase in distance from the farmer's house, i.e. fragment number (Chisholm, 1979:23). To a certain extent this point is evident in the preceding analysis where it was revealed that higher numbered fragments were likely to contain more idle land and a lower incidence of ownership. In the following analysis account is only taken of the presence of specific food or spice-producing trees and vegetable crops on a given piece of land. Reference is neither made to the actual number nor the area occupied by these crops, because had such information been requested many farmers would only have been able to provide guestimates. Thus, any subsequent analysis would be more complicated, but not necessarily any more meaningful. From collected data on tree crops, indices of occurrence were determined for each fragment number by means of comparing the declared number of different trees against the maximum number possible for a specific set of fragments. Likewise, indices of vegetable-crop occurrence were calculated for each fragment number (Tables 11 & 12). The results provide a quantitative method of assessing land-use practices associated with the constituent set of fragments in the survey.

Tree Crops

A typical vista of Grenadian small-scale agricultural holdings is characterized by mixed arboreal cultivation. On an island where steep slopes and heavy rains make soil erosion an omnipresent threat, particularly during the wet season, such a land-use practice is commendable since it restricts the regular disturbance of soil. In addition to providing farmers with an important source of food for their households, trees are the source of their principal cash crops. Although on any given fragment trees may be of limited number and commercial importance, their canopies, nevertheless, provide a dominating physical presence over all fragments, including the kitchen gardens on F_1. The profusion of different varieties of trees results in this most accessible fragment having the highest index of occurrence, 0.38 (Table 11). The most ubiquitous trees on F_1 include non-export bananas (principally bluggoes and plantains), breadfruit, cocoa, coconut, mango and nutmeg, all of which are found on more than half the total number of parcels. This selection reflects the preference of farmers to combine food-crop production with that of cash crops. In the case of cocoa and nutmeg, their cultivation underlines the fact that kitchen gardens regularly are the initial piece of land occupied by a farmer and on which he/she acquires the knowledge, expertise and interest in agriculture, that may lead to the expansion of the farm onto other fragments where the emphasis is usually on the cultivation of Grenada's traditional export crops, bananas, cocoa and nutmeg.

Another conspicuous feature of F_1 is the presence of trees whose fruit is valued and therefore particularly prone to larceny. Examples of such trees include annonaceous fruits, especially soursop, avocado pear, citrus fruit, papaya and sapodilla; all usually numbering less than five in any one kitchen garden, but located within line of sight from the farmer's home. In the case of papaya plants, they were frequently situated either in the centre of F_1 or in a relatively inaccessible spot. It is these varieties of trees in particular, whose frequency of occurrence diminishes considerably on all subsequently numbered fragments (Table 11).

It is difficult to make specific generalizations with respect to the planting arrangements of trees on F_1, owing to the numerous combinations of mixed cropping, interplanting, intercropping and interculture[7] that exist. Some of these combinations can be of a localized nature and be restricted to a particular valley, while others can be more widespread.[8] Nevertheless, three basic points emerge with respect to the distribution of trees. First, there is some variety of evergreen that is found in close proximity to the farmer's house in order to provide year-long shade. Secondly, trees frequently encompass and/or are interspersed with areas of vegetable cultivation to supply both shade and shelter from wind. Lastly, tall or sizeable trees, such as coconut and breadfruit, can denote property boundaries, especially the corners of fragments. The latter two traits are not solely associated with kitchen gardens and can be found on other fragment numbers.

As the distance separating the farmer's home and fragment increases, so the trend is for the variety of tree crops to dwindle. Evidence of this more specialized land-use practice is borne out by the respective indices of occurrence for F_1, F_2 and F_3 which exhibit marked declines from .38 to .20 (Table 11). A comparison between F_1 and F_2 reveals a shift in the emphasis of tree-crop production from one of food-crop prominence to that of export cash crops, namely cocoa and nutmeg. Small farmers who possess two or more fragments will generally devote the majority of their cultivated land to export crops. Where bananas for export are present, they will often be intercropped with cocoa during the early stages of the latter's growth.

	\multicolumn{8}{c}{Fragment Number}							
	1	2	3	4	5	6	7	8
Number of fragments	**186**	**158**	**97**	**50**	**14**	**4**	**1**	**1**
Tree Crops								
Annonaceous fruits[2]	64	18	9	2	–	–	–	–
Avocado pear	91	48	28	14	5	–	–	–
Banana (Export varieties)[3]	54	52	22	13	4	–	–	–
Banana (Domestic use)	170	85	33	18	5	2	–	–
Breadfruit/Breadnut	121	74	33	10	3	1	1	1
Cashew	12	13	8	2	1	–	–	–
Cocoa	126	101	49	23	7	–	–	–
Coconut	129	97	49	23	3	1	–	–
Golden apple[4]	38	17	4	1	–	–	–	–
Lime	39	9	3	1	2	–	–	–
Mango	119	81	29	11	9	1	1	1
Nutmeg	114	107	46	32	3	–	–	–
Orange	82	36	12	7	3	–	–	–
Other citrus[5]	41	23	8	4	3	–	–	–
Papaya	13	2	–	–	–	–	–	–
Sapodilla	30	17	5	3	–	–	–	–
Spices[6]	21	39	10	7	–	–	–	–
Other fruits[7]	4	1	–	–	–	1	–	–
Index of occurrence	0.38	0.29	0.20	0.19	0.18	0.05	0.11	0.11

1 Index of occurrence $I = \dfrac{\Sigma a}{P}$,

where a = individual occurrence of a crop

P = maximum potential occurrence (i.e. total number of tree crops multiplied by total number of parcels in a fragment number)

2 Mainly soursop, but also includes sugar apple and custard apple.

3 Although not botanically a tree, bananas are regarded in this study as such because they are cultivated more in the manner of a tree than a vegetable. Domestic varieties include plantains and bluggoes.

4 Also referred to as Jew Plum and June Plum.

5 Includes citron, grapefruit and tangerines.

6 Includes cinnamon, cloves, pimento and tonka bean.

7 Includes guava, starapple, pimento and tamarind.

Table 12: Distribution of vegetable crops by fragment number and index of occurrence

	Fragment number							
	1	2	3	4	5	6	7	8
Number of fragments	186	158	99	50	14	4	1	1
Classes of Vegetables								
Tropical Roots and Tubers								
Cassava	28	15	10	3	–	–	–	–
Dasheen	96	46	25	8	2	1	1	1
Eddo	12	4	–	–	–	–	–	–
Sweet potato	71	27	13	4	1	1	–	–
Tannia	110	51	26	19	4	–	1	1
Yam	113	55	33	9	4	–	–	–
Temperate Roots								
Beetroot	7	1	–	–	–	–	–	–
Carrot	27	6	6	–	–	–	–	–
Onion	2	–	1	–	–	–	–	–

Green Leaf	—	—	—	—	—	—	—	—
Cabbage	—	—	—	1	2	9	17	44
Celery	—	—	—	—	—	1	—	3
Lettuce	—	—	—	—	—	2	4	41
Fruit and Pods	—	—	—	—	—	—	—	—
Corn	—	—	—	1	6	21	43	72
Cow pea	—	—	—	—	—	2	2	7
Cucumber	—	—	—	—	1	3	12	30
French bean	—	—	—	—	3	5	24	55
Melongene	—	—	—	—	—	2	11	19
Okra	—	—	—	—	2	5	15	39
Pepper	—	—	—	2	8	8	14	68
Pigeon peas	—	—	—	2	—	23	49	85
Pumpkins/Melons	—	—	—	—	—	1	1	10
Tomatoes	—	—	—	—	4	9	22	76
Others	—	—	—	—	—	—	—	—
Chive and thyme	—	—	—	—	—	2	2	25
Sugar cane	—	—	—	—	1	2	12	12
Index of occurrence	0.08	0.08	0.02	0.05	0.06	0.09	0.10	0.24

Cultivated in this manner bananas serve a dual role by supplying necessary shade for young and immature cocoa plants, and at the same time providing an interim source of income. Ultimately, bananas are phased out to leave pure stands of cocoa. Other varieties of trees found on F_2, and all subsequently numbered fragments, are generally few and of limited number, and hence have little commercial value.

Indices of occurrence for fragments F_3 to F_5 display little variation denoting that the nature of tree-crop cultivation is not significantly affected by distance beyond a radius of 1.92 km from the farmer's home (the mean distance of F_3 in this regard). While the nature of cultivation, that of the triumvirate of export crops, may not appear to differ consistently with distance, it is usual for the intensity of agriculture of decline as per unit area inputs of capital and labour drop off. As was mentioned earlier, the sample size for fragments F_6 to F_8 is inadequate for deducing any generalizations.

Vegetable Crops

Despite their small size and the dominating presence of trees, kitchen gardens contain a variety of vegetables that in the final assessment can be regarded as the hallmark of this critical component of small farm holdings. Scattered about this fragment are beds of vegetables, where variations of mixed cropping, interplanting and intercropping are practised,[7] alongside pure-stand cultivation which is commonly employed with temperate crops, such as cabbage and lettuce. These cultivation practices permit a wide range of vegetables to be grown on F_1 (Table 12). Some indication of the principal ingredients of the rural Grenadian diet can be gleaned from those vegetables which occur most frequently, namely ground provisions (dasheen, sweet potatoes, tannias and yams), corn, peppers, pigeon pea, and tomatoes; all present in more than one-third of the gardens. As a rule, about two-thirds of the area assigned to vegetable cultivation each year is devoted to tropical roots and tubers. On higher numbered fragments, the tendency is for this proportion to increase, so that ground provisions are customarily the only vegetables grown on F_5 and higher numbered fragments.[8]

A marked difference exists between F_1 and F_2 in the nature of vegetables cultivated. This fact is reflected by their indices of occurrence which are 0.24 and 0.10 respectively (Table 12) and is attributable to the very noticeable reduction in the cultivation of those crops which require special vigilance throughout their period of growth,[9] so that their produce is prized. For instance, tomatoes are present on 41 per cent of F_1 fragments, yet occur on only 14 per cent of F_2; similarly, for lettuce where the corresponding percentages are 22 and 3. In addition to the basic tenets of von Thünen, whereby the intensity of cultivation is a function of the distance between the fragment and the house, there is the problem of praedial larceny, already noted as being a serious issue at the time of the survey. Thus, as fragments become increasingly removed from the farmer's home the tendency is to plant crops, such as ground provisions, corn and pigeon peas, which require minimal attention during their growth and whose ubiquity gives them low market value.

In sum, the impact of fragmentation upon land-use patterns is more pronounced for vegetable cultivation than for arboriculture.

Conclusion

The structural composition of small farms into scattered fragments deters the efficient utilization of Grenada's land. To what extent fragmentation directly contributes to the problem of idle land is uncertain, but its role in this regard should not be underestimated. Other factors, such as the nature of tenure, the age and physical fitness of the farmer, and the problem of praedial larceny, have been alluded to as ones influencing the nature and intensity of land use on individual fragments. Nevertheless, 35.5 per cent of the total land occupied by the sampled farmers lay idle in 1982 despite the efforts by the PRG at that time to combat this problem. Comparison of these results with those of a similar survey conducted in 1969 (Brierley, 1978) reveal some notable trends. First, that the degree of fragmentation has increased from an average of 2.38 to 2.75 parcels per small farm. Secondly, that mean farm sizes enlarged by 22.4 per cent, from 1.65 to 2.02 ha. Thirdly, that the extent of idle land grew from 17.0 to 35.5 per cent, a consistent feature noted for all fragment numbers for which there was an adequate sample size from which to make a meaningful deduction. As a result, whereas small farmers in 1969 cultivated an average 1.40 ha of land, their counterparts in 1982 worked 1.30 ha. Lastly, the indices of vegetable-crop occurrence reveal that less variety is grown outside the kitchen gardens (F_1) in 1982 than in 1969; a result ascribed to the increase in praedial larceny during the interim. However, the fact that more than one-third of the land occupied by small farmers lies in an unproductive state at a time when policies of economic self-reliance were being actively pursued by the PRG, underscores the difficulties of achieving development in Grenada's small-farm sector. In order that such advancement may occur, there is a need for studies that will shed more light on both the patterns and issues associated with land-use efficiency. It is in this regard that the subject of farm structure becomes a central theme; one warranting more focus and analysis than has heretofore been the case in the Caribbean.

Notes

1   In a recent address by Dr B. Yankey, Director of Caribbean Development Bank's Projects Department, it is interesting to note that no mention was made of farm fragmentation, yet his topic dealt with the depressed state of Caribbean agriculture and the need for its redevelopment. His emphasis was on the economics and management of technological change within the Region (1985:4–5).

2   The island of Carriacou, although part of the independent nation of Grenada, is a separate agricultural district and is excluded from consideration in this calculation.

3   CARDI (1980) in its profile of small farming indicates these points, Tables 38, 40 and 45.

4   Even though one-quarter of the farmers owned donkeys and a couple possessed motor vehicles, there was no tendency amongst them to work land regularly beyond a distance of 5 km, a point attributed to 1) donkeys generally being used as pack animals and a source of manure rather than as a means of personal transport in rugged terrain and 2) the poor condition and inadequacy of service roads in much of the interior of Grenada.

5   Sharecropping was noted to exist only in the few remaining sugarcane producing areas in Grenada, found principally in the south. The arrangement is one where commonly one-third of the harvested produce is turned over to the owner in lieu of rent.

6   A review of these factors is presented in a paper by the author entitled 'Idle lands and idle hands in Grenada, West Indies', forthcoming in *Rural Systems.*

7   Ruthenberg, H. (1971:28) provides a useful distinction between these terms:

   1)   Mixed cropping refers to the simultaneous and intermingled cultivation of two or more crops
   2)   Interplanting when short-term annual crops are planted between longer-term annuals or biennials
   3)   Intercropping is the simultaneous cultivation of usually two, but possibly more crops in alternate rows
   4)   Interculture is the growing of arable crops under perennials.

8   Ifill (1979:30–42) provides evidence of the permutations and combinations of these planting arrangements for Grenada.

9   A comparison between this study and the earlier one (Brierley, 1978) reveals that while the index of vegetable crop occurrence is of a similar magnitude for F_1, those for the subsequent fragment numbers are consistently lower. Whereas in the earlier study the difference in indices

between F_1 and F_2 was 0.6, this analysis reveals it to be 0.14; an increase attributed to the greater severity of petty theft which discouraged farmers from growing a wider range of vegetables on their dispersed fragments.

References

Bowler, I. 1983, Structural Change in Rural Geography. In *Progress in Rural Geography*. (ed.) M. Pacione, London: 46–73.
Brierley, J.S. 1978. Fragmentation of holding: A study of small farms in Grenada. *Journal of Tropical Agriculture*, Vol. 55:135–140.
(forthcoming) Idle hands and idle lands in Grenada, West Indies. *Rural Systems*.
Caribbean Agricultural Research and Development Institute 1980. *A Profile of Small Farming in Antigua, Montserrat and Grenada*. St Augustine, Trinidad, University of the West Indies.
Chisholm, M. 1979. *Rural Settlement and Land Use*. (3rd ed.) London. Hutchinson.
Edwards, G. 1961. *An Economic Study of Small Farming in Jamaica*, Kingston, Jamaica, University College of the West Indies.
Farmer, B.H. 1960. On Not Controlling subdivision in Paddy Lands, *Transactions of the Institute of British Geographers*, Vol. 28:225–235.
Grenada, Ministry of Agriculture 1982. *Agricultural Census 1981*, mimeographed copy, St George's.
Harewood, R.R. 1979. *Small Farm Development; Understanding and Improving Farm Systems in the Humid Tropics*. Boulder, Westview Press.
Ifill, M. 1979. *Report on a Farm Survey Conducted in Grenada*. Port of Spain, Trinidad, Economic Commission for Latin America.
King, R. and S. Burton 1982. Land fragmentation: notes on a fundamental rural spatial problem. *Progress in Human Geography*, Vol. 6:475–494.
Morgan, W.D. 1978. *Agriculture in the Third World: a spatial analysis*. Boulder, Westview Press.
Ruthenberg, H. 1971. *Farming Systems in the Tropics*. Oxford, Clarendon Press.
Wood, H.A. 1963. *Northern Haiti: Land Use and Settlement*. Toronto, University of Toronto Press.
Yankey, B. 1985. 'Farm Tech '85' first instalment of an address entitled The Economics and Management of New Technologies in Agriculture, *CBD News* Vol. 3, No. 1:4–5.

CHAPTER 10

Dimensions of opportunity for reducing the dependency factor in Caribbean food production

Frank C Innes

John Antle (1985) reviewing *Ill Fares the Land: Essays on Food, Hunger, and Power* by Susan George (1985) has recently called for a critical assessment of current development strategies and thereby added his voice to that of others equally concerned. He suggests pessimistically that development either implies massive applications of not always appropriate technology, and with it dependence on foreign capital and expertise, or it involves low key infusions of limited local resources with little or no immediate apparent effect. This chapter whilst tending towards the second alternative as being the preferable one, seeks, on the basis of experience with a field programme previously centred at McGill University in Montreal,[1] to take a more optimistic view and consider the possibility of accelerating indigenous development efforts in the Caribbean.

Whilst we know something of the dimension of West Indian societies in terms of broad urban, rural, plantation, and small farm divisions there are as yet no statistics identifying, in the region as a whole, those food producers who primarily produce for personal use or auto consumption, selling only occasional surpluses, and who by necessity, through lack of capital, or choice, severely limit their inputs of exogenous origin. Indeed inputs from external sources have historically not been available to this group and they have therefore had to show a great deal of ingenuity in solving the problems of food production in an often fickle environment. Field work has identified some of these individuals and recorded their survival tactics. By studying these peasant household survival strategies we may come to understand something of the possibilities of indigenous development.

The field evidence

Andrew Royer of Giraudel, in Dominica, is one such individual. His Anronat Farm is situated on steeply sloping land at 300 metres elevation. It is about half a hectare (1.2 acres) in size which is the average for a small farm in this island. However, unlike others Mr Royer has not tied his fortunes to the banana industry but has rather developed a mixed farm with emphasis on production of food for himself, his wife, two children and a young nephew. He terraced his land and with one full-time and one part-time assistant produces some forty different crops over a year. In doing so he is cognizant of inter-species competition and nutritive requirements and manages his production system organically without recourse to imported chemicals or herbicides. Four cows, two pigs, two goats and about 140 fowl provide organic wastes for the cropping system. The cows, however, are fed some coconut meal bought from a local factory and some imported food is given to the poultry. The main tool employed is the hoe and yields have been sufficient to provide a surplus of marketable value worth over $1,500 per month.

Marketing was carried out utilizing public transport to the Roseau market, but now eggs on Thursdays and a wide variety of produce on Saturdays are transported in a recently acquired pick-up truck. No contractual arrangements ensure business but rather Mr Royer sells on a first come first served basis at his stall in the market (Royer, 1981).

Mr Cohen on Mount Prospect, Jamaica, farms because 'I love it'. He has approximately four hectares (9 acres) divided into three plots: his house spot and two others three-quarters of an hour walking distance away. This fragmentation has obvious disadvantages but he claims it gives him different soil types and, due to relief, different climatic conditions. In addition, he notes that his commuting time is not much different from that of others going to work. Although chemical fertilizer is employed on this farm, 'as recommended by agricultural extension people', organics are also employed in the production of yams, sweet potatoes, thyme, pimento, escallion, bananas, and other, primarily, root crops. His cropping pattern is carefully planned. Since 'sweet potatoes kill yams', these are not grown together and neither are yams and cocoes or cassava. Itinerant higglers are the main means of marketing whilst every three years or so the family cow is sold to the local butcher. No non-family labour is used. A tractor is, however, occasionally hired for tillage. Thus again a family of five is largely self-sufficient and yet contributes a surplus to the market place (Iton, 1969).

Ina Sparkes, a thirty-six year old farmer in Knockpatrick, Jamaica, with five plots of land, finds it best 'not to borrow' to finance her agricultural operations and regards offers of subsidy by Government 'too unreliable'. She does, however, undertake part-time dress-making and occasional nursing to raise funds and her brothers contribute from their earnings from time to time. This way she can employ a tractor for the heavy land preparation, whilst some 'day for day' labour exchanges are also used. Pigs, sheep, goats, and cows are kept and a crop mix is selected which provides for her household and a marketable surplus of livestock, Irish potatoes, sweet potatoes, coffee and citrus fruits (Iton, 1969).

Many other examples could be cited of self-sufficient farmers in these islands. Large numbers of such farmers support themselves and provide small off-farm sales, without dependency on outside assistance. Indeed, their historical roots have always emphasized their own entrepreneurial skills. As Edwards (1961:26–27) reminds us:

> Since then [emancipation], thousands of small farms have been created by the descendants of the slaves. These small farms now use a considerable part of the resources employed in agriculture and produce a considerable part of the total output. Farms of from one to less than 25 acres in extent — these are small farms for the purpose of this discussion — occupy 38 per cent of the area of land in agricultural use in Jamaica and provide almost one-half of the total agricultural product.

Yet as will be noted below, these facts and the significance of this activity have largely been ignored and overlooked in discussing the future development of the Caribbean region.

Recent evaluations

It is typical of much post World War II writing, that agriculture, and notably indigenous agriculture, as opposed to export driven plantation type agriculture, has been virtually written off (Braithwaite, 1968 and Levitt & Best, 1975). Thus the International Bank for Reconstruction and Development in its report on Jamaica in 1952 describes this sector as 'in general — the most inefficient, partly because they have the least desirable land, partly because their agricultural techniques are the most backward'. Levitt and Best saw development as a process of drawing labour from a backward, traditional, agricultural sector into urban and industrial activities. Traditional small scale agriculture was considered to represent a pool of unskilled labour, often disguising chronic unemployment in excess of 10 per cent and perhaps more realistically in Jamaica, over 30 per cent.

Those who have examined the indigenous sector closely, whilst admitting some of these features, would, however, argue in protest about many of the stereotypes regarding these farmers. In the Commonwealth Caribbean such small holders who make up from 46 to 98 per cent of all farmers have available to them only between 6 and 27 per cent of the agricultural land and yet contribute a substantial proportion of the total agricultural product, especially in basic foodstuffs for internal consumption (Beckford, 1975 and Nurse, 1973). However, problems are encountered in measuring this production as both barter exchange and subsistence production are common occurrences on the islands. Studies made by field workers are accumulating to support the view that justice has not been done to the significant contribution of small scale agriculturalists not only to the food supply but also to the development process itself (Momsen, 1973b; Innis, 1980; Paquette, 1982).

Some constraints, real or imaginary

Commonly it is claimed that poor land resources resulting from the historical sorting process of land acquisition in the West Indies, have tended to confine peasant farmers to sub-marginal land and hence a resource base that cannot be the basis for viable farming in this sector (Momsen, 1973a). Evaluation of this claim for Barbados was made by mapping the distribution of peasant land and superimposing the land classification system employed by the University of the West Indies. In this way it was discovered that peasants farmed a fair proportion of the better land. Thus this claim of resource marginality can be rejected in specific cases and further study of this question, taking into account the small farmer's mode of operation, suggests that more generally one can state that the techniques employed and the inherent land typology are well matched. In other words, where intensive farming methods based on human labour are employed (Edwards (1972) cites 600 man/hours per acre of crop land per year) the inherent land quality ceases to have crucial significance. Measures and classifications have to be made in terms of local appraisals of technology as was done in Momsen's (1973b) study which was based on farmer's perceptions of soil quality.

A further constraint on the development of this section is seen to be the size and fragmentation of the land holdings (Edwards, 1961). In Jamaica only one-third of the small farms consisted of a single piece of land, a further third of two pieces of land and the remainder of more than two pieces, whilst the author, in studying small farms in Barbados, found it not unusual for a ten acre small holding to consist of three or more parcels of land. The immediate reaction is to regard this as little short of catastrophic with respect to the running of a farm. The usual response is to call for consolidation within the context of land reform. The assumption throughout is, however, in the context of monocropping, with given levels of advanced technology implying capitalization and commercialization appropriate to the Western and temperate lands. In an unpublished but thought provoking paper by Hills, Iton, and Lundgren (1972), the specific case of the Commonwealth Caribbean was examined. This argues that 'under certain circumstances fragmentation of the farm is a necessity and may be economically and socially advantageous'. Whilst many reasons for fragmentation into two or more parcels of land in the area are mentioned, some are listed as follows:

> When a farmer adds a parcel of land to the land he already has use of, he may be trying to reduce the risks involved in the farm operation by diversifying the available environmental resources, or he may primarily, or as a result of diversification, be attempting to increase the markets open to his operation, or he may be trying to provide additional collateral in order to improve his credit rating, or he may simply be safeguarding against old age, in that a parcel of land is in most cases readily convertible into cash (*Idem.* 1972).

In one of the author's field studies, the Kelman Green farm in Barbados, the farm was in three fragments: one, the house-spot intensively farmed in vegetables, was also the site of a chicken farm with some 300 birds; the second plot housed a few pigs and the third plot some one and a half kilometres distant was almost entirely dedicated to sugar cane. As a result Mr Green had a diversified operation providing maximum security by its high 'diversity index', to borrow an ecological term from biology. Thus in the context of Caribbean small scale farming it is probably unwise to assume that fragmentation is a serious constraint and it may indeed be a strength in the system, given its contextual relationships. Indeed my McGill colleagues concluded that:

> it is only in carefully integrated agricultural rationalization programs for larger regional and national development plans that a consolidation policy can be justified (*Idem.* 9).

Monocropping versus multicropping

Another characteristic of small scale tropical farming is multicropping usually involving intercropping, resulting in multiple land use within each unit of land. This was a characteristic of the Amerindian 'conuco' and the tradition from that source was probably strengthened by the importation of an African cultural strand by the slaves. Thus slave gardens or provision grounds were generally admixtures of root crops, grains, beans and fruits all intercultivated. This has continued as a normal feature of much small scale farming and is characteristic of what are sometimes referred to as 'kitchen gardens' and 'provision grounds' (Brierley, 1974).

This form of cultivation is not merely followed to ensure year round dietary requirements through continued harvesting and even spread of the temporal demands for labour, although it does all this. It has also been found that this system is ecologically meaningful. Constant ground cover diminishes the danger of soil erosion, although vegetative bunds, terracettes and microdrainage systems can also be identified in the fields. The intermixture of crops itself is not haphazard (Innis, 1980). Small farmers know that legumes will help a non-leguminous crop, so in Jamaica, kidney beans and Irish potatoes are usually grown together, whilst chick peas and a range of beans are frequently planted around a yam mound. On the other hand, yams and sweet potatoes or cassava are not interplanted.

Using data from India, and Africa, as well as the West Indies, Innis (1980) has demonstrated that such intermixtures raise the *total* yield substantially — in one example six intercropped items produced 17,600 lb of produce compared with 14,996 lb of output from the same acre divided into three successive pure stand crops over the same year and a half. The implication then is that small farming techniques are often more efficient and productive than they are given credit for being, and that given the conditions they maximize the resource base and inputs applied to it. It has also been found that not only do correctly selected 'companion plants' not compete with, but rather enhance each other, but also that such techniques have value in pest control. Thus the scent or effusion, from one plant can provide a biological deterrent to a pest which would otherwise strike its companion (Hill, 1978). Furthermore, Kapoor and Ramakrishna (1975) have shown that a 'weed' when tolerated in a wheat crop can, if leguminous, improve the wheat yield by providing nitrogen. Thus a much closer examination of the intercropping practices of West Indian smallholders is called for, as it is likely that in the hard school of experience they have already learnt, and have been applying these lessons, whose scientific value and merit is only now being discussed in the literature. In promoting pure stand cropping it might now well be argued that there has been a lack of 'knowledgeable intervention' and it has certainly reduced self-reliance and imposed dependence.

Thus a careful and detailed inventory of the planting practices of traditional farmers is urgently needed so that the lessons they have learned can be recorded and strategies for development used that will build on this wisdom. Personal field experience on this question indicated that the local explanation may be far fetched, relating to the phase of the moon, or the almanac but the pragmatic results are telling. Ecological education should provide the reasons for the present long established practices.

Problems of measurement

The traditional measure of yields per acre, employed in developed Western Societies, is now held as suspect, when applied generally. When land is scarce in relation to capital and labour it perhaps still makes sense. When, however, as is increasingly true given the world-wide retreat from the land, land itself is not the scarce commodity, yield per acre must often be replaced by measures of yield per man-hour employed. In the Caribbean small farm sector, a higher dependency on external inputs in order to increase yields per acre would only aggravate the balance of payments problem caused by the high cost of imported fossil fuels. Yet agricultural development planning, where it has existed, or is being promoted, has usually advocated this increased dependency together with imports of machinery. As has been noted by another Caribbeanist (Innis, 1980):

> Proponents of modern agriculture sincerely believe that the best thing the developed countries can do for other countries is to replace traditional farms with *modern* farms. But they seldom measure the inputs which are necessary to produce the enormous yields of which they are so proud. First, fossil fuels and fertilizers ... are being used to step up production for a couple of centuries, till the supply runs out; second, the calories harvested from a modern field are usually much less than the calories which were used up in growing the crops. The reasons for this are that modern commercial farmers use machines which consume calories in the form of fuel and which also take a lot of fuel to manufacture. When calorie input-output is used to define efficiency, traditional methods are much more efficient than modern methods.

Development implications

The above review indicates that indigenous methods offer a viable system of livelihood providing food and shelter and the dignity of work without the fetters of dependency. This latter point is most significant, for it has been said that 'subsistence farming without purchased inputs has the great virtue of being relatively safe. The farmer is largely independent of the outside world' (Millikan and Hapgood, 1967). But does this imply that this system is self-limiting or can it be harnessed to a development plan? If so, what kind of development process is appropriate?

Traditional meanings for this process have included the transfer of people from agricultural tasks to industry and commerce; the raising of levels of skill and education, and the provision of paid employment within a cash economy, and hence the ability to increase the potential tax base so government might more effectively provide services to people. Perhaps now is the time to challenge this model, especially in view of the evident ability of the masses to provide much for themselves, and the equally cogent evidence that big government is increasingly unable to respond to individual needs in a meaningful way.

The World Bank (1979) has recognised this problem, albeit in a slightly different way, by stating in its 1979 annual report that there is, and should be, a movement from the financing of capital infrastructure towards placing more emphasis on investments that can directly affect the well-being of the poor in developing countries by making them more productive. Such a move surely implies identification of constraints and the provision of appropriate technology. The rural environment of the Caribbean has then to be re-examined in detail.

Two categories of situation can be seen. Firstly, those territories where there is still land available which offers the potential for additional application of labour, and secondly those societies where land is not easily available to the small farm sector. Where large tracts of land are under-utilized, the normal response is to call for land reform. Mr. Royer of Dominica claims this is not a solution, for he feels that many people do not know how to use the land. He himself has clearly shown that but a half hectare, organically farmed, and properly managed is enough for an individual. Thus, more intensive use of land is needed rather than reallocation of the resource itself.

Furthermore, land that is growing plantation type crops aimed at export markets must be redeployed to provide foodstuffs and inputs to locally based agricultural industries. Where this has not been done, land reform movements have merely integrated traditional farmers into development, making farmers wage-dependent peons of agro-plantations, or driving them to migrate to urban areas, and reducing their ability to feed themselves. The result is a fall in food consumption as these, now low wage, workers must buy food instead of growing it for themselves, and the variety and quality drops and what Chossudovsky (1981) calls 'the political economy of malnutrition' sets in.

Unfortunately a recent World Bank report does not see this danger and calls rather for 'the revival of the principal agricultural export crops in which the region continues to have a comparative advantage' as well as 'the development of sources of supply within the region for currently imported food' (Chernick, 1978). A more effective development policy would work within the prevailing systems of peasant agriculture, and attempt to upgrade the systems, rather then replace them. Such upgrading has, almost certainly, to start with education. Most small scale farmers in the Caribbean have but a few years of elementary schooling together with an extensive apprenticeship on the land. The two should not be incompatible. Rather the formal teaching should emphasize the value of self-reliance, of field observation, of explanation of what is experimentally seen, and of application. Thus traditional knowledge of 'companion planting' and of the symbiotic value of different plants in combination should be confirmed wherever possible with test plots and scientific analysis. Likewise an understanding of the local pharmacopoeia should be imparted and value placed on this knowledge rather than it being discounted as folk medicine or worse. Prescription, beyond this is perhaps folly. Fieldwork shows that Third World peoples are working out their own solutions to the problems of development.

Theoretical implications and conclusions

The Caribbean area like other Third World regions has been subject to much analysis at a macro-scale utilizing economic models such as diffusion development and dependency theory. Social measures have not been considered, and essentially much research has been done from the perspective of the academic and the outsider. This outsider view from the core of the world economy is aptly criticized by the Brazilians Becker and Bernardes (1976) who indicate that the periphery is not merely an area of innovation adoption but is also capable of indigenous innovation which may be more effective in preserving the environment.

To undertake a pragmatic solution this discussion suggests the rhetoric of academia must be put aside. The 'praxis' of the local dweller, the insider, should be validated and micro-level study and research in rural areas should seek to understand the culture and traditions of peasant farmers. In this regard, we might draw a parallel with Liberation theology with its emphasis on grassroots organisation rather than its origin in the ivory towers of theological schools.

Notes

1   Caribbean Project 1967–70, Dept. of Geography, McGill University, Montreal. Funded by the Canada Council and organized by T.L. Hills, F.C. Innes and J.O. Lundgren.
2   In April 1987 when Mr Royer was interviewed by Janet Momsen he was growing 42 different crops and using the organic waste from his farm to fuel a biogas plant, one of the first in the region.

References

Antle, J. 1985. Food for Thought. In *Resources*, Resources for the Future, Washington, Number 80:14–15.

Becker, B.K. and Bernardes, N. 1976. Considerations on Regional Development and the Spatial Location of Economic Activities in the Developing Countries. *Geoforum*, Vol 7:223–232.

Beckford, G. 1975. Caribbean Rural Economy. In Beckford (Ed.), *Caribbean Economy*. I.S.E.R. University of the West Indies, Jamaica.

Braithwaite, L. 1968. Social and Political Aspects of Rural Development in the West Indies. *Social and Economic Studies*, Vol 17, No. 3, December: 264–275.

Brierley, J. 1974. Small Farming in Grenada, West Indies. *Manitoba Geographical Studies*, Vol. 4, Winnipeg Department of Geography, University of Manitoba.

Chernick, S.E., (ed.) 1978. *The Commonwealth Caribbean, the Integration Experience*. A World Bank Economic Report, John Hopkins University Press, 19.

Chossudovsky, M. 1981. Capitalist Development and Agriculture in Latin America. In *Dependant Agricultural Development and Agrarian Reform in Latin America*. L.R. Alschuler, (ed.) Ottawa University Press: 13–28.

Edwards, D. 1961. *An Economic Study of Small Farming in Jamaica*. I.S.E.R., Mona, Kingston: 26–17.

1972. The Development of Small Scale Farming: two cases from the Commonwealth Caribbean. *Caribbean Quarterly*, Vol. 18, No. 1:59–71.

George, S. 1985. *III Fares the Land: Essays on Food, Hunger, and Power*. Washington, Institute for Policy Studies.

Hill, S.B. 1978. Biological Approaches to Pest Control. In *Proceedings of the P.E.I. Conference on Ecological Agriculture*, Charlottetown, P.E.I.: 174–196.

Hills, T.L., Iton, S. and Lundgren, J. 1972. *Farm Fragmentation in the Commonwealth Caribbean, some preliminary observations and analysis.* Mimeo, McGill Univ., Geog. Dept., unpublished.

Innis, D.Q. 1980. The future of traditional agriculture. *Focus*, Vol. 30, No. 3, New York, American Geographical Society.

Iton, S. 1969. Interview, McGill Geography Department, Caribbean Project supported by grant to the author from the Canada Council.

Kapoor, P. and Ramakrishna, P.S. 1975. Studies on Crop-legume behaviour in pure and mixed stands. *Agro-Ecosystems,* Vol. 2, No. 1.

Levitt, K. and Best, L. 1975. Character of Caribbean Economy. In Beckford, G., (Ed.), *'Caribbean Economy'.* I.S.E.R. Jamaica 34–59.

McGee, T.G. 1974. In Praise of Tradition: towards a Geography of Anti-Development. *Antipode,* Vol. 6, No. 3:30–47.

Millikan, M. and Hapgood, D. 1967. *No Easy Harvest: the dilemma of Agriculture in underdeveloped countries.* Boston, Little, Brown and Co.

Momsen, J.D. 1973a. Small Scale Farming in Barbados, St Lucia and Martinque. In *Proceedings of the Fifth West Indian Agricultural Economic Conference,* St. Augustine, U.W.I. 78–84.

 1973b. A Model for Agricultural Change in Developing Areas. In L.G. Reeds (ed.) *Agricultural Typology and Land Use.* Hamilton, McMaster University: 221–230.

Nietschmann, B. 1971. The Substance of Subsistence. In *Geographic Research on Latin America: Benchmark 1970.* Proceedings of the Conference of Latin Americanist Geographers, Vol. 1 (ed.) Lentnek, Carmin and Martinson. Muncie. Ball State University: 167–181.

Nurse, J.O.J., 1973. Small Scale Farming in Barbados. In *Proceedings of the Fifth West Indian Agricultural Economics Conference,* St Augustine, U.W.I. 85–102.

Paquette, R. 1982. *Désengagement paysan et sous-production alimentaire.* Montreal, Les Presses de l'Université de Montreal.

Royer, A. June, 1981. Unpublished interview.

Index